Practitioner Series

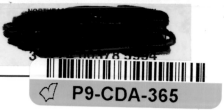

Springer

London
Berlin
Heidelberg
New York
Barcelona
Budapest
Hong Kong
Milan
Paris
Santa Clara
Singapore
Tokyo

Other titles in this series:

The Politics of Usability
L. Trenner and J. Bawa
3-540-76181-0

Electronic Commerce and Business Communications
M. Chesher and R. Kaura
3-540-19930-6

The Project Management Paradigm
K. Burnett
3-540-76238-8

Distributed Applications Engineering
I. Wijegunaratne and G. Fernandez
3-540-76210-8
Publication due Autumn, 1998

Finance for IT Decision Makers
M. Blackstaff
3-540-76232-9
Publication due Autumn, 1998

Using Interface Development: Using Entity-Relationship Modeling for
Information Artifacts
D. Benyon, D. Bental and T. Green
1-85233-009-0
Publication due Autumn, 1998

John Hunt and Alex McManus

Key Java

Advanced Tips and Techniques

Springer

John Edward Hunt
Alexander George McManus
Department of Computer Science, University of Wales, Aberystwyth,
Dyfed, SY23 3DB

ISBN 3-540-76259-0 Springer-Verlag Berlin Heidelberg New York

British Library Cataloguing in Publication Data
Hunt, John
　Key Java : advanced tips and techniques. - (Practitioner series)
　1.Java (Computer program language)
　I.Title II.McManus, Alexander
　005.1'33
　ISBN 3540762590

Library of Congress Cataloging-in-Publication Data
Hunt, John, 1964-
　Key Java : advanced tips and techniques / John Hunt and Alexander McManus.
　　p.　cm. -- (Practitioner series)
　Includes bibliographical references and index.
　ISBN 3-540-76259-0 (alk. paper)
　1. Java (Computer program language)　I. McManus, Alexander, 1972-
. 　II. Title.　III. Series: Practitioner series (Springer-Verlag)
　QA76.73.J38H87　1998
　005.13'3--dc21　　　　　　　　　　　　　　　　98-6380

Typesetting: Ian Kingston Editorial Services, Nottingham
Printed and bound at the Athenæum Press Ltd, Gateshead, Tyne and Wear, UK
34/3830-543210 Printed on acid-free paper

Dedication

---

*To my daughter Phoebe for brightening every day with a smile and to my
wife Denise for giving me such a beautiful daughter.*

John Hunt

To my parents.

Alex McManus

Contents

Preface

The Java platform is such a rapidly evolving environment that it can be difficult for developers to keep abreast of progress. It has moved beyond being a language used just for creating Web-based applets to one that is being used for developing serious enterprise wide applications.

This book is aimed at developers who already know the language, its classes and its tools, but who want to get more out of Java. It explores some of the more significant and exciting developments in Java and covers techniques that will be fundamental to programmers developing significant applications. It looks beyond the mechanics of coding applications and explores the concepts that will prove vital to getting the most out of the Java language.

Some of the subjects that we cover include:

- How to design classes for reusable components
- Code optimization for speed and space
- How to use JavaBeans
- How to construct and document frameworks
- Testing code in an object-oriented language
- How to access databases with the JDBC from applets
- The evolution of Swing and the Java Foundation Classes

The individual chapters are listed below and are divided into four parts. Each part is self-contained and can be dipped into as required – it is envisaged that this book will be used as a reference, rather than read cover to cover.

Content Summary

Part 1: Java Development

Chapter 1: Introduction to Java Development
This chapter discusses Java's background and history. In particular it identifies three stages to Java's evolution and considers the impact of each stage. It then discusses the emerging Java platform and its use in the construction of Web-based applications. A number of case studies are presented to illustrate its use.

Chapter 2: Guidelines for Reusable Java Classes
This chapter discusses a set of guidelines for the development of reusable Java classes. These guidelines relate to the naming conventions used in JavaBeans as well as to the use of facilities such as private, final and packages.

Chapter 3: Persistent Storage of Objects
This chapter explains how objects can be permanently stored to disk files.

Chapter 4: Introductory JavaBeans
This chapter introduces Java beans, what they are, how they work, how you define a bean and how you use them.

Chapter 5: JavaBeans in Depth
This chapter describes how a bean info object is defined and how property editors and customizers are created, as well as how the introspection process works.

Chapter 6: Java Database Connectivity
This chapter introduces the JDBC API used to interface Java with databases.

Chapter 7: The Web and JDBC
In this chapter we consider the use of databases and JDBC within applets.

Chapter 8: File-Based Storage Classes
This chapter illustrates how the encapsulation methods in Java can be used to hide the implementation of a storage class. In particular, examples are presented which allow an in-memory approach or a file-based approach.

Chapter 9: Frameworks
A framework is a combination of two or more classes (which may be abstract) which cooperate with each other to provide some level of functionality. They are an important construct in any object-oriented systems but are notoriously hard to design and implement. This chapter discusses how frameworks can be constructed.

Chapter 10: Documenting Frameworks with Patterns
One of the hardest problems for the developer of a framework is how to document it. One solution which has received a great deal of interest in recent years is the concept of a pattern. This chapter explains what patterns are and illustrates how they can be used to document frameworks.

Part 2: Java Testing

Chapter 11: Testing Object-Oriented Code
Object-oriented systems may make code easier to reuse and may be supported by object-oriented analysis and design methods, but they do not guarantee that the code is correct. This chapter looks at some of the problems introduced by object orientation for software testing.

Chapter 12: Testing Java Code
The preceding chapter discussed the problems facing the tester of an object-oriented system (and in particular a Java system). This chapter considers

current best practice in testing object-oriented systems, with particular reference to Java.

Chapter 13: Assertions in Java
Assertions can be an excellent way of incorporating self-test features into your code with a minimum of runtime overhead. This chapter presents one way in which they can be added to Java programs.

Part 3: Java Performance

Chapter 14: Performance: Tooling Up
The most common criticism levelled at Java is its relatively poor performance. In this chapter we consider the reasons for this and how to get the most out of Java development tools and virtual machines.

Chapter 15: Optimizing for Speed
In this chapter we arm the reader with some essential information on the performance of Java code. With this information, improvements can be made that outclass the speed-up gained from a faster virtual machine.

Chapter 16: Optimizing for Memory
This chapter takes a detailed look at how Java stores objects in class files and in memory. We consider how we can reduce the size of class files in order to speed up applets, and how to reduce runtime memory overhead for the new breed of "serious" applications.

Chapter 17: Future Evaluators
Future operators are objects that can transparently take the place of another object that has yet to be computed. They are calculated ahead of schedule when the processor is free, which is computationally intensive. They are often used in client–server applications.

Chapter 18: Real-Time Systems in Java
Real-time systems can be implemented in Java if care is taken with the code. This chapter builds on the previous two chapters to consider what additional steps must be taken to guarantee response times.

Part 4: Graphic Java

Chapter 19: Evolution of Java UI
The speed with which Java's user interface framework is evolving has left many developers bewildered by the rate of change. In the chapter we examine the forces influencing the need for change and put the recent developments, such as the Internet Foundation Classes and the Java Foundation Classes, in context.

Chapter 20: The Internet Foundation Classes
The Internet Foundation Classes (IFC) from Netscape provide a sophisticated user interface framework that is available in a stable form today. This chapter takes a closer look at the advantages it offers over the AWT.

Chapter 21: Swinging with the Java Foundation Classes
The Swing user interface classes in the Java Foundation Classes (JFC) provide a rich set of components with unparalleled flexibility, thanks to their use of the Model–View–Controller architecture. This chapter explores the concepts behind the framework that will revolutionalize user interfaces in Java.

Chapter 22: Graphical Java Media
The new Java Media frameworks provide Java with advanced graphical capabilities that will make a new range of applications possible. In this chapter, we take a look at Java 2D, Java 3D and the Java Media Foundation (JMF) classes.

Chapter 23: UI design and Java
This chapter attempts to provide guidance on the principles of good user interface design, whichever toolkit is used. This is a subject often overlooked by texts on building Java applications.

Obtaining Source Code Examples

The source code for the examples in this book is available on the Web at the URL `http://www.springer.co.uk/comp/support/`. Each chapter has its own directory within which the class files are listed individually. The source code has all been tested using the JDK 1.1. As new versions of the JDK are released all examples will be tested against those. Any changes necessitated by a new release will be noted at the above Web site.

Typographical Conventions

In this book the standard typeface is Minion; however, `Courier` is used to identify source code, for example `a = 2 + 3;`.

Trademarks

HotJava, JDBC, Java, Java Development Kit, Solaris, SunOS and SunSoft are trademarks of Sun Microsystems, Inc. MS-Windows and Windows 95 are registered trademarks of Microsoft Corporation. Apple is a registered trademark of Apple Computer, Inc. Unix is a registered trademark of AT&T. All other brand names are trademarks of their respective holders.

Acknowledgements

John would like to thank his wife Denise Cooke; yet again she has been a patient and thorough proofreader and critic. Without her support this book would not have been written.

Alex and John would like to thank their friends and colleagues in the Department of Computer Science for their help and support (in particular Fred Long, Professor Ian Pyle, Mark Neal, John Timmis, Neil Taylor and Chris Price).

Part 1
Java Development

1 Introduction

1.1 Introduction

This book considers issues important to the effective, efficient, safe, reliable and reusable construction of software systems in Java. Subjects range from the correct use of inheritance, to where and when to use Java components (as represented by JavaBeans). It also considers the difficulty inherent in testing object-oriented systems (and Java in particular) as well as highlighting the importance of such testing.

Java itself is one of the phenomena of the 1990s computing world. It sprang onto the scene in the mid-1990s and has grown from strength to strength. This growth has been seen in its acceptance by the developer community and in the interest shown in it by the lay community, as well as in its technical ability.

It is particularly interesting to note the contrast between the hype that has, admittedly, surrounded Java and the hype that surrounded Windows 95. Microsoft spent a (not so) small fortune convincing everybody and their granny that they needed to get Windows 95 (even if they didn't have an appropriate computer!). Indeed, in Japan it was reported that people who did not even own a computer were actually buying Windows 95. In contrast, when Sun released Java to an unsuspecting world at the beginning of 1995, they are reported to have doubled the Java marketing department from one person to two people. Thus it was actually the developer community that latched onto this new language and its potential. Obviously every company that markets a Java product is now pushing that product and its abilities through the hype barrier. However, this is as a response to the interest and expectations of developers. This is possibly a unique situation!

The growth in the development of Java applications has been astounding. In 1997, over 1000 applications were reported to have been released in the USA that were written in Java. Meanwhile, in the UK the demand for Java developers far outstripped the actual supply. This resulted in contractors being offered incentives to retrain in Java so that agencies could meet this demand.

1.2 A Brief History of Java

Java was originally the language developed to support a larger project intended to develop "smart" consumer electronics devices (such as TV-top control boxes). The members of this project (codenamed Green) did not wish to use C or C++ due to technical difficulties with those languages (not least, problems associated with portability and the construction of high-integrity software). Like many people before them they decided that they could do better. It is interesting to note that those involved in this development had a diverse range of backgrounds that not only included experience with C and C++, but also languages such as Lisp, the P-System, Pascal and Smalltalk. They therefore brought a unique perspective to the whole enterprise, in particular familiarity with languages that did not require explicit memory management, which compiled to byte code and which ran on virtual machines.

August 1991 can be treated as the birth of this new language, as it was at this time that a basic set of classes and a compiler were made available (internally to the Green project). This new language was known as Oak. The derivation of the name Oak is now lost in the mists of (Java) prehistory, and a number of stories have grown up about its derivation. For example, one rumour has it that the language was named after the tree outside the team leader's office.

By the end of 1993, it became clear that the perceived market for the results of the Green project just wasn't there. Sun therefore decided to drop the project and disband the team. However, in mid-1993, the first Mosaic browser was released, and interest in the Internet, and in particular the World-Wide Web, was growing. A number of the original project team felt that although the hardware element of the Green project might not be useful, the software language they had developed might well be perfect for the Web. They managed to convince Sun that it would be worth funding the software part of the project for a further year, and Sun pumped $5 million into the software development during 1994.

In mid-1994, Oak was used to build a new Web browser, which went on to be called HotJava. This illustrated the potential of the language by allowing animated (rather than static) Web pages. This was the catalyst that really started things for the language. As the language was designed to be portable, secure and small, and to operate in real time, it was ideally suited to the sort of environment that the Web imposed.

During this period Oak was renamed Java. This was, apparently, because Oak was already the name of a programming language; however, it may also be because Oak was not a particularly exciting name, whereas Java conjures up the right images.

In early 1995 Java was launched on an unsuspecting public at the first Java Day. Its popularity has not just risen due to interest in the Web. It draws inspiration from many different programming languages. Indeed, there is very little new in Java. However, the resulting language is more than the sum of its parts. It supports concurrency, exceptions, dynamic linking of new code, interface definitions, automatic memory management, ordinary procedural statements, a built-in make-like facility, cross-platform GUI facilities, compilation to byte codes, platform independence and strong typing. It is also worth noting that it is an excellent object-oriented programming language in its own right. It is already becoming clear that Java will be far more influential as a language for building applications, which may well be web-based, than merely as a language for animating pictures on a Web page!

1.3 The Three Stages of Java

Java has already undergone three stages in its evolution. These have been its junior, adolescent and adult periods. They represent the facilities provided by the language and thus its ability to construct robust real-world enterprise-oriented systems. These three stages are considered below.

1.3.1 Stage 1: Web Page Programming Language

This was the initial stage in Java's evolution (and covers version 1.0 of the Java Developers' Kit – JDK). It was quite a small language containing only 200 or so classes. It provided basic graphical user interface facilities, rudimentary event handling and no database access, but was a compact safe language. Many of the classes supported either graphical components or provided basic data storage facilities. The language could be used to make Web pages come alive. It could also be used as a "personal programming" language. That is, it could be used to write small programs for an individual's personal use, but was not really suitable for large system development. This did not stop Java from being used in this way, and a number of successful systems were built. However, there were few intrinsic features that directly supported such development. Sun saw the potential of this market and knew it could do better.

1.3.2 Stage 2: Application Development Language

By Easter 1997 Sun released JDK 1.1. This was a major upgrade of the Java language. Not only did it include very many new classes (now well over 500) it also incorporated many language enhancements. For example:

- Reflection was added to the language. This allowed access to the internal definition of a class. This was particularly useful for tool developers.
- Delegation event model. This was a new, and far more powerful, event-handling model. It was used both in the GUI and in JavaBeans.
- JavaBeans were introduced. This is the Java software component model.
- Serialization of objects was made available. This was a facility embedded within the virtual machine which allowed objects (as opposed to ASCII text or numeric data) to be saved to a file. These objects could then be reloaded at a later date.
- The JDBC database interface was provided. This allowed access to very many database systems. This opened Java up as a client–server development environment.
- The Remote Method Interface was added. This allows objects executing in one virtual machine to directly call methods on an object in a different virtual machine.
- Signed applets. These allow applets to move outside the Java "sandbox" if the user trusts the supplier of the applet. This provides greater flexibility to the applet developer.

Other subtler, but equally significant, changes were made to many classes. In JDK 1.1 all classes[1] conformed to the JavaBeans naming conventions for accessing variables. For example, to set a value name a `set` method would be used, while to

---

1 Actually this should say "almost all". For example, to obtain the size of a vector you do not use `getSize()`, you use `size()`!

access a value a `get` method was used. This made the process of remembering the very many methods available easier.

At this stage Java was well suited to the construction of real-world systems. It was a relatively simple matter to implement a Java program that accessed a database, retrieved some information and presented that information graphically or in table form to a user. It also allowed the straightforward construction of distributed applications using RMI. These programs could be run as standalone applications or as applets. However, the actual GUI interfaces were quite basic. For example, it was not possible to place a graphic on a button, or to provide tool tips over a button. In addition there were no data-aware tables that could be used to directly display information obtained from a database. Third-party tools could be obtained to provide such facilities, but they were not part of Java. Again Sun would rise to the challenge.

1.3.3 Stage 3: Enterprise Development Language

During 1998 Sun released JDK 1.2. This was yet another major upgrade to the language. It contained many features that pushed Java from a simple application development language to an enterprise development language. That is, not only could relatively simple standalone systems be written, but also systems could now be implemented which integrate Java with business application middleware and back-end applications. As such, Java could be integrated with legacy systems (potentially written in non-object-oriented languages such as Cobol) via the Java IDL (an interface to CORBA-compliant object request broker ORBs).

In addition, the Java Foundation Classes (JFC) are included in JDK 1.2. These are a major extension to the basic AWT and also provide new facilities designed to simplify the construction of real-world applications. The JFC adopts the classic model–view–controller architecture for building user interfaces. It provides more sophisticated graphical components (such as buttons with graphics, tool tips and toolbars) and support for data-aware components (such as tables).

Many other classes have also been improved. In some cases these provide improved performance, while in others they represent an extension of the facilities previously available. For example, the basic data structure classes have been extensively revised and extended. There is now a much easier way of enumerating over all the elements of a collection, as well as a new set of classes which provide for operations such as sorting and ordering.

The JDK 1.2 is thus Java at its best, as a mature development language. However, it does not stop there, as extensions to the basic JDK are planned. The new Enterprise JavaBeans are components oriented towards client applications (as opposed to the original JavaBeans that were used to construct visual applications). Enterprise JavaBeans were intended to insulate business application developers fully from the complexity of the enterprise infrastructure. Associated with the Enterprise JavaBeans are a suite of Enterprise APIs that deliver a comprehensive set of Java interfaces to existing platforms and protocols (see Figure 1.1). These include:

- Java IDL: the Java IDL compiler that maps IDL to Java. It also includes a Java ORB and IIOP support. This will allow Java to be easily and simply integrated with CORBA-compliant ORBs.

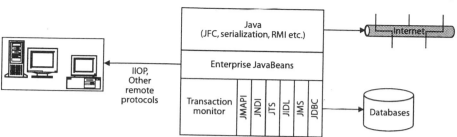

Figure 1.1 The Enterprise JavaBeans architecture.

- JTS: the Java Transaction Service, a low-level API which allows access to ORBs Object Transaction Services. It will enable developers to write Java code that interfaces with a variety of transaction processing infrastructures.
- JNDI: this is the Java Naming Directory Interface, which simplifies the process of accessing an enterprise naming and directory service. This API also includes an SPI (Directory Service Provider Interface) enabling service providers to connect and develop cooperative operations between various implementations.
- JMAPI will provide a uniform model for representing networked resources.
- JMS: the Java Message Service API will provide a Java API for message-based enterprise communication, such as publish and subscribe for smart communication between objects.

There will of course be subsequent releases of Java. However, it is likely that it is this period that will be noted as the point at which Java "came of age".

1.4 The Java Application Platform

The Java application platform is actually much more than just the language. It is a scalable environment that not only makes it easy to develop applications, but also to manage and deploy them. This platform is only really starting to emerge. It consists of client, middle and server tiers. It allows organizations to combine the Web's universal access and deployment with their own mission-critical business processes. However, to deliver applications like these online corporations must re-engineer their architectures to support this multiple tier structure.

In this multiple tier architecture (Figure 1.2), a user must first access a thin client. This thin client typically provides the basic GUI. It may be an applet running within a Web browser or it may be a standalone Java application. Of course, if the organization is to take full advantage of the possibilities offered by the Web, it needs to be an applet.

The applet then communicates directly with the application servlets (or business logic) using high-speed protocols. These servlets exist in the form of the components running in the middle tier.

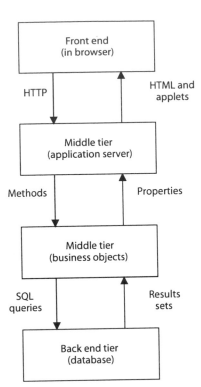

Figure 1.2 Multi-tier architecture.

The middle tier of this architecture implements the business logic of the application. It may be implemented in Java or it may be a legacy system etc. Indeed, the middle tier may actually be a number of tiers, providing various functions. However, for simplicity we shall continue to refer to this business logic as the middle tier. The middle tier in turn accesses the back-end components, for example a database. This may be done via JDBC-based methods or via existing servers.

It is interesting to note that Java is actually migrating its way right down into the databases themselves. It is beginning to appear as the stored procedure language in back-end DBMSs. This allows data-intensive procedures to be written in Java and executed inside the DBMS. Vendors such as Sybase, IBM, Tandem and Oracle are all working with JavaSoft and the ANSI SQL standards committee (and the JSQL consortium) to develop standards for running Java in a database.

With the advent of such a powerful application platform the potential has now been truly realized to enable organizations to fully reap the full benefits of portable, scalable and Internet-deployable applications.

1.5 Case Studies

To give an idea of the range of systems currently being developed within Java we present four recent case studies. These systems have been documented publicly and are therefore well known. They also represent a broad spectrum of the variety of systems currently being developed using the Java platform.

1.5.1 Bell Sygma

Bell Sygma, a subsidiary of Bell Canada, operates the National Circuit View (NCV) System. This system details information on the millions of voice and data circuits maintained by Canada's telecommunications companies. It provides users with a unified picture of Canada's telecommunication circuits. As such it is a powerful tool in the efficient management of services.

The NCV database has been made available to users all over Canada via the Internet and the Java platform. The system employs a three-tier architecture. The back end is the legacy data itself, stored in an Oracle database. The front end consists of any computing platform with a JDK 1.1-enabled browser running Java applets. These applets perform the presentation and data entry functions. The core of the system is the middle application tier. It is in this middle tier that the business logic is defined. It thus handles the circuit view system logic; it also handles security, user administration, event management, load balancing etc. It is also implemented in 100% pure Java. The systems architecture is illustrated in Figure 1.3.

Bell Sygma themselves have identified a number of advantages to this system. These include:

● Scalability (via distributed applications employing JavaBeans)
● Portability (as the Java elements of the system are 100% pure Java and any JDBC-compliant database can be used)
● Low-cost administration (it is easy and simple to distribute the application – you tell the user the URL)
● Usability (it is possible to produce a sophisticated graphical user interface for the system over the Web)
● Rapid deployment (it has been claimed that implementing in Java is faster than implementing in C or C++, and Bell Sygma's experience appears to bear this out)

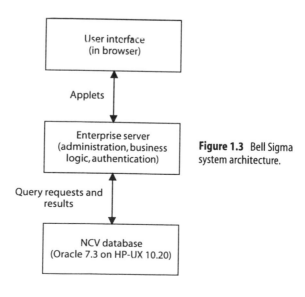

Figure 1.3 Bell Sigma system architecture.

In addition, Bell Sygma has found that the provision of the NCV system over the Web has opened up an important source of new revenue as more users subscribe to the system.

1.5.2 United States Postal Service

The United States Postal Service (USPS) allows bulk users to obtain discounts based on weight, quantity and preparation of their mailings. Postal customers (mailers) affix postage or deposit funds in advance and then fill out and submit detailed postage statement forms with each mailing.

Until late 1996, USPS customers had to type or print their information on a double-sided form and then calculate the total mailing cost based on the correct discount rates. Many of these forms arrived at the USPS incomplete or incorrect. This delayed the customers' mail shipments.

In an attempt to ease the situation the USPS provided the Postage Statement application. This application is a 100% pure Java application that can be downloaded onto a customer's computer. It calculates the costs of mailings for a customer. It includes a calculation engine, error-checking features and an "intelligent" form-filling interface (based on the original paper forms). It then automatically creates the required documentation for small-to-medium size USPS bulk mail customers.

By writing its application in 100% pure Java (JDK 1.0), the USPS was able to produce an application which would execute on any platform for which a Java Virtual Machine had been written. It is thus possible for the Postage Statement application to run on a diverse range of machines and operating systems, including PC, Macintosh, Amiga and Unix boxes without the need to recompile. Thus users do not need to know which version is the correct one for them, simplifying the distribution process. In turn, the Java Virtual Machine is also distributed to customers (although they have to download the correct one for their platform).

The actual application is comprised of individual Java applets that provide specific functionality. This approach has been adopted in order to maintain a manageable memory footprint (about 1.5 megabytes) on the customer's desktop. Current development of the system aims to provide an "intelligent" wizard to simplify the form-filling procedure still further.

It is interesting to note that this type of use of Java takes advantage of its cross-platform abilities. That is, it is not the fact that it can be accessed over the Internet (any executable can be downloaded in this way) that makes Java so good for the USPS, it is that fact that the "write once, run anywhere" nature of the language greatly simplified the development of the software.

1.5.3 American Information Systems

American Information Systems (AIS) has developed a sophisticated conferencing system, featuring online messaging and graphics, for use on the World-Wide Web. This system is known as Forum. It relies on Java-based clients and a server application. Java was selected as the appropriate implementation medium because of its portability, graphical user interface-building facilities and real-time interactivity. Forum provides three primary functional modules:

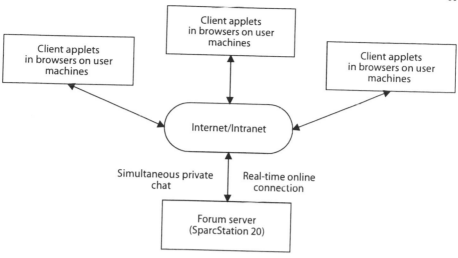

Figure 1.4 Forum multi-platform conferencing system.

- *Real-time chat* In the main viewing area of the user interface, all text messages are posted instantly and identified by author. To the side, a window displays all of the people in the chat room. During the session a participant may select anyone in the list and commence a simultaneous private conversation while staying in the main chat area.
- *Threaded discussion group* In this window, information on different topics (known as threads) can be posted in a bulletin board-style interface.
- *Advanced whiteboard capability* A prototype version of the whiteboard permits entry of text, graphics, line drawings and free-form diagrams that greatly enhance the quality and content of a multi-party communication.

The architecture of Forum is illustrated in Figure 1.4. The back-end server is a multi-threaded Java application that handles all communications. In turn, each client is implemented as an applet within a browser which maintains a permanent connection to the server. Each time a user requests or provides information, it is sent to the central server (over the Internet). The server then sends any response back to the user (broadcasting any general information to all users). Each of the clients may be on a PC, Macintosh or a Unix box displaying Forum within a Java-enabled Web browser.

Future work on this project aims to improve the graphics handling capabilities of the system, including streaming video. Also under consideration is a downloadable whiteboard that would continue to be active between sessions.

1.5.4 The First Tennessee Bank

The First Tennessee bank has deployed a Web-based banking system implemented using Java. This system includes an online ATM (automated teller machine), a bill payer/checking function, a balance and statement facility and a financial advisor (this system is similar to the system developed by the First Direct bank in the UK).

The system relies on Java's security mechanism as well as a multi-tiered architecture to provide secure access to the customers' accounts. Once again the benefits identified by the bank were portability, ease of distribution and, in this case, security.

1.6 Issues for Java Developers

Java has emerged as a significant force in today's software industry. However, the construction of any program in Java (whether a Web-based system or not) raises a number of issues for any developer. These include:

- how best to develop reusable components
- what influence JavaBeans have on component development
- what the best way to access a database system from Java is

Other issues are concerned with the performance of a Java system, as well as which of the user interface classes to use (for example, whether to use the original AWT classes or the newer JFC classes).

Testing is another major issue for developers. This is because the testing of a program written using an object-oriented language such as Java is different in nature to testing one written using a procedural language.

These are very real issues for Java developers. This book addresses these issues, providing key techniques for overcoming the problems encountered and tips on how to develop better applications.

2   *Inheritance and Reuse*

2.1 Introduction

Object orientation has been held up as the "silver bullet" of the software crisis by Brad Cox. However, many projects are still running over budget and behind time, and fail to provide the level of functionality originally specified. Of these projects many are now based on solid object-oriented philosophies. Indeed, it is not uncommon to hear the cry that "we used an object-oriented programming approach and still had problems". Such problems are of course, due to a variety of mistakes made by project leaders, designers and developers. In some cases it can be attributed to lack or training, lack of experience or poor methods.

A cry that can often be heard is that "all object orientation provides is a more suitable framework for software development". This may well be true, but inheritance is supposed to allow increased levels of reuse, providing improved quality and speed of development. However, this major claimed benefit of object orientation often fails to materialize, even when appropriate training has been provided and suitable design methods applied. Indeed, many project managers will state that they have achieved very low levels of reuse through inheritance. Why is this? In turn, many non-object-oriented languages (such as Ada83 and Modula 2) place a great deal of emphasis on compositional reuse. However, in many texts on object-oriented systems little or no mention is made of compositional reuse. This is possibly indicative of the emphasis placed on inheritance within the object-oriented community rather than the potential contribution of the two approaches.

This chapter considers whether inheritance in object-oriented programming languages (such as Java) is actually harmful or not. It explores what impact inheritance actually has on issues such as code reuse in practice, rather than in theory. This is based partly on the extensive experience of the authors in developing object-oriented systems. Given this exploration, an analysis is performed of why inheritance can, in some situations, be detrimental to reuse. From this, guidance can be provided to ensure that developers are able to maximize the benefits of inheritance while minimizing the drawbacks that can occur.

The remainder of this chapter is structured in the following manner. Section 2.2 considers what inheritance is and what the aims and benefits of inheritance are. Section 2.3 considers some of the potential drawbacks of inheritance if care is not taken with its application. Section 2.4 considers the balancing act that must be performed between inheritance, reuse and code dependency. Section 2.5 discusses compositional reuse (as opposed to reuse via inheritance) and how that is performed. It also considers its strengths and weaknesses. Section 2.6 considers approaches to promoting reuse within object-oriented systems. It does this by indicating that developers should try to minimize code dependency where appropriate by using compositional reuse, but should not try to duplicate code unnecessary and should use inheritance instead. Finally, Section 2.7 suggests that sophisticated tools support is required to maximize the use of inheritance and components in object-oriented systems.

2.2 Inheritance

2.2.1 What is Inheritance?

The *Dictionary of Object Technology* defines inheritance as:

> The definition of a derived class in terms of one or more base classes

That is, using inheritance it is possible to define one class as being like another class but with certain differences (e.g. extensions). For example, objects may have similar (but not identical) properties. One way of managing (classifying) such properties is to have a hierarchy of classes. A class inherits from its immediate parent class and from classes above the parent. The inheritance mechanism permits common characteristics of an object to be defined once but used in many places. Any change is thus localized.

If we define a concept *animal* and a concept *dog*, we do not have to specify all the things that a dog has in common with other animals. Instead, we inherit them by saying that dog is a *subclass* of animal. This feature is unique to object-oriented languages; it promotes (and it is claimed achieves) huge amounts of reuse. As is stated in the Fusion method book (Coleman *et al.*, 1994), it is "...widely viewed as the fundamental technique supporting reuse". This is backed up by Brad Cox, who says that "few programmers realize just how natural it can be to program using inheritance" in *Object-oriented Programming: An Evolutionary Approach.*

However, Brad Cox has also stated that "Inheritance is not a necessary feature of an object-oriented language, but it is certainly an extremely desirable one". This is an interesting statement, as inheritance is often taken as the defining characteristic of object-oriented systems. If we consider the four elements often presented as comprising object-orientation (encapsulation, polymorphism, abstraction and inheritance), various procedural programming languages can be seen to provide them all except inheritance. We briefly summarize each of these concepts below:

- *Encapsulation* This is the process of hiding all the details of an object that do not contribute to its essential characteristics. Essentially, it means that what is inside the class is hidden; only the external interfaces can be seen by other objects. The user of an object should never need to look inside the box!

- *Inheritance* Objects may have similar (but not identical) properties. One way of managing (classifying) such properties is to have a hierarchy of of classes. A class inherits from its immediate parent class and from classes above the parent (see the hierarchy in Figure 1.4).

- *Abstraction* An abstraction denotes the essential characteristics of an object that distinguish it from all other kinds of object and thus provides crisply defined conceptual boundaries, relative to the perspective of the viewer. That is, it states how a particular object differs from all others.

- *Polymorphism* This is the ability to send the same message to different instances which appear to perform the same function. However, the way in which the message is handled depends on the class of which the instance is an example.

Inheritance can be seen to be the unique element of object-oriented systems. It could be argued that without inheritance a programming language is at best object-based (e.g. Ada83) and not object-oriented.

48

2.2.2 Aims and Benefits of Inheritance

Inheritance in object-oriented programming languages supports reuse of existing code within new applications. It does this by allowing a developer to define new code in terms of existing code and new extensions. This is a different kind of code reuse from that found in non-object-oriented languages. For example, in Ada83 a programmer can reuse the TextIO package for input and output, but cannot extend any elements of the TextIO package directly in order to provide a new type of input–output operator. In contrast, the Java IO package provides a variety of classes designed for input and output (such as `FileReader`, `FileWriter`, `InputStream` and `OutputStream`). If developers wish to create an `InputStream` which only reads numbers then they can create a new subclass of `InputStream` with the appropriate `read()` methods defined. The remainder of the `InputStream` class's code would then be reused (without the need to copy any source code).

One significant benefit of this is the increased productivity such reuse can provide. A developer need only define the ways in which a new class differs from an existing class to have a fully functioning class. In addition, if a bug is found in the code inherited from the parent class, then it need only be corrected in the parent class. All of the parent class's subclasses receive the corrected version of the code automatically. This therefore reduces the maintenance effort required.

In Java, inheritance also provides for the implementation of, and typing for, polymorphism. This is a significant aspect of any object-oriented language. Polymorphism is a powerful concept that can greatly enhance the productivity of a developer by increasing the reusability of the code produced.

In languages such as Java, inheritance also allows for "enrichment of type". That is, given the type `Component` a developer can subclass `Component` and provide classes which are still of type `Component` but which provide additional functionality. Indeed, this is the way in which user interfaces are developed within Java, relying on the fact that the `add()` methods expect a type of graphic component to be provided. In some cases a component such as a `Button` may be presented, while in others a whole `Panel` might be provided. Again, this supports the implementation of polymorphism.

It can also be argued that inheritance can improve the reliability of code. This is because code that has been implemented and tested in a superclass has a greater chance of remaining valid in its subclasses than code that has effectively been cut and pasted from one source file to another.

It is important to note that this form of reuse is internal to the encapsulation wall normally present around an object[1]. This means that a subclass has access to the internals of a parent class in a way that objects are never allowed. This ability to break the encapsulation "bubble" can be useful as it provides for more flexible reuse than would otherwise be possible. In a component-oriented reuse model, a developer only gets access to the whole component, while via inheritance the developer can pick and choose which parts of the parent class are reused and which parts are rewritten.

2.2.3 The Role of Inheritance

The role of a subclass is to modify the behaviour of its parents. In particular this modification should refine the class in one or more of the following ways:

- *Changes to the external protocol*, the set of messages to which the instances of the class respond.
- *Changes in the implementation of the methods*, the way in which the calls are handled.
- Additional behaviour that references inherited behaviour.

If a subclass does not provide one or more of the above then it is not an appropriate subclass of the parent class. The exceptions to these rules are the subclasses of the class `Object`. This is because `Object` is the root class of all classes in Java. As you must create a new class by subclassing it from an existing class, you can subclass from `Object` when there is no other appropriate class.

2.3 Drawbacks of Inheritance

Inheritance is not without its own set of drawbacks. If inheritance is applied without due consideration problems can arise. In some situations it can:

- reduce the comprehensibility of code
- make maintenance harder
- make further development harder
- reduce reliability of code
- may reduce overall reuse!

---

1 In Java it is possible to introduce encapsulation to inheritance. For example, any variable or method, whether static or not, can be specified as private. This means that not only can no object outside the class access these variables or methods, but also that access to these variables and methods is denied to subclasses.

● access modifiers can affect potential for reuse

It is useful to consider what can cause these drawbacks. There are, in fact, a number of factors that come into play. In the following subsections we will consider each of the issues raised above and what factors contribute to their existence.

2.3.1 Reduces Comprehensibility of Code

The Yo-Yo Problem

Inheritance can pose a problem for a programmer trying to follow the execution of a system by tracing methods and method execution. This problem is known as the *yo-yo* problem (Figure 2.1) because, every time the system encounters a message which is sent to "this" (the current object), it must start searching from the current class. This may result in a developer jumping up and down the class hierarchy while trying to trace the system's execution path.

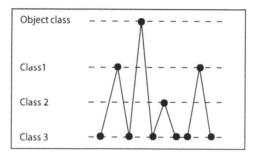

Figure 2.1 The yo-yo problem.

The problem occurs because the developer knows that the execution search starts in the current instance's class, even if the method that sends the message is defined in a superclass of the current class. In Figure 2.1, the programmer starts the search in Class3, but finds the method definition in Class1; however, this method sends a message to "this" which means that the programmer must restart the search in Class3. This time, the method definition is found in the class Object etc. Even with the browsing tools provided, this can still be a tedious and confusing process (particularly for those new to object orientation).

Code Dependency

Inheritance can potentially increase the dependencies between the code in the parent class and the code in all subclasses. This means that in order to evaluate a potential change to some class *X* it is necessary to consider the impact of this change in multiple subclasses. If care is not taken then it can be a simple matter to damage the operation of apparently unrelated parts of a system, while fixing an apparently simple "bug" in another part of a system.

This situation is exacerbated, as it may also be necessary to understand the implementation of the superclass when implementing a subclass. This can be because the implementation of the superclass:

- assumes a particular behaviour from one method or combination of methods
- assumes that subclasses will provide a specific behaviour in one or more methods
- relies on the state of one or more variables which become critical to the operation of the class
- contains an overly complex structure in order to allow for inheritance

The emergence of an overly complex structure can arise when a developer has tried to force the potential for reuse among a set of classes. This commonly occurs when a developer has implemented a number of classes, has then noticed that they have some common features and has tried to create a suitable parent class to represent the commonalities. In these situations the developer is familiar with the structure of the subclasses and can design around them. They can therefore develop a parent class that is flexible enough to allow each subclass to provide the specialization required. However, for any other developer examining this parent class at a later date it may be far from obvious what the purpose of the class is or why the class is structured in the way that it is.

The result is that, in order to extend the parent class, the developer must gain a detailed understanding of the structure of the parent class (this may be because instance variables are referenced, internal methods executed or internal states relied upon).

From analyzing many class hierarchies in which this has occurred, it is possible to identify the programming cliques which most often given rise to inappropriate dependencies between subclasses and parent classes. These can be described as:

- subclasses which override methods used by other inherited methods (which are thus reliant on the behaviour and results of the overridden methods)
- subclasses which extend inherited methods using super. In this way, other inherited methods rely on the extended method. In addition the subclass must ensure that its use of the super method as well as its extensions are appropriate
- subclassed behaviour that relies on or changes the state of key instance variables

2.3.2 Makes Maintenance Harder

One of the aims presented above for inheritance was the minimization of the maintenance task. However, in reality, if care is not taken, inheritance can make the maintenance task harder. This is due to a number of contributory factors. Firstly, it may be necessary to examine two or more classes (in the class hierarchy) in order to determine the behaviour of a single class. This situation is made worse by the need to do the same for any objects referenced by the class under consideration.

In part this is because subclasses can break the encapsulation "bubble". It is therefore not sufficient merely to consider the published protocol of a class; it is also necessary to consider its implementation. Within the encapsulation bubble the subclass may have made any number of changes.

The maintenance issue is also affected by the yo-yo problem and to the code dependency issue already discussed. Thus the maintenance issues can be summarized as:

- the need to analyze two or more classes to determine behaviour of an object
- the need to understand the implementation of descendant classes before maintenance of a superclass
- the need to analyze any superclass(es) before modification of a subclass

2.3.3 Makes Further Development Harder

In many situations it is necessary to understand how a parent class was intended to be extended before it is possible to define a subclass. However, as the implementation of one class is now reliant on an understanding of the implementation of a parent class the resultant code may be opaque, leading to inherent maintenance and possible reliability problems. In addition, methods which may be available to the subclass may reference variables which are hidden from that subclass (for example private instance variables in Java). If a subclass attempts to define an instance variable with the same name as the hidden variable, the behaviour of the resulting subclass may be erroneous. This is because any inherited methods will execute within the scope of the superclass. They will therefore access and update the hidden variable. However, any methods defined in the subclass will access and update the local variable. Therefore the same object may possess code accessing instance variables with the same name but apparently different values (because they are in fact different variables). This can have a detrimental effect on comprehensibility, maintenance, reliability etc.

2.3.4 Reduces Reliability of Code

Identifying appropriate tests for a subclass can be problematic. However, for a long time there was a feeling that object-oriented systems required less testing than systems constructed with traditional procedural languages. This was because there was the impression that if a superclass has been thoroughly tested then anything inherited by a subclass from that superclass did not need testing. However, this is misleading, because in defining a new subclass a user has changed the context within which the inherited methods will execute. For example, inherited methods may call a method that has been overridden. This means that the correct operation of the inherited methods can no longer be assumed. Even if the inherited methods do not reference any methods defined in the subclass, the subclass may modify a variable inherited from the superclass. The inherited methods may then be found to be dependent on the state of this variable. Again, their correct operation cannot be assumed.

The problem is that each new subclass may not require any retesting and may very well function acceptably, but a developer is relying on a continuing hypothesis. Of course, this hypothesis may have held many times before, but there is no guarantee that it will hold in the future. Interestingly, the same problem also occurs with Ada generics. In this case, each instantiation of the generic package may work as intended, but equally it may fail (see Chapters 11 and 12 for further discussion of this issue).

In the worst possible case the whole of the subclass (the inherited methods and those defined in the subclass) may need to be tested. However, in most systems this would not be acceptable, as the full set of methods may run into the hundreds (and the developer may not have the knowledge or experience to be able to identify an appropriate set of tests for all methods). In practice, only a small percentage of the inherited methods actually need to be tested. The provision of regression tests with a class can be used to simplify the task of testing these methods. Of course, the identification of the appropriate methods is still fraught with difficulty

2.3.5 May Reduce Reuse

Due to reduced comprehensibility and increased code dependency resulting in increased difficulty of maintenance, developers may be led away from reusing existing classes. This can result in developers:

- reimplementing the wheel
- cutting and pasting required code
- failing to analyze superclass(es) sufficiently

This is a particularly important problem facing inheritance, as this negates one of the prime motivations for having inheritance in the first place.

2.3.6 Access Modifier Effects on Reuse

Java provides the developer with the ability to specify in detail what is available outside a class and to whom it is available. Thus a developer can hide almost everything within the encapsulation bubble (something must be available to other classes, otherwise the class is useless) or make everything available. In between, the developer can specify at the level of variables or methods how much access is allowed. Table 2.1 indicates the access modifiers available in Java.

Table 2.1 Access modifiers and their effects

Class	public	Available in all packages
	default	Available only in the current package
	final	Cannot subclass this class
Variables and methods	public	Available in all packages
	default	Visible only in current package
	protected	Visible in current package and in subclasses in other packages
	private	Visible only in current class
Variables	final	Once set the value cannot be changed
Methods	final	Cannot be overridden in subclasses

As this table shows, attempting to control the access that other objects have to an object's methods or data can also affect the access that subclasses can have to the parent's methods or data. For example, if a developer specifies an instance variable as being private, then subclasses of that class cannot access that instance variable either. Indeed, deciding to use the default access modifier for methods and variables has the subtle effect of allowing subclasses in the same package access but not subclasses in another package. Having such a fine level of control can be a two-edged sword. If it is used appropriately, parent classes can make sure that subclasses only have access to the appropriate aspects of the parent class. However, as some books on Java recommend that any implementation that uses more than the public and private modifiers it either very good or very bad, some developers may be put off using the most appropriate access modifiers.

A further subtlety is that if any methods are defined as final they cannot be overridden. This may initially seem a very good thing. as a subclass cannot harm the inherited functionality (at least in theory – see later in this chapter). However, it is very difficult to envisage all the ways within which a class may be used. For example, if we wished to create a specialized version of the class Vector in order to change the way in which the vector was printed we would need to be able to override the toString() method. However, this method is specified as final (as follows):

```
public final synchronized String toString()
```

This means that it is not possible to sensibly subclass Vector. We must therefore define a completely different class and start from scratch just in order to change the way the vector prints itself as a string! Not only does this result in a great deal of extra effort, it also means that our code will either have to be written for our own version of the Vector class or the default version, but not both (unless we rely on using parameters of type Object which are then cast to the appropriate class when we need to apply any operators).

We have therefore generated the following guidelines. These guidelines are intended to promote the greatest chance of reuse while maximizing the encapsulation of the executing objects.

1. Use protected as your default access modifier for methods – this leaves the way open for future extension within subclasses without letting all and sundry have access to the class.

2. Only use private when a method really is private to the current class. That is, there is no possible situation in which you can envisage anyone ever needing to access the method.

3. If you make an instance variable private, provide accessor methods that have protected access. This will allow subclasses to read and write the data without actually access the data item directly. This is actually a good technique to use in general, as it also buffers your code from changes to the way you are holding your data.

4. Never merely use the default access modifier. It means that anything within the same package can access the current element but that no subclass can access it (a dubious state of affairs). It also suggests that you haven't thought about what access requirements there are.

5. Always question whether you really need to make a method final. If you feel that it is essential to fix a particular method's implementation, then provide convenience methods that use the final method. These methods can then be overridden by a subclass if necessary (without affecting the core functionality). For example:

```
public void setPoint(Point p) {
  setPoint(p.x, p.y);
}

public final void setPoint(int x, int y) {
  ...
}
```

You should then use Javadoc documentation to make it clear what you expect a subclass to do – at least then others will know what you were thinking and can ignore you if they wish.

6. Use final to set critical variables so that subclasses can't change them. However, think carefully before you do this in order that you clearly understand why no subclass must ever change the variable's value.

2.4 Balancing Inheritance and Reuse

The discussion in Section 2.3 can be seen as quite damning for inheritance. However, this is not the end of the story, as it is important to consider what conclusions can be drawn from the results of this discussion. There are at least four possible conclusions. These are summarized below:

- Inheritance *is* extremely useful (consider classes such as Frame or Panel in Java).
- Reuse *promises* higher levels of productivity, maintainability and reliability.
- Inappropriate reuse by extension (inheritance) can have detrimental effects on productivity, maintenance and reliability.
- But inheritance is not the only form of reuse.

From this is it clear that inheritance has an important part to play in the development of complex software systems. However, it is also clear that it needs to be used with greater caution than is often the case. In particular, object-oriented systems developers need to pay greater attention to the other primary form of reuse – compositional reuse. One way to distinguish between inheritance-based reuse and compositional reuse is that inheritance-based reuse is primarily developer-oriented reuse ("developer" here refers to those developing the functionality of the elements which might comprise a component). In contrast, compositional reuse is user-oriented reuse (that is, no further development of the component takes place). The next section discusses compositional reuse in more detail. In particular it selects the JavaBeans component model as an example of a compositional approach (JavaBeans are discussed in more detail in Chapters 5 and 6).

2.5 Compositional Reuse

Compositional reuse relates to the "combination of independent components into larger units". These components can be combined in different ways as long as their interfaces are compatible (in a similar manner to a jigsaw puzzle). In general, no further development of the components themselves takes place. Instead, a user of a component is allowed to customize the behaviour of a component via predefined properties or methods. JavaBeans exemplify this approach.

JavaBeans is an architecture for the definition and reuse of software components. The goal of JavaBeans is to define a *software component model* for Java. Examples of beans might be spreadsheets, database interfaces, word processors and graphical components, such as buttons or business graphs. It would then be possible to add such beans to your application without the need to refine the beans. It is intended that most beans should be reusable software components that can be manipulated visually in some sort of builder tool. Thus, in the case of the word processor bean we might select it from a menu and drop it onto an application, positioning its visual representation (i.e. the text-writing area) as required. The key issue here is that you should be able to use a bean without ever having to examine its implementation, subclass it or otherwise modify its code. That is not to say that you cannot change it in some way. However, it is expected that the user of a bean does so via its published interface (by changing property values, sending it events or by directly calling methods).

2.5.1 Strengths of Compositional Reuse

Software components designed for compositional reuse have great potential. They can greatly improve a developer's productivity and the reliability of software. For example, in Java, Buttons, TextAreas and Labels are all beans. They can therefore be used within a `Panel` or a `Frame` without further development. Similarly a `Panel` or `Frame` uses a component (a layout manager) to determine how graphical elements are displayed. Thus a graphical user interface can be developed without the need to subclass any existing classes. Instead, all a developer must do it to write the code which will glue all of these elements together. If a tool builder such as the Bean Box is used, even this task can be simplified.

An important question to ask is how is this achieved? Why is it that compositional reuse can be so effective? Part of the answer to this is "low software dependency". That is, when a developer uses a software component the only dependency between the developer's code and the component is the component's interface. The developer cannot get inside the encapsulation bubble. There is therefore no dependency between the code and the internals of the component (i.e. its structure or internal state). This is very significant. It means that as long as the interface to the component remains the same, the user will experience no problems with the component even if its internals are completely altered.

2.5.2 Weaknesses of Compositional Reuse

If compositional reuse is so good, what is the point in having or using inheritance? Herein lies the problem – compositional reuse allows the developer to use a component, but it is a take it or leave it approach. That is, you get what you see and are not allowed to change the internals of the component. In contrast, inheritance allows for far greater flexibility (and of course it is this very flexibility which can be a problem). Without inheritance but with compositional reuse a developer would end up with a great deal of duplication of code in situations where they require similar (but slightly different) behaviour from that which already exists. Of course, by duplicating code they would be introducing "implicit" dependency between the duplicated code. That is, if a bug was found in one piece of code that had been duplicated, it would be necessary to find all the duplicated pieces of code and to correct that bug individually in each. Not only is this a tedious task, it is also prone to error. For example, one of the duplicates may be missed, or a mistake may be made in one of the duplicates, which introduces a completely different bug into that duplicate. Of course these were specifically the issues which originally led to the introduction of inheritance. It is therefore clear that what is required is a combination of both inheritance-oriented and compositional reuse. However, as was indicated in the introduction, compositional reuse is paid scant attention in much of the object-oriented community (although this may well be changing due to initiatives such as JavaBeans). The next section considers the implications of the results of this and the last section.

2.6 Promoting Reuse in Object-Oriented Systems

There is a (natural) tension between code minimization and code dependency. Developers tend to want to minimize the amount of code being written and the dependency between elements of that code. The less code that has to be written, the greater the productivity (at least theoretically). In turn, the lower the dependency, the easier it will be to maintain, test and reuse. It is important to note that implicit dependency exists even when a "cut and paste" approach has been used to reuse code (and that such an approach certainly does not lead to code minimization).

From Section 2.5 it is clear that an approach based purely on compositional reuse is insufficient. Equally, it is clear that problems can arise with inheritance due to misuse. It is therefore proposed that the judicious use of composition and inheritance has the potential to provide the greatest benefit. That is the strengths of the two approaches should be combined to minimize the weaknesses.

In order to achieve the above aim, guidance needs to be provided on when to use each approach. Some very general guidelines which embody the main philosophy are relatively easy to identify:

● Use composition and inheritance to promote reuse. Do not focus on one approach while ignoring the other.

- Attempt to minimize dependency between subclass and superclass (don't access variables etc.). Consider the interface that a class presents to potential subclasses. Try to force more encapsulation during inheritance. For example, make key instance variables only accessible by accessor methods (i.e. by using the private modifier in Java).

- Design for "pluggable" extension rather than "method" extension, as exemplified by Frame and Panel in Java. The way in which they lay out the graphical components they display is dependent on the behaviour of a layout manager. This is an object that is plugged into the frame or panel. It alters the way that they operate without the need to subclass.

- Complete structural, but non-functional, classes are ideal for inheritance (e.g. Applet, Canvas, and Object). These are classes that provide the entire infrastructure required for a specific type of behaviour. The user then specifies their own extensions which fit into (but do not alter) that infrastructure. For example, the Applet class provides a powerful (and complex to implement) framework within which developers can implement their own functionality (e.g. the methods init(), start(), stop(), suspend()) without the developers ever needing to know how that framework is implemented (or how to modify it). The Canvas class is similar: cf. the paint() method.

- Complete functional classes are ideal for composition (e.g. Button, ObjectOutputStream). These are classes that require no extension in order to provide a fully functional object. For example, to obtain a labelled button in Java requires only the instantiation of the Button object with the appropriate string passed to its constructor as a parameter. In terms of JavaBeans these classes are Beans.

- Provide structural classes with gaps for functional classes (e.g. the class Thread with Runnables in Java). This approach orients the design process around the creation of structural classes (which are intended for inheritance) which may be customized by functional classes (which are presented to them as objects with which they cooperate). This reduces dependency and is intended to increase reuse.

2.7 Tool Support

Tool support is required to simplify the processes required by the approach described in Section 2.6. These tools need to operate within the scope of inheritance. Thus a basic text editor is insufficient. It cannot provide the required views of class hierarchies, method and variable inheritance etc. Some editors are available which do take some of the issues associated with inheritance into account. However, many systems separate out the compositional aspect of development from the inheritance aspect. Indeed many of them only consider composition for the graphical user interface and ignore its use in the main body of software development.

Development environments, however, need to go further. No system allows the developer to consider limited scope views (such as private, protected, default or public views in Java). Thus there is no easy way to consider what interface is being presented to a subclass nor to examine how a superclass is expected to be viewed. Indeed, there is no easy way of incorporating information intended to direct those considering extension into the source code (other than keywords such as `abstract` in Java or method calls such as `subclassResponsibility()` in Smalltalk or via comments).

Development environments need to go further if they are to take the provision of support for inheritance seriously. They need to provide tools that will allow the visualization and analysis of interaction paths. Such tools would simplify the process of tracking method execution and variable access in object-oriented programs.

Finally, such environments also need to support the identification and execution of regression tests. These would allow a developer to ensure that the behaviour of a subclass matches the behaviour of a parent class even if its implementation differs.

2.8 Conclusions

In this chapter we have considered the benefits and drawbacks of inheritance within an object-oriented programming language. We have challenged the general perception that inheritance is by its very nature always good and have considered when it should and should not be used. We have reassessed compositional reuse and made the case that it is as important, in an object-oriented language, as inheritance in order to achieve the maximum possible reuse. We can therefore provide a summary of our findings that can be used as a set of guiding principles for object-oriented development:

● Avoid code dependency except on published protocol.
● For structural inheritance direct extension is fine.
● For functional inheritance compositional extension is to be encouraged.
● Avoid inheritance if it is going to damage code cohesion.

Thus the final conclusion of this chapter is that inheritance can be harmful to a development project's long-term chances of success if it is misused. In such situations inheritance can be harmful. However, in general it is essential for the power it provides to object-oriented systems.

2.9 Further Reading

Coleman D., Arnold P., Bodoff S., Dollin C., Gilchrist H., Hayes F. and Jeremes P. (1994) *Object-Oriented Development: The Fusion Method*, Prentice Hall International, Englewood Cliffs NJ.

Cox B.J. (1986) *Object-Oriented Programming: An Evolutionary Approach*, Addison-Wesley, Reading.

Cox B.J. (1990) There *is* a silver bullet. *BYTE*; October, 209–218.

Firesmith D.G. and Eykholt E. M. (1995) *Dictionary of Object Technology*, SIGS Books, New York.

3 *Persistent Storage of Objects*

3.1 Introduction

Prior to serialization it was necessary to explicitly write each data element in an object. You then needed to reconstruct the data into objects when you read the file, which meant that you had to indicate that certain data were associated with certain objects and that certain objects were related. This was a very time-consuming and error-prone task. Also, unless you used existing file formats, it was unlikely that your data could be used by other applications.

This was the only way of creating persistent data in the JDK versions 1.0 and 1.0.2. However, in JDK version 1.1 serialization was introduced to the java.io package to simplify this operation.

Serialization allows you to store objects directly to a file in a compact and encoded form. You do not need to convert the objects or reconstruct them when you load them back in. In addition, everyone else who uses serialization can read and write your files. This is useful not only for portability but also for sharing objects.

This chapter first reviews the concept of streams in Java. It then introduces serialization in more detail and describes the classes and interfaces used in serialization before considering how to control what is and is not serialized. The final section considers the drawbacks of serialization.

3.2 Streams

3.2.1 What Is a Stream?

Streams are objects that serve as sources or sinks of data. At first this concept can seem a bit strange. The easiest way to think of a stream is as a conduit of data flowing from or into a pool.

There are a number of types of stream in the Java system, and each has a wide range of uses. These stream classes are all defined within the java.io package. The abstract InputStream and OutputStream classes are the root classes of the stream hierarchies. Below them are stream classes for reading, writing, accessing external files, etc. and for reading and writing objects. Figure 3.1 illustrates the classes most closely associated with the serialization process.

A stream may be input-only (InputStream) or output-only (OutputStream); it may be specialized for handling files (FileInputStream);

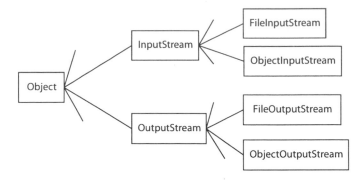

Figure 3.1 Stream classes relevant to serialization.

it may be an internal stream (which acts as a source or sink for data internal to the system) or an external stream (which is the source or sink for data external to the system).

Streams are often combined to provide the required functionality (as illustrated in Figure 3.2). For example, a stream designed to access a file may be wrapped inside a stream designed to write objects. Thus an object-writing stream is generic and can be used with different types of streams in different situations (for example, in this way objects can be sent across a network using socket to socket communications and the socket input and output streams).

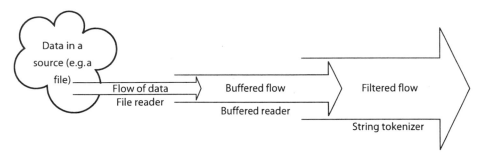

Figure 3.2 Building streams.

3.3 Serialization

The name "serialization" comes from situations that can arise when saving more than one related object to a file. For example, in Figure 3.3 four objects are related by references and are held by another object Family (within a vector).

If, when we want to save the whole family to file, we merely save each object independently, we also have to save copies of the objects that they reference. In the above example, we would end up with multiple copies of Phoebe. If we can determine whether an object has already been saved to disk, then we can record a

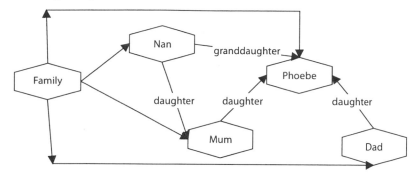

Figure 3.3 Related objects.

reference to the previously saved object, so that the original structure can be restored at a later date. This reference is referred to as a serial number (hence the name "serialization").

Each object is stored to disk with its own serial number. If an object has been stored, then a reference to its serial number is included with any object that references it. For example, if Phoebe has serial number 1 then, when Mum, Dad or Nan are saved, they merely record that they reference the object with serial number 1.

3.3.1 Saving Objects

To save an object to file, you use the ObjectOutputStream class. However, an ObjectOutputStream must use a stream, such as FileOutputStream, to actually write data into a file:

```
String filename = "data.ser";
try {
  FileOutputStream file = new
  FileOutputStream(filename);
  ObjectOutputStream output - new
    ObjectOutputStream(file);
  output.writeObject(family);
  output.close();
} catch (IOException e) {
  e.printStackTrace();
}
```

The above code results in all the objects held by family being saved to the file data.ser using serialization. This illustrates that, although you may find the concepts confusing, serialization is easy to work with.

There are a number of points you should note about the above code. Firstly the file that the objects were saved to was called "<filename>.ser". This follows a convention adopted by the JavaBeans component model which looks for a ".ser" file in order to find a serialized bean (see later in this book).

Secondly the `writeObject()` method throws the `IOException` in the event of an error.

3.3.2 Reading Objects

To read objects that have been saved to file back into an application, you need to use the `ObjectInputStream` class. You must also use a more primitive input stream, such as `FileInputStream`, to read the actual (byte) data from the file:

```
String filename = "data.ser";
try {
  FileInputStream file = new
    FileInputStream(filename);
  ObjectInputStream input = new
    ObjectInputStream(file);
  Family family = (Family) input.readObject();
  input.close();
} catch (Exception e) {
  e.printStackTrace();
}
```

Notice that you must cast the object retrieved by the `readObject()` method into the appropriate class (just as with vectors and hash tables). In addition the `readObject()` method can also throw both the `IOException` and the `ClassNotFoundException` (hence the use of the superclass `Exception`).

3.4 The Object Input/Output Streams

As you can see from the above example, two streams are provided which understand how to read and write objects to a file. These are the ObjectOutputStream and the `ObjectInputStream`. These objects are illustrated in Figure 3.4. This figure shows that the two streams implement the `ObjectOutput` and `ObjectInput` interfaces. These interfaces define the methods required to perform the reading and writing of objects.

3.4.1 The Serializable Interface

Any class whose objects are to be used as part of a serializable application must implement the `Serializable` interface (if you examine the documentation supplied with Java you can see that many classes, such as `Vector`, implement the `Serializable` interface) or the `java.io.Externalizable` interface. The serialization interface acts as a flag indicating that a class can be serialized. It means that user-defined classes can also be serialized without the need to define any new methods. All the instance variables of an object are written onto the output stream automatically. When the object is restored the instance variable information is automatically restored.

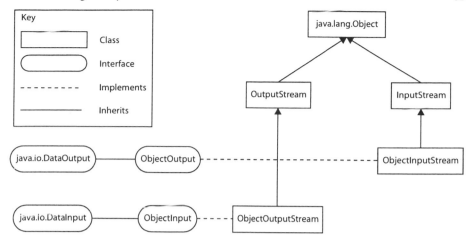

Figure 3.4 The object serialization classes and interfaces.

If you try to save an object that is not serializable, then the NotSerializable-Exception is thrown. This exception identifies the class of the non-serializable object.

Notice that the way in which you define how an object can be saved to a file or restored from a file is classic object orientation. That is, the object itself defines how it should be saved to a file. The parameter to writeObject is the stream that is linked to the file, but the stream does not decide what is written.

3.4.2 The Externalizable Interface

Object serialization actually uses the Serializable and Externalizable interfaces. Each object to be stored is first tested for the Externalizable interface. If the object supports it, then the externalize methods are used. If the object does not support Externalizable and does implement the Serializable interface the object is saved using ObjectOutputStream. The input process is similar.

From the above you can see that the JVM attempts to perform the externalize methods before the serialize methods. Why is this? It is because Externalization allows a class to specify the methods to be used to write the object's contents to a stream and to read them back. The Externalizable interface's writeExternal() and readExternal() methods are implemented by a class to give the class complete control over the format and contents of the stream for an object and its supertypes. These methods must explicitly coordinate with the supertype to save its state. Note that by default the Serializable interface requires no work from the developer, whereas Externalize requires the developer to determine how the object should be saved. This is summarized in Table 3.1.

Table 3.1

void writeExternal(ObjectOutput out) **throws** IOException	The object implements the writeExternal method to save its contents by calling the methods of DataOutput for its primitive values or calling the writeObject method of ObjectOutput for objects, strings and arrays.
void readExternal(ObjectInput in) **throws** IOException, ClassNotFoundException	The object implements the readExternal method to restore its contents by calling the methods of DataInput for primitive types and readObject for objects, strings and arrays. The readExternal method must read the values in the same sequence and with the same types as were written by writeExternal.

3.5 Controlling What is and is not Saved

In some situations, you may not need to save the information held in all the instance variables, but only those which cannot be regenerated or which should not be saved. This minimizes the size of the serialized objects on disk as well as improving the performance of the serialization process.

To indicate to the JVM that an instance variable should not be serialized, use the keyword transient. This indicates that the associated file should not be saved. For example, a variable holding a thread, or a reference to a file stream etc. would not normally be stored. In addition, under JDK 1.1, images are not serializable. Thus a class containing such variables might have the following definition:

```
public class Test implements java.io.Serializable {
    public transient Image icon;
    private transient Thread thread;
    ...
}
```

If the image to be held in the icon field is packaged within a JAR file along with the serialized file, then both files can be distributed together, thus allowing the serialized object to access the icon from the JAR file when it is restored. This could be done by defining the readObject() method to perform this restoration once the object has been read from an objectInputStream.

Note that class variables (static variables) are not written as they are part of the class rather than the object.

3.6 Version control

When an object is serialized, information is recorded with that object about the class from which it was created. This enables the correct class to be used to restore the object. This information contains both the fully qualified name of the class and a version number. It is this version number which determines whether a serialized object can be deserialized or not. The version number is generated from the signature of the class – this means that it changes if any variables or methods are added, deleted or renamed. A check is made to see that the serialized object has the same version number as the current version of the class. If it does not have the same version number an exception is thrown.

If you have made small changes to a class which should not affect whether an object can be deserialized or not, then you can get around the version number problem by supplying your own. The version number of a class is actually stored in a constant long field named `serialVersionUID`. In your own classes you can redefine this field. This means that it is not automatically updated. Thus if you serialize an object, you can decide whether it should be possible to deserialize it or not (by leaving the `serialVersionUID` constant the same or not). You can use the `serialver` program that is provided with the JDK to generate an initial value for this constant. This number can then be left unchanged until you decide to change it (when you rerun the `serialver` program to get a new number). The `serialver` program can either be given a class name on the command line or a graphical interface can be displayed using the `-show` option. This interface is illustrated in Figure 3.5.

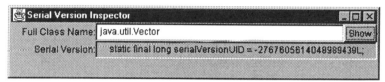

Figure 3.5 The `serialver` GUI.

3.7 Problems with Serialization

Although serialization makes the process of saving an object to a file much easier, it is not without its own drawbacks. Firstly, the serialization files produced can be quite large. This means that it would be conceivable that a developer might use up more disk space than expected.

Secondly, there is no concept of version control for serialized files. If you needed to preserve older versions of data files, it would be relatively easy to read in the wrong version of a serialization file and find that you had lost the latest changes made to an object's data. The only way round this is to provide your own code to check that you are reading the most recently saved data.

Thirdly, serialization also has problems with different versions of classes. As described in the previous section it is possible to handle minor changes in a class. However, major changes can result in a serialized file failing to be loaded. You would therefore find it impossible to access the serialized objects. This is a significant issue for developers, as it implies that transitional code must be written to read the data in the old format and then convert it into the new format before saving a new serialization file.

Fourthly, the actual serialization process is quite slow. If performance is important in your application then you may need to implement your own form of serialization.

This is a particularly good option if the structures you are saving are not complex and primarily hold basic data types (as opposed to reference types such as `Strings` or other objects). For example, let us assume that you have a vector of objects, each of which contains an employee's details in the form of strings, integers and doubles. You would be better off using the `DataOutputStream` and `DataInputStream` to save the basic data types explicitly than using serialization. This is because you do not need the cross-reference benefits of serialization. To do this you would provide some form of delimiter between each record to indicate that a new instance of employee was now required.

Finally, serialization does not allow you to alter the way that a parent class saves its data. For example, you can't subclass `TextArea` to make it save a filename rather than the whole text it displays.

3.8 Further Reading

The reader might also want to look at the following for further details on streams and serialization:

Hunt J. (1998) *Java and Object Orientation: An Introduction.* Springer-Verlag, Berlin (ISBN 3-540-76201-9).

3.9 Online References

The Object Serialization specification:

```
http://www.javasoft.com/products/jdk/1.1/docs/guide/
    serialization
```

4   *Introductory JavaBeans*

4.1 Introduction

Many developers have now heard of JavaBeans, but may be unsure of what they are or how to write a JavaBean (often referred to just as a Bean). JavaBeans are a relatively new addition to Java, having been added to the JDK 1.1 release, with additional facilities being available in the Beans Development Kit (BDK). The goal of JavaBeans is to define a *software component model* for Java. Examples of Beans might be spreadsheets, database interfaces, word processors, and graphical components such as buttons and business graphs.

4.2 Overview

4.2.1 Background

JavaBeans is an architecture for the definition and reuse of software components. The Beans Development Kit 1.0 (BDK) was first released in February 1997. The BDK contains the JavaBeans API sources (the class files are already part of the JDK 1.1), the BeanBox test container (see Figure 4.1) and some examples, as well as tutorial documentation.

What is the JavaBeans architecture for? The primary aim is to allow developers and third-party software vendors to supply reusable components in a simple to use and unified manner. For example, you might wish to incorporate a simple word processor into your application. This word processor might be available as a "Bean". It would then be possible to add this bean to your application without the need to refine the bean. Sun intends that most beans should be reusable software components that can be manipulated visually in some sort of builder tool. Thus in the case of the word processor bean we might select it from a menu and drop it onto an application, positioning its visual representation (i.e. the text writing area) as required. Of course, the facilities provided by a builder tool will depend both on the types of components being used and on the intended use of the builder. Examples of such builders, cited in the JavaBeans 1.0 API Specification, include visual application builders, GUI layout builders, Web page builders or even server application builders. Indeed, sometimes the "builder tool" may simply be an editor (such as a word processor) that is including some beans as part of a larger document. Beans can also

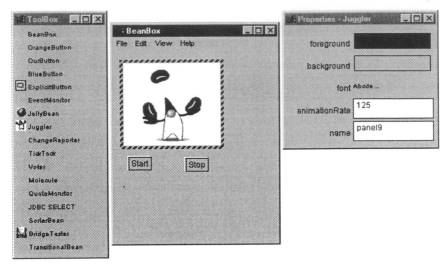

Figure 4.1 The demonstration BeanBox application builder.

be used directly by programmers (as indeed anyone who uses any of the components in the AWT is already doing).

JavaBeans may vary in size and complexity. Simple ones may be buttons or sliders; other more complex examples may be database viewers, word processors or spreadsheets. In practice, it is expected that bean components will be small to medium-sized controls.

4.2.2 JavaBeans and Other Component Models

The Beans component model is intended to be similar in concept to Visual Basic's VBX and OCX component architecture and to Delphi's VCL, but without the need to follow a rigid programming model. This makes the generation of Beans simpler, but at times requires the developer to define numerous methods for accessing Bean properties.

Beans differ from class libraries in that they are intended for visual manipulation and customization via their properties, while class libraries are intended for programmatic use and for customization either through instantiation or via subclassing[1]. Thus the new JDBC API is not a bean, although a database access bean for Sybase would make sense. Such a bean would be built on top of the JDBC.

It is intended that JavaBeans should be architecture-neutral, except where they interface to the underlying platform. Thus beans which handle buttons will be independent of the platform on which they will be run. In contrast, a bridge between JavaBeans and Microsoft's ActiveX has already been released (March 1997) and allows a bean to use the ActiveX facilities. Other bridges are being actively developed to Live Connect (for Netscape Navigator) and Live Object (née OpenDoc). The

---

1   Having said this, it is still possible to use beans programmatically.

intention is that a given bean will use the appropriate platform features but will present a common face to the Java environment. This has actually been one of the largest constraints on the development of JavaBeans and has taken a lot of work to ensure that the various bean APIs can be cleanly converted to these component models.

4.2.3 The JavaBeans Package

One of the most confusing elements in JavaBeans is the use of the `java.beans` package and the BDK. The `java.beans` package provides classes and interfaces which are primarily useful to programmers who are developing tools to support and manipulate Beans. The BDK provides additional support for the JavaBeans API, a test Bean development tool (the "BeanBox"), sample Beans and documentation. In the example presented here, you will notice that no classes or interfaces provided by either are used. The only element used is the BeanBox tool. This is because any class can be treated as a Bean as long as certain naming conventions are followed, although any Bean which will have a visual representation must be a descendent of `java.awt.Component`.

4.2.4 Bean Terminology

A JavaBean is defined via its interface. That is, the interface presented by the bean to its user indicates what it can be made to do. There are three things that comprise this interface: its properties, its events and its methods. These are discussed briefly below.

Properties

These are the attributes of the Bean that can be modified by anything outside of the Bean. They are often referred to as being "published" or "exposed" by the Bean. In effect, a property is an instance variable which is accessed via specific get and set methods. For example, if we have a property `max`, then we would have:

- an instance variable `max`
- `setMax(-)` and `getMax()` methods

Note that the methods which are used to set and get the value of the property `max` have the format `set<property name>` and `get<property name>`, with the name of the variable starting with an upper-case letter. This will be discussed again in more detail later.

Events

These are used to allow one component to communicate with another component. The event model used is the Delegation Event model introduced to the AWT (Abstract Window Toolkit) in JDK 1.1.

Methods

These are public methods (which do not match the naming conventions used in Beans) that can be used to directly request some service of a Bean.

4.2.5 Creating a Bean

To make a class into a Bean you must follow a set of naming conventions for the methods you define. For example, if you define a property such as name (an instance variable holding a single value) then this is indicated by defining set and get methods (e.g. setName and getName). If a Bean needs to provide additional information or does not follow the conventions then a class implementing the BeanInfo interface must be provided. This works in association with the Bean to provide information on its properties, methods and events.

One of the JavaBeans model's greatest strengths is thus its simplicity. In addition, because all that distinguishes a Bean from any other Java class is the naming convention, there is no overhead associated with defining creating, defining or using a bean.

In the remainder of this chapter we shall review the concept of JavaBeans and then consider how a JavaBean is defined. We shall also examine one particular example of how a simple Java class can be converted into a Bean and used within the Bean Box developer tool.

4.3 Implementing JavaBeans

A JavaBean is an ordinary Java class that must describe itself following a specified naming convention or by using a BeanInfo object. This approach is in contrast with some other component models (notably Delphi's VCL), in which components must inherit from a particular ancestor class. This can be a point of confusion for JavaBean developers, who might well attempt to find the Bean class upon which to construct their bean. Instead, any class in Java can be converted into a Bean as long as it follows the Bean's naming conventions or defines a BeanInfo object (the only caveat being that if a Bean has a visual appearance which can be used within a tool builder then the Bean must inherit from the AWT class Component or one of its subclasses). The great advantage of this approach is its simplicity. The disadvantage is that, at first sight, it appears that there is nothing concrete that defines a Bean.

4.3.1 The Beans Conventions

There are a number of conventions associated with JavaBeans. The first of these was mentioned above and relates to properties; others relate to methods, events, the BeanInfo object and the visual representation of beans.

Properties

To make a private instance variable into a published property, "getter" and "setter" methods should be provided which match the following format:

```
public <property type> get<Property Name> ( )
public void set<Property Name> (<property type>
    parameter)
```

In addition, if the property is a boolean property then by convention this is indicated by `is` followed by the (capitalized) property name, for example:

```
public boolean is<property name>
```

Note that a `get<Property Name>` method should not be defined for a boolean property. The BeanBox does not enforce this; however, other bean builders might well. It is therefore best to define `is<Property Name>` and `set<Property Name>` methods.

Properties can be read, read/write or write-only and can be simple, indexed, bound or constrained.

- *Simple* This is the most basic property type and contains a single value. Changes in this value are independent of changes in any other property.
- *Bound* A bound property is one in which a change to the property results in a notification of that change being sent to some other Bean.
- *Constrained* A constrained property is one in which an attempt to change the property's value is validated by another Bean. The second Bean may reject the change if it is not acceptable.
- *Indexed* An indexed Bean property is one that supports a range of values instead of a single value (that is, the property is actually an array of values).

Simple properties will be used in the example presented below. The other types will be discussed later in this chapter.

Events

Event handling in JavaBeans is exactly the same as event handling in JDK 1.1 of the AWT. This means that there are sources of events (in this case Beans), event objects and receivers of events (or listeners). However, JavaBeans imposes some restrictions on the naming of the methods associated with events in order that it can determine the events fired by a Bean automatically. This means that the methods used to register event listeners must match the following conventions:

```
public void add<listener type> (<listener type>
    listener)
public void remove<listener type> (<listener type>
    listener)
```

Note that this assumes that an appropriate listener interface has been defined.

Beans also introduce a number of special events used by the bean mechanism.

Methods

Any method that is public, but does not match the above conventions, is assumed to be one that is published by the Bean. Such methods may be called by other beans directly or any Java code. Note that a limitation in the BeanBox used in the example presented below is that it can only deal with public methods that return no value and take no parameters.

Graphical Beans

Any Bean which has a visual representation that can be used within a Bean development tool, such as the BeanBox, must subclass the `Component` class or one of its subclasses. This will allow it to use the standard AWT facilities to draw itself in the development tool. Note that non-visual beans can also be used in tools such as the BeanBox; it is just that they have no appearance.

`BeanInfo` Object Naming

The `BeanInfo` object, if present, is expected to have a name that matches the following convention:

```
<BeanName>BeanInfo
```

4.3.2 The `BeanInfo` Object

A `BeanInfo` object is an object that provides information on a bean's properties and methods. This can be used if the developer of a bean has not followed the Bean's naming conventions or if the developer wishes to provide additional information (for example an icon). `BeanInfo` is actually an interface that must be implemented by any class providing Bean information. A convenience class, `SimpleBeanInfo`, defined in the JavaBeans API, provides default implementations for the methods specified in the `BeanInfo` interface.

In many situations the JavaBeans API can quite adequately provide all the information required by a builder tool. However, there a number of situations in which a `BeanInfo` object can be useful in addition to those mentioned above. The following list indicates situations in which a `BeanInfo` object can be useful:

- to limit a long list of properties or events
- to provide an icon for the builder tool's component pallette
- to provide descriptive, human-readable and possibly localized names for properties
- to provide facilities for novice and expert operating modes
- to specify "wizard" style customizers for beans
- to map a class to the bean naming conventions

The `BeanInfo` interface and the `SimpleBeanInfo` class are discussed in more detail later in the next chapter.

4.4 Defining JavaBeans

Listings 4.1 and 4.2 define two simple JavaBeans that are intended to work together. These beans act as a simple counter and a simple alarm. The counter bean increments a visual counter whenever its increment method is called. When the counter reaches its maximum value, if the rollover property is false then an event is triggered. This event is sent to a bean (or any Java class) which implements the `MaxValueListener` interface. When the alarm bean receives this event it is triggered (which results in its visual representation changing from a white square to a red square).

Listing 4.1 *The `Counter.java` file.*

```
package counter;
import java.awt.*; import java.util.*;
public class Counter extends java.awt.Panel {
  private long count;
  private Vector listeners = new Vector();
  private Label label;
  private long initialValue, maxValue;
  private boolean rollOver = true;

  public Counter() {
    setBackground(Color.blue);
    setForeground(Color.white);
    label = new Label(" ");
    add(label);
  }
  public Dimension getMinimumSize() {
    return new Dimension(30, 30);}
  public void setInitialValue(long init) {
    initialValue = init;}
  public long getInitialValue () {
    return initialValue;}
  public void setMaxValue(long max) {maxValue = max;}
  public long getMaxValue () {return maxValue;}
  public void setRollOver(boolean state) {
    rollOver = state;}
  public boolean isRollOver () {return rollOver;}
  public synchronized void addMaxValueListener
    (MaxValueListener l){
    listeners.addElement(l);
  }
  public synchronized void removeMaxValueListener
    (MaxValueListener l) {
    listeners.removeElement(l);
```

```
  }
  public void reset() {count = initialValue;}
  public void increment() {
    if (count != maxValue) {
      count++;
      label.setText(count + "");
    }
    else {
      if (isRollOver())
        reset();
      else {
        MaxValueEvent mve = new MaxValueEvent(this);
        synchronized (this) {
          MaxValueListener ml;
          Enumeration e = listeners.elements();
          while (e.hasMoreElements()) {
            ml = (MaxValueListener)e.nextElement();
            ml.maxValueReached(mve);
          }
        }
      }
    }
  }
}
```

Listing 4.2 The Alarm.java file.

```
package counter;
import java.awt.*;
public class Alarm extends Canvas implements
    MaxValueListener {
  private boolean triggered = false;
  public Alarm () {
    setBackground(Color.white);
  }
  public boolean isTriggered() {return triggered;}
  public void setTriggered(boolean state)
    {triggered = state;}
  public Dimension getMinimumSiźe() {return new
    Dimension(30, 30);}
  public void maxValueReached(MaxValueEvent e) {
    setTriggered(true);
    setBackground(Color.red);
  }
}
```

The Counter Bean

The first Bean, the Counter Bean, counts up to a maximum value and then either resets its counter or notifies an Alarm Bean (via an event), depending on the state of the property rollOver, that it has reached its maximum value.

The initial value and the maximum values for the counter are also properties. Notice that the naming conventions imposed by JavaBeans have been followed and thus no BeanInfo object is required. We therefore know that the private instance variables count, listeners and label are not properties, as they do not have the necessary get or set methods.

The increment() method in the Counter Bean is used to increment the value of the count instance variable. If this reaches the maxValue, the counter is either reset or the MaxValueEvent is generated. This is then sent to any objects that have registered themselves as listeners of this event with the Counter.

The class Counter actually extends the class Panel in order that the Bean can have a visual representation in a "BeanBox"-style tool. Panel has been used so that not only can we set the background and foreground colours (features inherited from Component via Panel), we can also add other components to the display (in this case a simple text label object). This text label will be used to display the current value of the count variable (via the setText() method). We have also defined a getMinimumSize() method which will be used by a development tool to determine the minimum size to allocate to the visual representation of the Bean. The Counter Bean is illustrated in Figure 4.2.

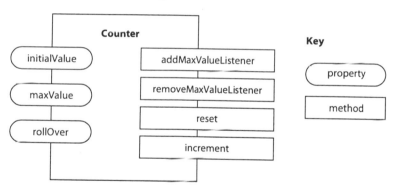

Figure 4.2 The Counter Bean.

The Alarm Bean

For the Alarm Bean we have subclassed Canvas, as we only need to display a coloured square in one of two colours, depending on whether it has been triggered or not. Triggered is a property which can either be set via the property tool editor or when the maxValueReached() method is executed. The result is that the box displayed by the Alarm bean is white when not triggered and red when triggered.

The *MaxValueEvent* and *MaxValueListener* classes

Two additional classes are defined in Listings 4.3 and 4.4. These classes are not Beans but are auxiliary classes used by the previous two beans. They define a simple event and an event listener interface. The event class, MaxValueEvent, defines the event which will be generated by the Counter Bean but caught by the Alarm Bean. It extends the java.util.EventObject class, which is the root class of all event classes.

Listing 4.3 *The MaxValueEvent.java file.*

```
package counter;
public class MaxValueEvent extends
java.util.EventObject {
  public MaxValueEvent(Object object) {
    super(object);
  }
}
```

Listing 4.4 *The MaxValueListener.java file.*

```
package counter;
public interface MaxValueListener
    extends java.util.EventListener {
  void maxValueReached(MaxValueEvent m);
}
```

In turn, the MaxValueListener defines an interface which specifies that any object registering itself as a MaxValueListener (a receiver of an event) must define the maxValueReached() method. For example, the Alarm Bean will act as just such a listener for the Counter Bean, and therefore it implements the maxValueReached() method (see Listing 4.4).

Finally, in order for the Alarm Bean to register as a listener with the Counter Bean, the Counter Bean must define the appropriate addMaxValueListener() and removeMaxValueListener() methods. These methods add or remove listeners from a vector (held in the instance variable listeners). As we want to ensure that no one tries to update the list of listeners while we are informing them of the occurrence of MaxValueEvent these methods must be synchronized, as must the part of the increment() method which calls the maxValueReached() method on each of the listeners.

Packaging the Beans

We are now in a position to package up the two beans (and auxiliary classes) so that they can be used by the BeanBox tool. The BeanBox tool expects beans to be placed in a JAR file within a directory called jars (beans can be loaded from other directories using the "load jar" option from the BeanBox file menu). A JAR file is a ZIP format archive file with an optional manifest file (JAR stands for Java archive file). For tools such as the BeanBox the manifest file is required, as it provides the BeanBox with information on which files are beans (see Listing 4.5). The statement `Java-Bean:` `<boolean>` is used to indicate whether the preceding class is a bean or not.

Listing 4.5 *The* `manifest.tmp` *file.*

```
Name: counter/MaxValueListener.class
Java-Bean: False

Name: counter/MaxValueEvent.class
Java-Bean: False

Name: counter/Counter.class
Java-Bean: True

Name: counter/Alarm.class
Java-Bean: True
```

Constructing the JAR file, and placing the JAR file in an appropriate directory, can be done manually or by using a make file. The actual jar tool can be used to construct a JAR file for the example classes described above using (note this assumes that the `*.class` files are held in a subdirectory called `counter`):

```
jar cvfm c:\bdk\jars\counter.jar manifest.tmp
    counter\*.class
```

The options specify that a new JAR file should be created and the `*.class` files added to it. The first parameter specifies where the JAR file should be placed, the second parameter specifies the name of the manifest file and the third parameter specifies where to look for the files to archive.

Using the Beans

The result of running the BeanBox tool, having created the JAR file, is illustrated in Figure 4.3. As you can see, the two beans have been added to the ToolBox menu. The BeanBox window itself demonstrates the functionality of the two beans. Each bean has been added to the window, the properties of the `Counter` bean have been set in the Property editor (e.g. the `maxValue` is 4 and the `rollOver` property is false). Note that the property editor is generated automatically by the BeanBox, with the properties displayed with the appropriate types. A third bean, a button bean, has been added and used to call the `increment()` method on the `Counter` bean. In turn, the `Counter` bean has been connected to the `Alarm` bean via the event `MaxValueEvent`. In the figure, the `Counter` has reached its maximum value and the event has been sent to the `Alarm` Bean, which has changed its colour to red (from its default white).

The relationships between the three beans are illustrated graphically in Figure 4.4.

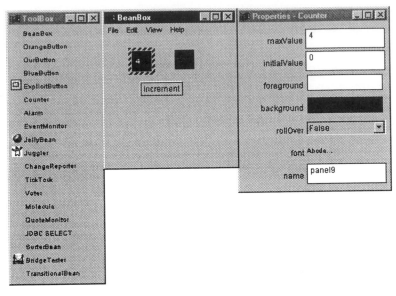

Figure 4.3 The BeanBox with the `Counter` and `Alarm` beans.

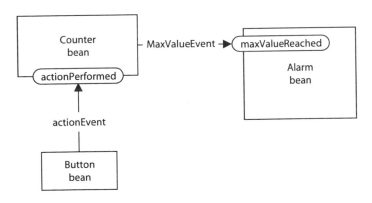

Figure 4.4 Bean relationships.

4.5 Using the BeanBox and Jar Files

The BeanBox tool provided as part of the BDK is only intended as an experimental environment. Indeed, Sun state that the BeanBox is provided as a tool to allow developers to test their beans. We have used it in this chapter as it is widely (and freely) available. However, it is very limited in what it can do and is certainly not a production-strength development editor. That is, you would not want to use it as the basis of your development. There are of course a wide variety of commercial development tools that support JavaBeans, including IBM's VisualAge for Java, Symantec's Visual Café, Borland's JBuilder and Sun's own Java Workshop. These tools are far superior to the BeanBox and should be used if you intend to develop serious Beans software.

4.6 Further Reading

The reader might also want to look at the following for issues relating to beans:

Hunt J. (1998) *Essential JavaBeans Fast*, Springer-Verlag, London.
Englander R. (1997) *Developing JavaBeans*. O'Reilly & Associates, Cambridge MA.
Brookshier D. (1997) *JavaBeans Developer's Reference*. New Riders Publishing.
Vanhelsuwe L. (1997) *Mastering JavaBeans*. Sybex, Soest, Netherlands.
Kassabgi G. (1998) *The Professional Developer's Guide to JavaBeans*. Que Corp., Carmel IN.

The reader might also like to look at the following book for information on the BDK:

DeSoto A. (1997) *Using the Beans Development Kit 1.0: A Tutorial*. JavaSoft, `http://splash.javasoft.com/beans/`.

For an introduction to events in Java see:

Hunt J. (1998) *Java and Object Orientation: An Introduction*. Springer-Verlag, Berlin.
Flanagan D. (1997) *Java in a Nutshell*. O'Reilly and Associates.

4.7 Online References

You can maintain contact with JavaBeans via a Web page relating to the JavaBeans project at:

`http://splash.javasoft.com/beans/`

5 *JavaBeans in Depth*

5.1 Introduction

The last chapter provided a brief introduction to JavaBeans. This chapter looks in more detail at a number of features of JavaBeans. In particular, it examines how a builder tool finds out about the properties, methods and events associated with a Bean. It then discusses the more complex property types "bound", "constrained" and "indexed". It then considers the construction of a BeanInfo object and the serialization of beans, as well as property editors and customizers. Finally, a critique of the whole JavaBeans approach is presented.

5.2 Introspection

Some component models require that a component's interface be explicitly defined via some interface definition language. However, JavaBeans merely requires the developer to follow a predefined set of naming conventions and "automagically" the builder tool is informed what properties are available, what methods can be called etc. How is this possible? It is actually achieved via a process known as introspection. The introspector allows a builder tool or a developer to examine the component at runtime to determine how it can interact with other components. The intention is that this minimizes the amount of extra work required by a Bean developer in order to make the Bean available for use by others.

So what is introspection? Put simply, it is the process which queries Beans and BeanInfo objects for the list of properties, methods, events etc. associated with the Bean. To do this, introspection uses reflection and the BeanInfo classes. Reflection is the means by which one class can obtain information about another class's fields, methods, constructors etc. By combining reflection with a rigid set of naming conventions it is relatively straightforward to determine a bean's details. For example, if a public method with the name setType() is found then there will be a property type etc.

Introspection is initiated by the getBeanInfo() method of the class Introspector (in the java.beans package). The introspector follows an elaborate plan for filling out what are called Descriptors that describe the properties, events and methods of a Bean. The plan operates in roughly two separate stages.

Firstly, the introspector locates any descriptor information that has been explicitly supplied by the developer through BeanInfo classes. These classes are identified by naming conventions. The introspector will identify a class called

*MyComponent*BeanInfo as the `BeanInfo` object for the Bean named *MyComponent*.

Secondly, the introspector uses various facilities of the core Reflection API to determine the names of all the methods in any given Bean class. It then applies the naming conventions to determine what properties the Bean has, the events to which it can listen and those that it can send. To learn more about the core Reflection API see the `java.lang.Class` class and the `java.lang.reflect` package.

Essentially, the process results in a fully filled in `BeanInfo` object (note that if no `BeanInfo` object has been supplied by the developer the introspector still creates a new one and fills in the details itself).

The actual steps involved are initiated when the `java.beans.Beans.instantiate()` method loads a Bean. Next a call is made to the method `getbeanInfo()` on the introspector class which looks for classes whose names look like *BeanName*BeanInfo. For example:

```
Counter bean = (Counter) Beans.instantiate
                              (classLoader, Counter);
Class beanClass = Class.forName("Counter");
BeanInfo beanInfo =
  Introspector.getBeanInfo(beanClass);
```

Note the second argument to the `instantiate` method could refer to a serialized file, a class or an applet, depending on how the Bean has been packaged. The `instantiate` method will first look for a file called `Counter.ser` and then for a file called `Counter.class`. The call to `getBeanInfo()` then initiates the introspection process.

A note of caution is necessary here. If you are using the BeanBox tool provided with BDK (up to and including April 1997) then you should be wary of using the `Beans.instantiate()` method to load serialized beans. At present it seems to raise problems with packages and `CLASSPATH`. This may be fixed in future releases of the BDK.

Finally, security applies to the introspection process just as it applies to other aspects of Java. The security manager always has control.

5.3 Property Data Types

Earlier in this chapter we said that there were four different types of Bean property: simple, indexed, bound or constrained. So far we have only looked at simple properties. In this section we shall look at the bound, constrained and indexed data types in more detail.

5.3.1 Bound Properties

A bound property possesses the same set of accessor and updator methods as a simple property (namely `set<Property name>` and `get<Property name>`)

plus event registration methods for objects which will respond to the PropertyChangeEvent. These objects must implement the Property-ChangeListener. This interface defines a single method propertyChange() (which takes the PropertyChangeEvent as an argument). When the bound properties value is altered each of the objects which has registered itself with the property as a property change listener is sent a property change event by calling its property change method.

To simplify this process the JavaBeans API provides a utility class called PropertyChangeSupport that makes the creation of a bound property easier. This class can maintain a list of objects interested in the bound property and can inform these objects of a change in the bound properties value. This is done using the add/removePropertyChangeListener methods and the firePropertyChange() method. For example, if we were to make the maxValue of the Counter class a bound property, then the code might be modified in the following manner:

```
public class Counter extends java.awt.Panel {
  private PropertyChangeSupport support = new
  PropertyChangeSupport(this);
  ...
  // Event listener registration methods
  public void    addPropertyChangeListener
                       (PropertyChangeListener l) {
    support.addPropertyChangeListener(l);
  }
  public void    removePropertyChangeListener
                       (PropertyChangeListener l)
  {
     support.removePropertyChangeListener(l);
  }
  ...
  public void setMaxValue(long max) {
    int oldMaxValue = maxValue;
    maxValue = max;
    support.firePropertyChange("maxValue",
        new Integer(oldMaxValue),
        new Integer(maxValue);
  }
  ...
}
```

Note that the firePropertyChange() method takes a string and two objects as parameters. We therefore need to wrap the basic int types held by oldMaxValue and maxValue in integer objects.

Now that the maxValue has been modified to represent a bound value we are in a position to link it to one or more beans that will be notified by a change in its value. In the BeanBox this is done from the Bind property option from the Edit menu.

5.3.2 Constrained Properties

With a constrained property a separate bean validates the changes made. This means that when a change is performed on a constrained property, a separate bean is informed of this change via the event-handling mechanism. This second bean either accepts the change or rejects it. The bean containing the constrained property is responsible for catching any exceptions raised (when the value is rejected) and reverting the property to its previous value. Thus the order in which things happen to a constrained property, within the set<Property name> method are very important. They must following this pattern:

- Save the current value of the property.
- Notify listeners of the new value.
- If no listener vetos the change (that is raises an exception) then change the value of the property.

Defining a constrained property is similar to defining a bound property in that you need to register beans that will listen for changes to the property. However it differs from bound properties in that the listeners may raise a PropertyVetoException. This indicates that the new value has been rejected. This means that the set<Property name> method throws the PropertyVetoException. For example:

```
public void setMaxSize(int s) throws
    PropertyVetoException{...}
```

The beans that listen for the changes in the constrained property must implement the VetoableChangeListener interface. This interface defines a single method vetoablePropertyChange() which takes a single argument PropertyChangeEvent. This method should check the new value of the property and either raise a PropetyVetoException or return null.

To simplify the maintenance and notification of the listeners the JavaBeans API provides a utility class called VetoableChangeSupport. This class defines methods for adding and removing listeners (addVetoableChangeListener() and removeVetoableChangeListener) and a notification method fireVetoableChange(). As with the bound property, the notification method takes a string (indicating the property that has changed) and two objects that represent the old value of the property and the proposed new value of the property:

```
public void fireVetoableChange(String propetyName,
    Object oldValue, Object newValue) {...}
```

As an example consider the following partial class definition for a constrained property maxSize:

```
public class Square extends Canvas {
    // Set up veto support
    private VetoableChangeSupport vetos = new
        VetoableChangeSupport(this);
```

```
  ...
  // Registration methods for vetos
  public void
    addVetoableChangeListener(VetoableChangeListener l)
  {
    vetos.addVetoableChangeListener(l);
  }
  public void
  removeVetoableChangeListener(VetoableChangeListener
  l) {
      vetos.removeVetoableChangeListener(l);
  }
  public void setMaxSize(int size) throws
      PropertyVetoException {
    vetos.fireVetoableChange("maxSize",
                                new Integer(maxSize),
                                new Integer(size));
    // no veto - otherwise would have raised exception
    maxSize = size;
    repaint();
  }
}
```

Note that the above approach assumes that the component that requested the bean to change its value (e.g. a property sheet) should be the one to deal with the exception.

An interesting question is what should happen if the bean holding the property wishes to validate changes to that property. It would certainly be possible to register the bean as the listener for its own property. However, this would not be very efficient. It would therefore be better to check the value of the property within the set<Property name> method directly.

As an example of a vetoer, consider the following source code for a SquareVetoer class:

```
public class SquareVetoer implements
    VetoableChangeListener {
  public void vetoableChange(PropertyChangeEvent e)
      throws PropertyVetoException {
    int newValue =
      ((Integer)e.getNewValue()).intValue();
    if (newValue > 100) throw new
      PropertyVetoException("Size > 100", e);
  }
}
```

As you can see from the code, the vetoer implements the VetoableChange-Listener. Within the vetoableChange() method it checks the new size and raises a PropertyVetoException if the new size is more than 100.

5.3.3 Indexed Properties

In some situations a property actually needs to hold a number of values. In JavaBeans this is achieved using an indexed property which holds an array of values or objects. With an indexed property it is possible to read or write a single element of the array or the whole array. This means that an indexed property is defined by the following get and set methods:

```
public PropertyElement get<Property name>(int index) {
   ... }
public PropertyElement[] get<Property name>() { ... }
```

and

```
public void set<Property name> (int index,
   PropertyElement element) { ... }
public void set<Property name>(PropertyElement []
   elements) { ... }
```

It is important to note the differences between the two different types of method. One type deals with an element of the array, the other type with the whole array.

5.4 Creating a `BeanInfo` Object

A developer can either chose to implement the `BeanInfo` interface or subclass the `SimpleBeanInfo` class. In general, most developers will subclass `SimpleBeanInfo`, as all this class does is provide null implementations of all the methods specified in the `BeanInfo` interface. This means that you only have to implement the methods you are particularly interested in. This produces more compact and comprehensible code. Note that if during introspection a `BeanInfo` method returns null, the introspector assumes that the `BeanInfo` object does not wish to deal with this aspect of the bean. The introspector therefore falls back on reflection to provide details about the bean.

The methods in Table 5.1 allow you to modify every aspect of your Bean. For example, the `getPropertyDescriptors()` method allows you to decide which properties will be presented to the user and what label will be associated with those properties. For example, let use assume that we do not want the `Counter` bean to have a property called `maxValue`. Instead we want the property to be called Alarm Trigger. This can be done by defining a `PropertyDescriptor` that changes the label. This is illustrated in the following source code:

```
public class CounterBeanInfo extends SimpleBeanInfo {
   public PropertyDescriptor[] getPropertyDescriptors()
   {
      PropertyDescriptor pd = null;
      // Create a new PropertyDescriptor instance for
      // MaxValue
```

Table 5.1 Methods specified by the `BeanInfo` interface

`getAdditionalBeanInfo()`	This method allows a `BeanInfo` object to return an arbitrary collection of other `BeanInfo` objects that provide additional information on the current bean. This means that you can force reflection to provide most of the details, with only a few elements filled in by the additional bean info.
`getBeanDescriptor()`	This returns a `BeanDescriptor` object which is used to specify a bean's customizer.
`getDefaultEventIndex()`	A bean may have a "default" event that is the event that will most commonly be used by humans when using the bean. This could be used by a builder tool to indicate the default event option.
`getDefaultPropertyIndex()`	A bean may have a "default" property that is the property that will most commonly be initially chosen for update by humans who are customizing the bean.
`getEventSetDescriptors()`	This returns an array of `EventSetDescriptors`. Each event descriptor controls how a builder tool allows the user to interact with the Bean's events.
`getIcon(int)`	This method returns an image object that can be used to represent the bean in toolboxes, toolbars, etc.
`getMethodDescriptors()`	This method returns a set of `MethodDescriptors`.
`getPropertyDescriptors()`	This method returns an array of `PropertyDescriptors`. Each property descriptor represents special information that the Bean provides on a specific property.

```
    try { pd = new PropertyDescriptor("maxValue",
      Counter.class);
    } catch (IntrospectionException e) {}
    pd.setDisplayName("Alarm Trigger");
    PropertyDescriptor result[] = { pd };
    return result;
  }
}
```

Now that we have a `BeanInfo` class for the `Counter` bean, when the introspector attempts to find out the `Counter` bean's details it will load the `CounterBeanInfo` class. It would find that all the methods return null (as they are inherited from `SimpleBeanInfo`) with the exception of the `getPropertyDescriptors()` method. It would therefore use the results obtained from this method to identify the `Counter` bean's properties. Unfortunately this means that the "Alarm Trigger" property would be the only one presented to the user. This is because the other properties such as the initial value were not mentioned by the `getPropertyDescriptors()` method.

Fortunately, this is where the `getAdditionalBeanInfo()` method comes in. Instead of defining the `getPropertyDescriptors()` method in a `CounterBeanInfo` class, you define it in a `CounterAdditionalInfo` class.

An instance of this class is then returned by the `getAdditionalBeanInfo()` method defined in the new `CounterBeanInfo` class. The introspector now obtains all the property information for the Counter bean by introspection, but replaces the `maxValue` property details provided by reflection with the property details provided by the method in the `CounterAdditionInfo` class. This is illustrated in the listing below:

```
public class CounterBeanInfo extends SimpleBeanInfo {
  // Indicates to the introspector to look elsewhere
  // for additional information
  public BeanInfo[] getAdditionalBeanInfo() {
    // Note an array of additional info classes is
    // returned
    return new BeanInfo[] { new
      CounterAdditionalInfo() };
  }
}


class CounterAdditionalInfo extends SimpleBeanInfo {
  public PropertyDescriptor[] getPropertyDescriptors()
    {
    PropertyDescriptor pd = null;
    // Create a new PropertyDescriptor instance for
    // MaxValue
    try { pd = new PropertyDescriptor("maxValue",
      Counter.class);
    } catch (IntrospectionException e) {}
    pd.setDisplayName("Alarm Trigger");
    PropertyDescriptor result[] = { pd };
    return result;
  }
}
```

In the above listing we have made the assumption that the `AdditionalInfo` class is in the same file as the `BeanInfo` class. There is no need to do this as the `AdditionalBeanInfo` class can be public (and would thus be defined in its own file).

The result of adding the above bean info classes to the `Counter` bean (and adding them in the `counter.jar` file) presented in the last chapter, is illustrated in Figure 5.1.

5.5 Serializing a Bean

In some situations it is desirable to save the state of a Bean instance. For example, once we have set the properties on a counter bean (for example by setting the Alarm trigger property to 5) we might want to reuse this configuration many times. We do

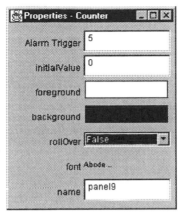

Figure 5.1 The result of applying a `BeanInfo` class.

not want to have to reset the Alarm trigger property every time. So how do we manage this (remember that if you have purchased a bean you may not have access to its source code)? In JavaBeans the way this is achieved is by serializing the bean; that is, storing the bean to a file in a format which allows it to be restored at a later stage. Chapter 3 discussed serialization in some detail. We will therefore merely point out that a bean is serialized in exactly the same way as any Java object as long as it implements either the `Serializable` or `Externalizable` interfaces. It should be noted that any visual bean will have inherited from `java.awt.Component`. This class implements the serializable interface. Thus any visual bean can be serialized. However, for efficiency it is better to specify that your Bean implements this interface as the JVM (supplied with Sun's JDK) does not then need to search back up the inheritance hierarchy to determine whether the bean can be serialized or not.

5.6 Property Editors

This section very briefly describes how the property sheet window displayed with each Bean can be modified. By default, the way that a property is displayed in this window is determined by a number of built-in property editors. A property editor defines how an individual property is changed. Thus a property sheet is made up of one or more property editors. If we look at Figure 5.1, we can see that this figure is made up from seven different property editors. For example, a BoolEditor is used for the flag `rollOver`, a StringEditor is used for the property `name` and an IntEditor is used for the Alarm Trigger value and the `initialValue` properties. Table 5.2 lists the full set of editors provided by JavaBeans.

These property editors are managed by the `PropertyEditorManager` class.

Table 5.2 Property Editors

BoolEditor	ByteEditor	FontEditor	DoubleEditor
ColorEditor	FloatEditor	StringEditor	IntEditor
NumberEditor	LongEditor		

The property editors are displayed within different types of views. For example, the colour property editor is displayed within a `PropertyCanvas` view, while the boolean editor is displayed within a `PropertySelector` view and a string editor is displayed within a `PropertyText` view. To determine which view to use, the property sheet checks the methods defined for the property editor associated with the property:

- The `PropertyCanvas` view is used if the associated property editor defines `isPaintable()` and `supportsCustomEditor()` as non-null.
- The `PropertySelector` view is used if the property editor defines `getTags()` as non-null.
- The `PropertyText` view is used if the property editor defines `getAsText()` as non-null.

The property sheet checks for these methods in the order presented above. The first methods satisfied specify the view that will be used.

Of course, in some situations you will want to define your own property editor. You can do this either by implementing the `PropertyEditor` interface or by extending the utility class `PropertyEditorSupport`. As with other utility support classes, this class merely provides null implementations for most of the methods in the `PropertyEditor` interface. As you have already seen, using the support classes can be much easier than working from scratch. Therefore to give you some guidance on which to use we have identified a number of rules:

- Use the `PropertyEditor` interface when you need a custom editor in a new window (see the source code for `FontEditor` and `ColorEditor` as examples).
- Use the `PropertyEditor` interface if you are extending an editor developed outside of the Beans conventions.
- Use the utility support class when you only need to change a simple property editor that will be displayed within a property sheet (see the BoolEditor or StringEditor as examples).

If you are implementing the `PropertyEditor` interface then you will need to:
- define the methods specified in the interface (although some may do nothing except return null)
- provide a null argument constructor
- support the addition and removal of `PropertyChangeListeners`

There are 12 methods specified by the PropertyEditor interface. Space precludes a detailed description of each of these (they are listed for your information in Table 5.3). However, the key method in this interface is the `setValue()` method. This method is used to modify a property of a Bean. It is passed an object. The method should then cast the object to the appropriate type and then set the property to this object. As an example, the following skeleton code illustrates the steps to be performed:

```
private PropertyChangeSupport support = new
PropertyChangeSupport();
private Color color;
public void setValue(Object obj) {
```

Table 5.3 The `PropertyEditor` interface methods

`Object getValue()`	Returns the value of the property
`setValue(Object)`	Set (or change) the object that is to be edited.
`String getAsText()`	Returns the property value as a String.
`setAsText(String)`	Set the property value by parsing a given String.
`String getJavaInitializationString()`	This method is intended for use when generating Java code to set the value of the property. For example, `"new Color(127, 127, 127)"` or `"Color.red"`.
`boolean isPaintable()`	Returns true if the property editor supports the `paintValue()` method.
`paintValue(Graphics, Rectangle)`	Paint a representation of the value into a given area of screen real estate.
`String[] getTags()`	If the property value must be one of a set of known tagged values, then this method should return an array of the tags.
`Component getCustomEditor()`	A property editor may choose to make available a full custom component that edits its property value.
`boolean supportsCustomEditor()`	Returns true if the property editor provides a custom editor specified through a user-defined GUI.
`addPropertyChangeListener (PropertyChangeListener)`	Register a listener for the `PropertyChange` event.
`removePropertyChangeListener (PropertyChangeListener)`	Remove a listener for the `PropertyChange` event.

```
    // Cast the object to the appropriate type#
      Colour c = (Colour)obj;
      // Change the properties value
    changeColor(c);
  }
  public void changeColor(Color c) {
    // Reset property
    color = c;
    // Change GUI representation
    ...
    // Inform listeners of change
    support.firePropertyChange("", null, null);
  }
```

You may note that the `firePropertyChange()` method has a null property name and values. This may seem strange; however, it is a convention used to indicate that an (unspecified) change has taken place. It would have been good style for the JavaBeans developers to have provided a null parameter `firePropertyChange` method.

To register your property editor with the `PropertyEditorManager` you can register it explicitly through the `getPropertyDescriptors()` method of the Bean's `BeanInfo` (by setting the appropriate property descriptor object using the `setPropertyEditorClass()` method). If you do not do that, then you can call the editor *datatype*Editor and save it in the package directory of the bean or any other package on the `CLASSPATH`. Using the `BeanInfo` approach is cleaner and eliminates the chance of "picking up" the wrong dataTypeEditor.

5.7 Customizers

In some situations even defining your own property editor is not sufficient. In these situations customizers can be defined. These are similar to "wizards" in that they take the user through a series of decisions which have the combined effect of setting one or more properties in one go. As with everything in JavaBeans there is a naming convention associated with customizers. This convention is that the customizer will be called *BeanName*Customizer. Thus if we wished to define a customizer for the Counter bean, then it would be called `CounterCustomizer`.

There are a number of steps required to use a customizer. These are:

- Define a BeanInfo file to specify the customizer. That is, define the `getBeanDescriptor()` method:

```
public class CounterBeanInfo extends SimpleBeanInfo {
  ...
  public BeanDescriptor getBeanDescriptor() {
    return new BeanDescriptor(Counter.class,
      CounterCustomizer.class);
  }
}
```

- Extend `java.awt.Component` or one of its subclasses (such as `Panel`).
- Implement the `Customizer` interface.
- Provide a null argument constructor for the customizer.
- Support the addition and removal of a `PropertyChangeListener`.
- Define the `setObject(Object obj)` method.

Of course, customizers can also implement any event handlers required by the actual customizer as well as methods such as `getMinimimSize()` and `getPreferredSize()`.

5.8 A Critique of JavaBeans

The Beans component model is very simple, thus ensuring that the creation of beans is straightforward. Communication is via methods or event delegation, and standard

Java resources such as JAR and Interfaces make it work. This makes it very easy to produce Beans. For example, in the simple example developed above, the only element of BDK and the Beans API used was the BeanBox. This was because we followed the naming conventions and thus did not need to use a `BeanInfo` object. This nicely illustrated that any class can be treated as a Bean as long as certain naming conventions are followed. However, it also illustrates a weakness, in that naming conventions are not good at ensuring specifications are met, providing definitions etc. During development a property did not appear in the BeanBox, on more than one occasion, in the way we expected. This was due to typographical errors and human error (for example, just forgetting to define both a `set<Property name>` and a `get<Property name>` method). In such situations having a bean specification against which the bean was checked, and via which others could reference the bean, would have been useful.

Thus the biggest disadvantage of the JavaBeans approach is that everything is done by naming conventions. This has the potential to introduce errors into the beans' definitions (e.g. set or get methods spelt incorrectly). Many component models deal with this by requiring an interface definition. This definition is then used when compiling the component to ensure that it matches its public interface. This would be a very useful addition to the Beans model. Of course, JavaBeans has the advantage that there is no overhead in creating a bean, as a bean is just a class that has followed the appropriate naming conventions.

In addition, our simple beans did not do very much. However, by the time we had defined set and get methods (plus some `is*` methods) the bean classes were quite verbose. The source code was thus longer and less clear than we would have wished (not to mention the tedious nature of defining all these methods). The result is that a programmer might well be better off if Java's designers had required them to specify somewhere that certain variables were properties (and whether they were read, write or read/write properties). It is of course possible to do this sort of thing through in a `BeanInfo` object by explicitly stating that a property is read-only. However, the `BeanInfo` object is intended more as an access mechanism (which allows things like the bean to be customized beyond the scope of the simple naming JavaBeans conventions) than as a bean specification.

The other main weakness is the lack of explicit object aggregation facilities. However, this is being addressed in the next release of JavaBeans (code named Glasgow). Aggregation relates to the ability to package a number of classes up explicitly into a single bean.

A very big advantage with JavaBeans is that it is not necessary to learn very much in order to create a bean which works in the BeanBox. Basically, all we have to do is:

- learn the naming conventions
- work with events and listeners (which you do in the AWT anyway)
- work out how to use the `jar` tool (not difficult)
- place the resulting JAR file into the correct jars directory

As more and more tools are appearing for Beans the influence and effect of Beans will undoubtedly grow. Such tools will also simplify the task of defining a Bean, minimizing the need for manually defining set and get methods.

5.9 Summary

As you can see from this and the last chapter, it is very easy to define a JavaBean. The model used is very simple: communication is via methods or event delegation, and standard Java resources such as JAR and Interfaces make it work. As more and more tools are appearing for Beans, the influence and effect of JavaBeans will undoubtedly grow. Such tools will also simplify the task of defining a Bean, minimizing the need for manually defining set and get methods.

It is probable that the JavaBeans architecture will become very influential and that many software vendors will package their products as beans. Thus the futures of Java and of JavaBeans will be tied inextricably to each other.

Finally, the great advantage of this approach is its simplicity, but the disadvantage is that, at first sight, it appears that there is nothing concrete that defines a Bean.

6 Java DataBase Connectivity

6.1 Introduction

Officially JDBC is not an acronym. However to all intents and purposes it stands for Java DataBase Connectivity. This is the mechanism by which relational databases are accessed in Java. Java is an (almost) pure object-oriented language, however. Although there are some object-oriented databases available, many database systems presently in commercial use are relational. It is therefore necessary for any object-oriented language which is to be used for commercial development to provide an interface to such databases. However, each database vendor provides their own proprietary (and different) API. In many cases they are little more than variations on a theme, but they tend to be incompatible. This means that if you were to write a program which was designed to interface with one database system, it is unlikely that it would automatically work with another.

Of course, one of the philosophies of Java is *"write once, run anywhere"*. This means we do not want to have to rewrite our Java code just because it is using a different database on a different platform (or even on the same platform). JDBC is Sun's attempt to provide a vendor-independent interface to any relational database system. This is possible, as most vendors implement most (if not all) of SQL, thus providing a common denominator. SQL (or Structured Query Language) is a standard language for interacting with databases. An introduction to SQL is listed in the references for this chapter.

One potential problem with such an approach is that although the developers' interface is the same, different implementations of an application would be needed to link to different databases. In the JDBC this is overcome by providing different back-end drivers. Developers are now insulated from the details of the various relational database systems that they may be using and have a greater chance of producing portable code.

In the remainder of this chapter we consider in more detail JDBC and these database drivers. We then look at some examples of typical database operations.

6.2 What is JDBC?

The JDBC allows a Java developer to connect to a database, to interact with that database via SQL, and of course to use those results within a Java application or applet. The combination of Java and JDBC allows information held in databases to be easily and quickly published on the Web (via an applet). The first version of the JDBC was released in the summer of 1996. It is an important addition to Java's armoury, as the JDBC provides programmers with a language and environment that is platform and database vendor-independent. This is (almost) unique. The Open Database Connectivity (ODBC) standard has a similar aim.

The Open Database Connectivity (ODBC) standard is a database access standard developed by Microsoft. This standard has been widely adopted not only by the vendors of Windows-based databases but by others as well. For example, a number of databases more normally associated with Unix-based systems or IBM mainframes now offer an ODBC interface. Essentially, ODBC is a basic SQL interface to a database system that assumes only "standard" SQL features. Thus specialist facilities provided by different database vendors cannot be accessed.

Most developers who use the ODBC C API are database vendor-independent, but find it non-trivial to port their C application to a different platform due to windowing differences, hardware-dependent language features etc.

In many ways JDBC has similar aims to ODBC. However, one major difference is that JDBC allows the application to be vendor- and platform-independent.

At present, the JDBC only allows connection to, and interaction with, a database via SQL. Features such as those found in tools such as Delphi and Visual Basic are not available. For example, there are no database controls, form designers, query builders etc. Of course, it is likely that such tools will become available either from Sun or third-party vendors. This situation is already changing to some extent with the JFC components (or Java Foundation Classes), which are moving towards becoming data-aware. These are discussed in detail in Part 4 of this book.

The JDBC is able to connect to any database by using different (back-end) drivers. These act as the interfaces between the JDBC and databases such as Oracle, Sybase, Microsoft Access and shareware systems such as MiniSQL. The idea is that the front end presented to the developer is the same whatever the database system, while the appropriate back end is loaded as required. The JDBC then passes the programmer's SQL to the database via the back end. Java is not the first system to adopt this approach; however, a novel feature of the JDBC is that more than one driver can be loaded at a time. The system will then try each driver until one is found that is compatible with the database system being used. Thus multiple drivers can be provided and at runtime the appropriate one is identified and used.

This is illustrated in Figure 6.1, which shows some of the most commonly used methods provided by the JDBC along with two database drivers (namely the MiniSQL driver and the ODBC driver). Such a setup would allow a Java program to

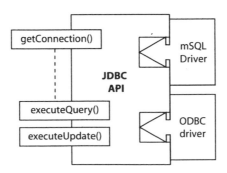

Figure 6.1 The structure of the JDBC.

connect to an mSQL database via the mSQL driver and to any database which supports the ODBC standard through the ODBC driver. The `getConnection()`, `executeQuery()` and `executeUpdate()` methods will be looked at in more detail later in this chapter.

There are an increasing number of database drivers becoming available for JDBC. At present, databases such as Oracle, Sybase and Ingres all have their own drivers. This allows features of those databases to be exploited. However, even databases that are not directly supported can be accessed via the ODBC driver, thus making a huge range of databases available to the Java developer.

There is a very definite series of steps that must be performed by any JDBC program. These involve loading an appropriate driver, connecting to a database, executing SQL statements and closing the connection made. These are discussed in more detail later in this chapter.

6.3 What the Driver Provides

What actually is a driver? In practice it provides the concrete implementation for a number of interfaces and classes defined in the SQL package (such as `Driver`, `Connection`, `Statement` and `ResultSet`). Each of these will be considered in more detail later. However, essentially they manage connections to a database, passing SQL statements to be executed to that database and examining the results returned. Note that, unlike some object-to-relational database interfaces, JDBC does not try to objectify the results of querying a relational database. Instead, the results are returned in a table-like format within a results set. It is then up to the developer to decide how to handle the information retrieved.

6.4 Registering Drivers

As part of the JDBC API a JDBC driver manager is provided. This is the part of the JDBC that handles the drivers currently available to a JDBC application. It is therefore necessary to "register" a driver with the driver manager. There are three ways of doing this:

1. Passing a command line option to a Java application using the `-Dproperty =value` parameter. For example:

   ```
   java -Djdbc.drivers=jdbc.odbc.JdbcOdbcDriver queryDB
   ```

2. For applets it is possible to set the `jdbc.drivers` system property. In HotJava this can be done in the properties file of the `.hotjava` directory. For example:

   ```
   jdbc.drivers=jdbc.odbc.JdbcOdbcDriver:
       imaginary.sql.iMsqlDriver
   ```

3. Programmatically by requesting the class of the driver using the static method `forName()` in the class `Class`. For example:

```
Class.forName("sun.jdbc.odbc.JdbcOdbcDriver");
Class.forName("COM.imaginary.sql.msql.MsqlDriver");
```

This will cause the associated class (in this case the driver) to be loaded into the running application.

As was mentioned earlier, you can install more than one driver in your JDBC program. When a request is made to make a connection to a database, each one will be tried in turn until one accepts that request. However, using more than one driver will slow down both system startup (as each must be loaded) as well as your runtime (as each may need to be tried in turn). For this reason, it may be best to select the most appropriate driver and stick with that one.

The JDBC ODBC driver is provided as part of Sun's JDK 1.1. However, other drivers can be obtained and used with the JDBC. For example, the mSQL driver mentioned above was downloaded from the Web and installed in an appropriate directory. In this way database vendors can supply their own proprietary database drivers which developers can then utilize in their own applications.

6.5 Opening a Connection

Listing 6.1 presents a simple class that uses the ODBC driver to connect to a Microsoft Access database. We must first make the JDBC API available. This is done by importing the SQL package. Next the application loads the JDBC ODBC driver and then requests that the `DriverManager` makes a connection with the database `testDB`. Note that to make this connection a string (called `url`) is passed to the driver manager along with the user id and the password.

***

Listing 6.1 `TestConnect.java`

```
import java.sql.*;
public class TestConnect {

  public static void main (String args []) {
    // URL specifies the type of access and its name
    String url = "jdbc:odbc:testDB";

    try {
      // Load the driver and request a connection
      Class.forName("sun.jdbc.odbc.JdbcOdbcDriver");
      Connection con =
        DriverManager.getConnection(url);
      // If the connection was successful close it
      con.close();
      System.out.println("All okay");
    } catch (Exception e) {
      // If a problem occurred - handle the exception
```

```
            System.out.println(e.getMessage());
            e.printStackTrace();
        }
    }
}
```

The string specifying the database to connect to is formed from a JDBC URL. This is a URL that is comprised of three parts:

1. the JDBC protocol indicator (jdbc:)
2. the appropriate sub-protocol such as odbc:
3. the driver-specific components (in this case JdbcOdbcDriver)

URLs are used as the Java program accessing the database may be running as a standalone application or may be an applet needing to connect to the database via the Web. Note that different database drivers will require different driver-specific components. For example, the mSQL driver requires a URL of the following format:

```
jdbc:msql://hal.aber.ac.uk:1112/testDB
```

In this case it is necessary to provide the host name, the port on that host to connect to and the database to be used.

Once a connection has successfully been made to the database, the program then does nothing other than to close that connection. This is important, as some database drivers require the program to close the connection, while others leave it as optional. If you are using multiple drivers it is best to close the connection.

Note that the attempt to load the driver and make the connection was placed within a try {} catch{} block. This is because both operations can raise exceptions and these must be caught and handled (as they are not runtime exceptions). The forName() method raises the ClassNotFoundException if it cannot find the class which represents the specified driver. In turn, the getConnection() static method raises the SQLException if the specified database cannot be found.

An example of using this application is presented in Listing 6.2.

6.6 Obtaining Data from a Database

Having made a connection with a database we are now in a position to obtain information from it. Listing 6.2 builds on the application in Listing 6.1 by querying the database for some information. This is done by obtaining a Statement object from the Connection object. SQL statements without parameters are normally executed using Statement objects. However, if the same SQL statement is executed many times, it is more efficient to use a PreparedStatement. In this example we will stick with the Statement object.

Listing 6.2 *TestQuery.java*

```
java TestConnect
import java.sql.*;
public class TestQuery {

  public static void main (String args []) {
    String url = "jdbc:odbc:testdb";

    try {
      Class.forName("sun.jdbc.odbc.JdbcOdbcDriver");
      Connection con =
        DriverManager.getConnection(url);

      // Build up a statement to execute. The string
      // to execute should contain SQL
      Statement statement = con.createStatement();
      ResultSet results = statement.executeQuery(
        "SELECT address FROM addresses
          WHERE name = 'John' ");

      System.out.println("Addresses for John:");
      // The results are held in a results set.
      // next() is used to move the cursor.
      while (results.next()) {
        System.out.println(results.getString(
          "address"));
      }
      statement.close();

      con.close();
    } catch (Exception e) {
      System.out.println(e.getMessage());
      e.printStackTrace();
    }
  }
}
```

Having obtained the `Statement` object we are now ready to pass it some SQL. This is done as a string within which the actual SQL statements are specified. In this case the SQL statement is:

```
SELECT address
  FROM addresses
  WHERE name = 'John'
```

This is pure SQL. The `SELECT` statement allows data to be obtained from the tables in the database. In this case the SQL states that the address field (column) of the table addresses should be retrieved where the name field of that row equals 'John'. SQL is a large topic in its own right and is beyond the scope of this chapter. Reference is therefore made to appropriate books at the end of the chapter.

This string is passed to the `Statement` object via the `executeQuery()` method. This method also generates an `SQLException` if a problem occurs. The method passes the SQL to the driver previously selected by the driver manager. The driver in turn passes the SQL to the database system. The result is then returned to the driver, which in turn returns it as an instance `ResultsSet`. `ResultsSet` is actually an interface, and thus what is actually returned is an object whose class implements the `ResultsSet` interface.

A results set is a table of data within which each row contains the data that matched the SQL statement. Within the row, the columns contain the fields specified by the SQL. A `ResultSet` maintains a cursor pointing to its current row of data. Initially the cursor is positioned before the first row. The `next()` method moves the cursor to the next row. Note that it is only possible to move the cursor forward through the results set; it is not possible to move backwards, nor is it possible to position the cursor using some form of seek operation.

The `ResultsSet` interface defines a variety of get methods for obtaining information out of the `ResultsSet` table, for example `getBoolean()`, `getByte()`, `getString()` and `getDate()`. These methods are provided by the JDBC driver and attempt to convert the underlying data into the specified Java type and return a suitable Java value. In Listing 6.2 we merely print out each address in turn using the `next()` method to move the table cursor on.

Finally, the `statement` and the `connection` are closed. In many cases it is desirable to immediately release a `Statement`'s database and JDBC resources instead of waiting for this to happen when it is automatically closed; the `close` method provides this immediate release.

6.7 Creating a Table

So far, we have examined how to connect to a database and how to query that database for information. However, we have not considered how that database is created. Obviously the database might not be created by a Java application; for example, it could be generated by a legacy system. However, in many situations it is necessary for the tables in the database to be updated (if not created) by a JDBC program. Listing 6.3 presents a modified version of Listing 6.2. This listing shows how a statement object can be used to create a table and how information can be inserted into that table. Again the strings passed to the statement are pure SQL; however this time we have used the `executeUpdate()` method of the `Statement` class.

Listing 6.3 `TestCreate.java`

```
import java.sql.*;
public class TestCreate {
```

```
public static void main (String args []) {
  String url = "jdbc:odbc:testdb";

  try {
    Class.forName("sun.jdbc.odbc.JdbcOdbcDriver");
    Connection con =
      DriverManager.getConnection(url);
    Statement statement = con.createStatement();

    // Create the tables in the database and insert
    // some data.
    statement.executeUpdate(
      "CREATE TABLE addresses
        (name char(15), address char(3))");
    statement.executeUpdate(
      "INSERT INTO addresses (name, address)
        VALUES('John', 'C46')");
    statement.executeUpdate(
      "INSERT INTO addresses (name, address)
        VALUES('Denise', 'C40')");

    statement.close();
    con.close();
  } catch (Exception e) {
    System.out.println(e.getMessage());
    e.printStackTrace();
  }
  }
}
```

The executeUpdate() is intended for SQL statements which will change the state of the database, such as INSERT, DELETE and CREATE. It does not return a result set; rather it returns an integer indicating the row count of the executed SQL.

6.8 Limitations

6.8.1 The SQLException

The JDBC approach possesses some inherent limitations. The first of these is that many operations performed in the JDBC raise the SQLException. This means that it can be difficult to determine what actually went wrong in a block of code. For example, was it a problem with making a connection to a database, with creating a table or with closing the connection? As these operations cannot be distinguished merely by catching different exceptions, it is necessary to determine the actual problem within the `catch` block. For example, in the listings in this chapter the exception message has been printed. The `SQLException` does support such operations to some extent:

- A string describing the error. This is used as the Java Exception message, and is available via the `getMessage()` method.
- An `SQLstate` string which follows the XOPEN SQLstate conventions. The values of the `SQLState` string as described in the XOPEN SQL specification.
- An integer error code that is vendor-specific. Normally this will be the actual error code returned by the underlying database.
- A chain to a next `Exception`. This can be used to provide additional error information.

However, the provision of different types of exception for different operations would have been a better solution.

6.8.2 The `ResultsSet`

The `ResultsSet` object maintains a cursor indicating the current position of the next read within the data retrieved from the database. However, as this cursor can only be moved one position forward (using the `next()` method) it is not possible to move backwards within the results set or to search for particular items of data. This is a facility provided by many similar data structures in other languages (such as Delphi). The means that if you need this functionality then you must extract the data from the results set and hold it within another type of object (for example, a `Vector`). This results in extra effort and duplication of data. It is probable that the results set operates in this way as a "lowest common denominator". That is, all drivers will provide the basic functionality, while some drivers may provide more advanced features.

6.9 Further Reading

Jepson B. (1997) *Java Database Programming*. John Wiley, Chichester.
Reese G. (1997) *Database Programming with JDBC and Java*. O'Reilly & Associates, Cambridge MA.
Hamilton G., Cattell R. and Fisher M. (1997) *JDBC Database Access With Java: A Tutorial and Annotated Reference*. Addison-Wesley, Reading.
Microsoft (1997) *Microsoft ODBC 3.0 Software Development Kit and Programmer's Reference*, Microsoft Press, Redmond WA.
Stephens R.K. (1997) *Teach yourself SQL in 21 days*, 2nd edn. Sams, Indianapolis.

6.10 Online References

Sun's JDBC home page can be found at:

```
http://java.sun.com/products/jdbc
```

Information on available JDBC drivers can be obtained from

```
http://java.sun.com/products/jdbc/jdbc.drivers.html
```

7   *The Web and JDBC*

7.1 Introduction

By default, applets are not allowed to load libraries or read and write files. In addition, applets are not allowed to open sockets to machines other than those they originated from. These restrictions cause a number of problems for those wishing to develop applets that work with databases. For example, many drivers rely on the ability to load native code libraries that actually generate the connection to the specified database. One way around these restrictions is to turn them off in the browser being used. This is acceptable for an Intranet being used within a single organization; however, it is not acceptable as a general solution.

Another possibility is to use drivers that are 100% pure Java, such as the mSQL driver (mSQL is described briefly in Section 7.2). However, even using an mSQL driver, the applet is still restricted to connecting to a database on the originating host. Thus the developers must ensure that the Web server that serves the applets is running on the same host as the mSQL daemon. This may or may not be a problem.

Another option is to use a separate database server application (note application and not applet) which runs on the same host as the Web server. Applets can then connect to the database server application, requesting that it connect to databases, execute updates, perform queries etc. The database server application is then the program that connects to and interacts with the database. In such a setup the applet does not directly communicate with the database system. In turn, the server application is not hindered by the restrictions imposed on applets and can therefore connect to any database it has access to. This approach is illustrated in the remainder of this chapter. We introduce the concept of sockets and discuss how they are implemented in Java before using sockets to enable a client applet to communicate with a server application. We conclude this chapter with a brief discussion of signed applets.

7.2 MiniSQL

MiniSQL or mSQL is a lightweight database server originally developed as part of the Minerva Network Management Environment. Its creator, David Hughes, has continued its development and makes mSQL available as a shareware product for a very small fee. MSQL provides fast access to stored data with low memory requirements through a subset of ANSI SQL (i.e. it does not support views or subqueries etc.). It is available for Unix-compatible operating systems as well as for Windows

95/NT and OS/2. However, it is worth noting that the Unix version tends to be ahead of the PC-oriented versions. The mSQL package includes the database engine, a terminal "monitor" program, a database administration program, a schema viewer and C and Java language APIs. A Java JDBC driver for mSQL is also available.

mSQL is a very popular choice among Java developers because it is available on a wide variety of platforms, the mSQL driver is 100% Pure Java (and thus there is no problem about loading a native library when writing applets) and of course it is shareware. The downside is that the performance of mSQL is not as good as that of commercial database systems. With regard to applets it is worth noting that an applet (by default) is not allowed to make a network connection to any other computer other than the machine from which it was loaded. Thus the Web server and the mSQL demon must be running on the same machine. For more information on mSQL see Jepson (1998).

7.3 Sockets in Java

A "socket" is an end point in a communication link between separate processes. In Java, sockets are objects which provide a way of exchanging information between two processes in a straightforward and platform-independent manner (see the classes in the `java.net` package). To achieve this, the streams model, already used for file access, is exploited. Associated with each socket are two streams, one for input and one for output. Thus to pass information from one process to another you write that information to the output stream of one socket and read it from the input stream of another socket (assuming the two sockets are connected). This is illustrated in Figure 7.1. This has the great advantage that once the network connection has been

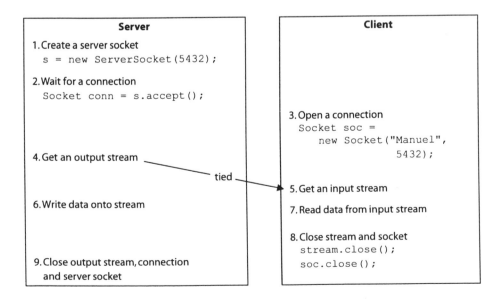

Figure 7.1 Socket-to-socket communication.

made, passing information between processes is not significantly different from reading and writing information with any other stream.

To set up the connection, one process must be running a program that is waiting for a connection while the other must try to reach the first. The first is referred to as a server socket, while the second is just referred to as a socket.

For the second process to connect to the first (the server socket) it must know what machine the first is running on and which port it is connected to. A port number is a logical point of communication on a computer. Port numbers in the TCP/IP system are 16 bit numbers in the range 0–65536 (a description of TCP/IP is beyond the scope of this book; see references at the end of this chapter for further information). Generally, port numbers below 1024 are reserved for predefined services (which means that you should avoid using them unless you wish to communicate with one of those services, such as telnet, SMTP mail or ftp).

For example, in Figure 7.1 the server socket connects to port 5432. In turn, the client socket connects to the machine on which the server is executing and then to port number 5432 on that machine. Nothing happens until the server socket accepts the connection. At that point the sockets are connected and the socket streams are bound to each other.

7.4 Web-Based Client–Server Architecture

7.4.1 The System Structure

Figure 7.2 illustrates the basic structure of the system we are trying to build. In this figure a user's browser has connected to the Web server and downloaded the client applet. The applet then connects to the database server application. The server application then connects to the database management system on this or another host. The client then passes a request for information to the server application via socket to socket communication. The server application then converts this request into the appropriate SQL for the database being used. A query is then made to the database. The database retrieves any relevant information and returns it to the server application. The server application then packages it into an appropriate form for transmission back to the client applet. The client applet is then able to present this information to the user.

The way that such an architecture can be implemented is described in the next few subsections. This is a very simple example of the three-tier architecture described in Chapter 1.

The actual application being implemented is a Web-based address book. The addresses of employees of a company are held in a database. This database was set up as in the previous chapter and contains names and addresses. The applet will allow a user to specify an employee's name, and the address will then be presented to the user.

7.4.2 Implementing the Server Application

We shall describe the server application first. This is the Java application program that will service requests from client applets for information. To do this it must

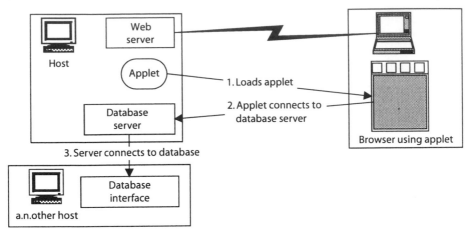

Figure 7.2 Using the JDBC within an applet.

provide both a server socket for clients to connect to as well as a database link. The database side of the server is essentially the same as that presented in the `TestQuery` application in the last chapter. However, it differs in that the actually query is from information provided by the client. That is, the basic SQL is provided by the server application, but the name to search on is provided by the client. Thus the SQL query is constructed at runtime. Listing 7.1 presents the annotated source code for the `Server` class.

Listing 7.1 *The server application*

```
import java.net.*;
import java.io.*;
import java.sql.*;

/**
 * Simple server class which provides addresses for
 * named people using a simple protocol
 * (e.g. name = 'John'). The socket to
 * socket communication facilities of Java are used
 * to connect a client to this server.
 */
public class Server {
   // Set up the url to the access database
   private String url = "jdbc:odbc:testDS";

   // Starts the server application
   public static void main (String args []) {
     Server s = new Server();
```

```
    s.start();
  }

  // Constructor to load the database driver
  public Server() {
  // Load the JDBC-ODBC driver
  try {
    Class.forName("sun.jdbc.odbc.JdbcOdbcDriver");
  } catch (Exception e) {
    System.out.println("Problem: ODBC driver");}
  }

  /**
   * Provides the main server loop:
   * 1. Wait for a connection
   * 2. Obtain a reuqest for an address
   * 3. Query the database
   * 4. Respond with a null string or the address
   */
  public void start() {
    // Set up the server socket
    ServerSocket serverSocket = null;
    Socket socket;
    InputStream socketIn;
    OutputStream socketOut;
    DataInputStream dataInputStream;
    DataOutputStream dataOutputStream;
    StringBuffer resultsString =
      new StringBuffer("");

    // Register service on port 1234
    try {
      serverSocket = new ServerSocket(1234);
    } catch (IOException e)
      {System.out.println("Server socket
        registration failed");}

    // Wait for a connection from a client
    while (true) {
      try {
        // Wait here and listen for a
        // connection
        socket = serverSocket.accept();
        socketIn = socket.getInputStream();
        dataInputStream =
          new DataInputStream(socketIn);
```

```java
    // Now build the search query from the
    // information provided by the client
    // e.g. SELECT address FROM addresses
    // WHERE name = 'John'
    String queryString =
      "SELECT address FROM addresses WHERE " +
        dataInputStream.readUTF();

    // Now obtain information from database
    try {
      // Make connection with the database
      Connection con =
        DriverManager.getConnection(url);
      Statement statement =
        con.createStatement();
      ResultSet results =
        statement.executeQuery(queryString);
      resultsString= new StringBuffer("");

      while (results.next()) {
        resultsString.append(
          results.getString("address"));
      }
      statement.close();
      con.close();
    } catch (Exception e) {
      System.out.println("Error reading
        database");
      System.out.println(e.getMessage());
    }

    // Return information to client
    // Get communications stream from socket
    socketOut = socket.getOutputStream();
    dataOutputStream =
      new DataOutputStream(socketOut);
    dataOutputStream.writeUTF(
      resultsString.toString());

    // Now close the connections,
    // but not the server socket
    dataInputStream.close();
    dataOutputStream.close();
    socketIn.close();
    socketOut.close();
    socket.close();
  } catch (IOException e) {
```

```
            System.out.println("Error: coms");}
    }
  }
}
```

Essentially, the server in Listing 7.1 loads the `JDBC-ODBC` driver and then waits for a client to connect to it. This is done by creating a `ServerSocket` (in this case on port 1234). It then enters a loop where it continually waits for connections, processes requests and waits for the next connection. When the connection is made, it uses the input stream of its socket to obtain the information provided by the client. It then constructs the SQL query string. Having done this it obtains a connection to the database, creates a statement object and executes the query (just as in the last chapter). It then concatenates each of the entries in the results set to form a single string which it passes back to the client via an output socket stream. Having done all this it closes its connection to the database and to the socket. It is now ready for the next query. As you can see from this, the program is actually very straightforward. This is thanks primarily to the Java `Stream` classes, which hide a great deal of the implementation details often associated with socket communications.

7.4.3 Implementing the Client Applet

The applet client is essentially just an applet that creates a link back to the host it was downloaded from. To do this it creates a socket that connects to the host machine. In our case this socket connects to the machine on which the server application is running, and in particular to socket 1234. It then uses an output stream to pass information to the server. Having done that, it waits for the server to provide a response. The response is the result of querying the database for the address associated with the supplied name.

In our client applet all of this is encapsulated within the `getAddress(String)` method. This method is called when the "Get Address" button is pressed. It is passed a string indicating the name of the employee. This name is then passed to the server. When a result is returned it is presented to the user.

As this is an applet we have defined a very simple graphical interface, illustrated in Figure 7.3. In this figure the appletviewer is being used to execute the `Client` applet. The interface allows a user to specify the name in the top field, to request the address using the bottom button, while results are displayed within the text area in the middle.

The annotated source code for the `Client` applet is presented in Listing 7.2.

Listing 7.2 The `Client` applet

```
import java.net.*;
import java.io.*;
import java.applet.Applet;
import java.awt.*;
import java.awt.event.*;
```

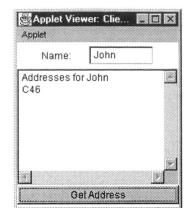

Figure 7.3 The Client
applet interface.

```java
/**
 * A simple applet client which allows a query to be
 * passed to a server object on the applets' host.
 */
public class Client extends Applet
     implements ActionListener {
  TextArea textArea;
  TextField textField;

  // Method used to initialize an applet.
  // Sets up the applet panel.
  public void init () {
    setLayout(new BorderLayout());
    // Set up panel with input field
    Panel p = new Panel();
    p.add(new Label("Name: "));
    textField = new TextField(8);
    p.add(textField);
    add(BorderLayout.NORTH, p);
    // Set up text area for results
    textArea = new TextArea(10, 10);
    add(BorderLayout.CENTER, textArea);
    // Set up button
    Button b = new Button("Get Address");
    add(BorderLayout.SOUTH, b);
    b.addActionListener(this);
  }

  /**
   * This method connects to the server at the
   * specified port, it then passes it a string
   * indicating the name to search on.
   * It then waits for the reply which constructs
```

```
 * into a displayable string.
 */
public String getAddress(String name) {
  String results = "";
  try {
    // First get a socket connection to the Server
    Socket socket = new Socket("manuel", 1234);
    OutputStream outputStream =
      socket.getOutputStream();
    DataOutputStream dataOutputStream =
      new DataOutputStream(outputStream);

    // Now send a query to the server specifying
    // the name to search for
    String query = "name = '" + name + "' ";
    dataOutputStream.writeUTF(query);

    // New get the response
    InputStream inputStream =
      socket.getInputStream();
    DataInputStream dataInputStream =
      new DataInputStream(inputStream);
    String result = dataInputStream.readUTF();
    results = "Addresses for " + name + "\n" +
      result;

    // Close streams and socket
    dataOutputStream.close();
    dataInputStream.close();
    outputStream.close();
    inputStream.close();
    socket.close();
  } catch (IOException e) {
    System.out.println("Error: socket comms");
    System.out.println(e.getMessage());
  }
  return results;
}

/**
 * Handles the button pressed event. It causes the
 * address of the named person to be displayed in
 * the textArea.
 */
public void actionPerformed(ActionEvent event) {

  textArea.setText(getAddress(textField.getText()));
```

```
    }
  }
```

The only aspects of the `Client` we have not yet covered are the `init()` method and the `actionPerformed(ActionEvent)` method. The `init()` method is run by a browser when it first accesses a Web page. It is therefore a good place to define the applet's display. We use one subpanel for the label and input text field, with a central text area and a single button at the bottom of the display. All this is handled by a `BorderLayout` (`FlowLayout` is the default). If you are not clear on concepts such as `Panels`, layout managers etc. please see an appropriate guide to the windowing facilities in Java.

The `actionPerformed()` method is necessary, as the `Client` applet implements the `ActionListener` interface.

7.4.4 The HTML Source

As the `Client` is actually an applet we need an associated HTML file. This file will specify the name of the applet to be run by any browser accessing this HTML file. It also defines how large an area in which to display the applet (there are actually a large number of parameters that can be specified within the `APPLET` tags; however, this is beyond the scope of this chapter). The HTML file for the `Client` applet is presented in Listing 7.3.

Listing 7.3 The `Client` HTML file

```
<html>
<title>Client Applet</title>
<body>
<applet code="Client.class" width=200
  height=200></applet>
<p>
<hr>
</body>
</html>
```

7.5 Signed Applets

With the advent of signed applets (in JDK 1.1) some of the above problems go away. The `javakey` tool is used: this can sign Java ARchive (`JAR`) files, which can contain classes and other data (such as images and sounds). The appletviewer and JDK 1.1-compliant browsers allow any downloaded applets in `JAR` files signed (using the `javakey` tool) by a trusted entity to run with the same full rights as local applications. That is, such applets are not subject to the "sandbox" restrictions of the original Java security model.

The command line `javakey` tool's primary use is to generate digital signatures for archive files. A signature verifies that a file came from a specified entity (a "signer"). In order to generate a signature for a particular file, the signer must first have a public/private key pair associated with it, and also one or more certificates authenticating its public key. Thus, `javakey` is also used to build and manage a persistent database of entities and their keys and certificates, as well as indications as to whether or not each entity is considered "trusted".

However, signed applets are far from universal. Firstly, the supplier of the applet must be registered with the user of the applet. Secondly the `javakey` tool is a very basic system which is quite limited. Thirdly, for many applications it would still be insufficient as a method of providing Web-based client–server applications. This may be because the database to be accessed is not directly accessible by the machine on which the applet is executing (for example, because it is behind a firewall). In addition, many organizations are using browsers which do not support them yet.

7.6 Further Reading

Parker T. (1994) *Teach Yourself TCP/IP in 14 Days*. Sams Publishing, Indianapolis.
Jepson B. (1998) *Official guide to Mini SQL 2.0*. John Wiley, Chichester.

7.7 Online References

mSQL is available by anonymous ftp from

    ftp://bond.edu.au/pub/Minerva/msql

The mSQL JDBC driver is available from

    http://www.imaginary.com/~borg/Java/java.html

8 File-Based Storage Classes

8.1 Introduction

This chapter deals with the problem of holding a large amount of (relatively) non-volatile data. It arose because of experiences with applications in which it was necessary to hold a very large amount of data but on a machine with a limited amount of memory. Due to financial and portability constraints a database was not an option. Indeed, as this was the only situation where large amounts of data were being held, it was not considered a viable option to purchase a database management system. This is a common situation, and one that many find that they face.

After much discussion and analysis it was decided that the only viable solution was to hold the data in a file. However, this had to be interfaced to existing code that assumed an in-memory data structure. This was because the same code was being used at different points in the system. In some situations only a limited amount of data was held. In these cases it was not necessary to store the data externally. However, the underlying software needed to be able to work with both types of data. The result was a file-based data structure.

A *file-based* structure is a data structure that holds its contents in a (serialization) file rather than in internal memory. Of course, there is a performance price to pay; however, the serialization system (discussed earlier in this book) gives reasonable performance, and this must be traded off against the impact on performance of the limited available internal memory.

8.2 File-Based Storage Classes

A `Bag` data structure is an unordered collection of objects which holds its data in an instance variable in internal memory. This is fine for very many applications and is essentially how the class `java.util.Vector` holds its data. However, a `FileBag` class holds its data in a file rather than in internal memory. This is useful for situations where you need to hold a very large amount of data (which is unlikely to change dramatically) in limited available memory; for example if you need to obtain a large amount of data from a remote process that must be displayed incrementally to a user, as might be the case in a browser.

In some situations you may not be able to state categorically whether you should use a `Bag` or a `FileBag` – it may depend on the amount of data you acquire. In these situations you do not want to have to write two versions of an application (one to use a `Bag` and one to use a `FileBag`). Nor do you want to have to use a `FileBag` even though you only have five data items. One way of dealing with this is to define the `FileBag` in such a way that the methods that use the data structures do not need to know whether they have a `Bag` or a `FileBag`. This can be done by ensuring that the `Bag` and the `FileBag` present the same protocol (set of methods). This is achieved by having both classes implement the same interface definition. This also means that methods that receive, or return the `Bag` or `FileBag`, can specify the interface as their return type, rather than a class.

In many ways a file collection is just the same as file-based data in other languages. The point to note is that whereas you would need to know that you are dealing with files (e.g. in C or Pascal), in Java you can easily encapsulate the file within an object. It is then the object that decides how the data is saved and where it is saved. The user of the object need never know that they are working with a file. This promotes the reusability, maintainability and clarity of the system. This is partly achieved due to the polymorphism and dynamic typing of Java.

8.3 Implementing a `FileBag` Class

In the remainder of this chapter we will consider the implementation of a `FileBag` class (and its supporting classes). A `FileBag` is a data structure that stores its objects in a file. This file only exists for the lifetime of the data structure object and is not used to make the data persistent or to share data between different Java runtimes.

To allow the use of either a `Bag` or a `FileBag` we first define a `Collection` interface. To support the development of the `FileBag` class two additional classes are defined. One is used to provide a ranged random number generator (this class is called `RangedRandom`). The second class, the `UniqueFilename` class uses the `RangedRandom` number generator to create a (semi)-unique filename for the file cache used by the `FileBag` class. A unique filename is required for the cache file as more than one Java virtual machine may be sharing the same cache directory. We therefore want to ensure that two file bags in different virtual machines do not try to use the same cache file. The `FileBag` class as well as the two supporting classes are defined in the `fbc` package (`fbc` stands for **File Bag Collection**).

8.4 The `Collection` Interface

This is an interface that specifies the methods provided by any object that can be treated as a unordered collection of objects (such as a `Bag` or a `FileBag`). The primary things which such a collection must be able to do is add and remove elements and allow iteration over these elements (note that JDK 1.2 provides an extended set of data structure classes and new methods of iteration). The interface thus defines the `addElement()`, `removeElement()`, `getSize()` and `isEmpty()`. It inherits `elements()`, `hasMoreElements()` and `nextElement()` methods from the `Enumeration` interface. The `Collection` interface is presented in Listing 8.1.

Listing 8.1 *The* `Collection` *interface*

```
package utilities;
public interface Collection extends Enumeration {
  public int getSize();
  public boolean isEmpty();
  public synchronized void
    removeElement(Serializable);
  public synchronized void addElement(Serializable);
}
```

8.5 The RangedRandom Class

The `RangedRandom` class is a subclass of `Random` and is capable of generating a number between a lower bound and an upper bound. The result of instantiating the class is not a random number but a random number generator which will generate numbers between the specified lower bound and the upper bound. Listing 8.2 presents the source code for this class.

Listing 8.2 `RangedRandom.java`

```
package fbc;
import java.util.Random;

/**
  * The class can be used to create random number
  * generators which return random integers in a
  * specified range.
  */
public class RangedRandom extends Random {
  private int lowerBound, expansion;
  /**
    * Creates a new RangedRandom object for the
    * specified range
    * from - lower bound of range
    * to - upper bound of range
    */
  RangedRandom (int from , int to) {
    lowerBound = from;
    expansion = (to - lowerBound) + 1;
  }

  /** Returns next value in the random sequence */
  public int next () {
    double temp = super.nextDouble();
    return lowerBound + ((int)(temp * expansion));
```

```
  }
}
```

The class possesses two instance variables, referred to as lowerBound and expansion. These will be used to hold the lower bound and the difference between the lower bound and the upper bound (respectively). The class possesses a single constructor that is used to specify the range within which the random numbers are to be generated.

There is one instance method, next, which returns a random number between the specified lower and upper bounds. It does this by generating a new random number from the nextDouble() method defined in the superclass and multiplying that by the expansion and adding the lower bound. Note that the nextDouble() method of the Random class provided with Java returns a random number between 0.0 and 0.9. This means that by multiplying it by the expansion we get a value which when added to the lowerBound provides a random number between the lower and upper bounds. For example, if the lower bound is 1 and the upper bound 10, and the superclass version of nextDouble() returns 0.5, then the result is 0.5 × 10 + 1, to give 6. The result is then cast to an integer.

We can test this class using the following test harness:

```
public class Test {
public static void main (String args []) {
  RangedRandom r = new RangedRandom(1, 6);
  for (int i = 0; i 10;i++)
    System.out.print(r.next());
  System.out.flush();
  }
}
```

The results of executing this test program are presented below:

```
C:fbcjava Test
1 5 2 3 6 6 3 3 3 4
```

8.6 The UniqueFilename Class

The UniqueFilename class is used to generate a unique filename to hold the objects placed in the file associated with the FileBag. Listing 8.3 presents the source code for this class. Note that the constructor for this class does nothing as it is not intended that instances can be constructed. Instead, the class acts as a convenient placeholder for the static method next(). This method returns a (semi-) unique random filename.

Listing 8.3 The UniqueFilename class

```
package fbc;
```

```java
/**
 *
 * This class generates unique filenames for use with
 * the FileBag class.To do this it uses the
 * RangedRandom class.
 * An example of using this class is presented below:
 *
 * <pre>
 *  public static void main (String args [] ) {
 *
 *     UniqueFilename f = new UniqueFilename();
 *     for (int i = 0; i 5; i++)
 *        System.out.println(f.next());
 *  }
 *
 * </pre>
 * @see RangedRandom
 */
public class UniqueFilename {
  static int FileIndex = 0;
  static char characters [] = {'a', 'e', 'i', 'o',
    'u', 'x', 'y', 'z'};
  static int sizeOfString = 5;
  static RangedRandom random= new RangedRandom(1,
    (characters.length -1));

  UniqueFilename () {
    // Note intended for instance creation
  }

  private static int nextIndex () {
    return FileIndex++;
  }

  /**
   * Returns the a new unqiue random filename.
   * @return result unique random filename.
   */
  public static String next () {
    StringBuffer result = new StringBuffer("");
    for (int i = 0; i sizeOfString; i++) {
      result = result.append(
        characters[random.next()]);
    }
    result.append(nextIndex());
    return result.toString();
```

```
    }
  }
```

To do this it uses the `RangedRandom` class to create a random number generator object to use in generating a unique filename. It then uses a list of characters (held in the static side of the class) to randomly select combinations of these characters to concatenate together to form a random string. A numeric identifier is added to the end of these file names to increase the uniqueness of the filename.

A test harness of this class can be written as follows:

```
public class Test {
  public static void main (String args [] ) {
    UniqueFilename f = new UniqueFilename();
    for (int i = 0; i 5; i++)
      System.out.println(f.next());
}}
```

The results of executing this test harness are presented below:

```
C:fbc>java UniqueFilename
euozi0
xyxyo1
eyxyu2
zziyy3
uioee4
```

8.7 The `FileBag` Class

The `FileBag` class is a data structure class based on a `Bag`. Such a data structure holds an unordered collection of objects. The `FileBag` holds this collection of objects in a file using the serialization mechanism introduced in Sun's JDK 1.1.

A `FileBag` can be used to store multiple copies of an object in any order. It is possible to add objects, remove objects and enumerate over those objects. However, as a bag is not guaranteed to have any particular order it is not possible to insert elements, remove elements or set elements at a particular point (as can be done with the class `Vector`). Listing 8.4 presents the source code for the class `FileBag`.

The instance variable `size` is used to record the number of objects in the `FileBag`. This actually indicates the number of objects currently held by the `FileBag` which have not yet been deleted. A second instance variable `total` indicates how many objects are actually held in the `FileBag` (some of which may have been deleted but have yet to be purged). This may seem a slightly bizarre way to hold data; however, if we wished to remove a deleted object immediately then we would have to rewrite the serialization file. This is time-consuming and unnecessary. Instead, a cache is maintained of all deleted objects. Once this cache reaches a certain size the serialization file is regenerated. Note the intention is that although elements may be added to a `FileBag`, it is rare that elements will be removed.

The `FileBag` class also defines the directory within which to hold the temporary cache file (this is a static variable), the name of this file and the `ObjectOutputStream`.

Listing 8.4 The `FileBag` class

```
package fbc;
import java.util.*;
import java.io.*;

/**
 *
 * A FileBag can be used to store multiple copies of
 * an object in any order. It is possible
 * to add objects, remove obejcts and enumerate over
 * those objects. However, as a bag is not
 * guaranteed to have any particular order it is not
 * possible to insert elements, remove elements
 * or set elements at a particular point (as can be
 * done with the class Vector).
 *
 * @author John Hunt
 * @version 6 June 1997
 *
 */

public class FileBag implements utilities.Collection {
    // The directory used to hold the cache files, the
    // name of the cache file and the stream to connect
    // to the file
    protected final static String directory ="C:/tmp/";
    protected String filename = "";
    protected ObjectOutputStream output;

    // Now provide for the modified type of enumeration
    protected ObjectInputStream input;
    protected boolean enumerationFlag = false;
    protected int currentPosition;

    // Counts for the current size of the file bag
    protected int size, total;

    // The removed elements vector and its maximum size
    protected int removedElementsMaxSize;
    protected Vector removedElements;

    /**
```

```
    * Constructs an empty file bag with a default
    * delete cache capacity of 10
    */
   FileBag () {
     this(10);
   }

   /**
    * Constructs an empty file bag with the specified
    * initial delete cache capacity.
    *
    * @param  removedCacheSize  the number of
    * elements which can be deleted before
    * the cache file is re-written.
    */
   FileBag (int removedCacheSize) {
     removedElementsMaxSize = removedCacheSize;
     removedElements = new Vector(
       removedElementsMaxSize);
     filename = newFilename();
     try {
       output = new ObjectOutputStream(
         new FileOutputStream(filename));
     } catch (IOException e) {
       System.out.println("Error opening cache
         file");
     }
   }

   protected static String newFilename() {
     String fileWithPath;
     UniqueFilename newfile;
     File dir;

     dir = new File(directory);
     if (!dir.exists()) {
       dir.mkdir();
     }
     fileWithPath = directory +
       UniqueFilename.next() + ".fv";
     return fileWithPath;
   }

   /**
    * Returns the current size of this file bag.
    *
    * @return int the current size of this file bag.
```

```
  */
public int getSize() {
  return size;
}

/**
 * Tests if this file bag has no components.
 *
 * @return <code>true</code> when file bag has no
 * components; <code>false</code> otherwise.
 */
public final boolean isEmpty() {
  return size == 0;
}

/**
 * Returns a string representation of file bag.
 *
 * @return String representation of this file bag.
 */
public String toString() {
  return "FileBag: cache file " + filename + " :
    holds " + size + " elements";
}

protected void incrementSize () {
  size++;
  total++;
}

protected void decrementSize () {
  size--;
}
protected void resetSize () {
  size = 0;
  total = 0;
}

protected void setEnumerationFlag() {
  enumerationFlag = true;
}

protected void resetEnumerationFlag() {
  enumerationFlag = false;
}

protected boolean isEnumeration() {
```

```
    return enumerationFlag;
}

/**
 * Adds the specified component to this file bag,
 * increasing its size by one.
 *
 * @param the serializable component to be added.
 *
 * @see java.io.Serializable
 */
public synchronized void addElement(
    Serializable object) {
  boolean append = false;
  try {
    output.writeObject(object);
    incrementSize();
    resetEnumerationFlag();
  }
  catch (IOException e) {
    System.out.println("Error within addElement
        for " + object);
  }
}

/**
 * Removes the first occurrence of the argument
 * from this file bag. The object to
 * be deleted is recorded in a deleted elements
 * cache. Once this cache reaches a specified size
 * the cache file is regenerated.
 *
 * @param   object   the component to be removed.
 *
 */
public synchronized void removeElement(
    Serializable object) {
  removedElements.addElement(object);
  decrementSize();
  if (removedElements.size() =
      removedElementsMaxSize)
    reCache();
  resetEnumerationFlag();
}

private synchronized Vector contents () {
  Vector result = new Vector(size);
```

```
      // Need to take a copy as we may have multiples
      // of an object but not all copies may have
      // been deleted.
      Vector elementsToIgnore = removedElements;
      Object element;

      try {
        ObjectInputStream input =
            New ObjectInputStream(
            new FileInputStream(filename));
        for (int i = 0; i < total; i++) {
          element = input.readObject();
          if (elementsToIgnore.contains(element))
            elementsToIgnore.removeElement(
            element);
          else
            result.addElement(element);
        }
        input.close();
      } catch (ClassNotFoundException e) {
        System.out.println("Error reading objects");
      } catch (IOException e) {
        System.out.println("Error accessing file");
        System.out.println(e.getMessage());
      }
      return result;
  }

  /**
   * Ensures that the file bag is ready for an
   * enumeration. It appears to work in a similar
   * manner to elements() in the class vector, but
   * the internal implementation is very different.
   */
  public Enumeration elements () {
    try {
      currentPosition = 0;
      input = new ObjectInputStream(new
        FileInputStream(filename));
      setEnumerationFlag();
    } catch (IOException e) {
      System.out.println("Error accessing cache");
      System.out.println(e.getMessage());
    }
    return this;
  }
```

```java
/**
 * Returns the next element in the enumeration
 * sequence
 * @returns Object Next element
 * @exception FileBagEnumerationException Indicates
 * that an element has been added or deleted while
 * the enumeration was in progress.
 * @exception java.util.NoSuchElementException if no
 * more elements exist.
 */

public Object nextElement() throws
     FileBagEnumerationException,
   NoSuchElementException {
 Object element, result = null;
 Vector elementsToIgnore = removedElements;
 if (isEnumeration()) {

    try {
      if (currentPosition == total) {
        input.close();
        throw new NoSuchElementException();
      } else {
      while (result == null) {
        currentPosition++;
        element = input.readObject();
        if
          (elementsToIgnore.contains(element))
            elementsToIgnore.removeElement(
            element);
        else
          result = element;
        }
      }
    } catch (ClassNotFoundException e) {
      System.out.println("Error reading
        objects");
    } catch (IOException e) {
      System.out.println("Error accessing
        file");
      System.out.println(e.getMessage());
    }

  } else {
  try {
    input.close();
  } catch (IOException e) {}
```

```
      throw new FileBagEnumerationException();
   }

   return result;
}

/**
 * Returns true if there are more elements to
 * enumerate.
 * @returns boolean
 */
public boolean hasMoreElements() {
   return currentPosition != total;
}

/**
 * Removes all cached elements from the
 * contents of the file and resaves the file
 */
private synchronized void reCache() {
   try {
     output.close();
     Vector allElements = contents();
     (new File(filename)).delete();
     resetSize();
     filename = newFilename();
     output = new ObjectOutputStream(
         new FileOutputStream(filename));
     Enumeration e = allElements.elements();
     while (e.hasMoreElements()) {
       addElement(
         (Serializable)e.nextElement());
     }
     removedElements =
       new Vector(removedElementsMaxSize);
   }
   catch (IOException e) {
     System.out.println("Problem in reCache");
   }
}

/**
 * Deletes cache file associated with file bag.
 */
public void dispose () {
   try {
     output.close();
```

```
      (new File(filename)).delete();
      output = null;
    }
    catch (IOException e) {
      System.out.println("Exception raised when
        disposing of cache file");
    }
  }

  /**
   * Runs when the object is garbage collected.
   * Checks to see if the output file has already
   * been disposed.
   *
   * @exception java.lang.Throwable  May be generated
   * by parents finalize or by disposal of resources.
   */
  protected void finalize() throws Throwable {
    super.finalize();
    if (output != null)
      dispose();
  }
}
```

8.7.1 Using a `FileBag` Constructor

The class `FileBag` provides two constructors. One is a convenient way of calling the
other. That is, the zero parameter constructor calls a constructor which takes a single
parameter, with an appropriate default value. This single parameter indicates the size
of the cache of deleted objects (called `removedElements`) and is maintained in
the variable `removedElementsMaxSize`. The second constructor (the single-
parameter constructor) sets these instance variables and calls the static (class)
method `newFilename()` which uses the `UniqueFilename` class to provide a
cache serialization file within a temporary directory (which it creates if necessary).
An example of using the constructors is presented below:

```
FileBag fb = new FileBag();
fb = new FileBag(5);
```

8.7.2 The Housekeeping Methods

There are a number of housekeeping methods, such as `incrementSize()`,
`decrementSize()` and `resetSize()`. These methods handle the `size` and
`total` instance variables appropriately. Note that `decrementSize()` does not
alter the value of `total`.

Another internal method, contents(), returns a vector of the elements held in the serialization cache file. To do this it reads objects from an ObjectInputStream. These objects are then added to the vector returned from the method if they are not members of the list of objects that have been removed.

The reCache() method is an important housekeeping method, which is used when it is necessary to regenerate the serialization cache file. This occurs when the number of objects that have been deleted but not yet purged from a filebag exceeds the removedElementsMaxSize. The reCache() method obtains a vector of objects from the existing serialization cache file, deletes that file and resaves the objects into a new cache file.

8.7.3 `FileBag` Collection Interface Methods

There are a number of methods involved in adding, removing and testing elements in the FileBag (as defined by the Collection interface). These include addElement(), removeElement(), getSize() and isEmpty(). These are briefly described below:

- addElement() This method allows serializable objects to be added to a FileBag. To do this it writes the object out onto the ObjectOutputStream (held in the instance variable output). It then increments the size of the file bag.
- removeElement() This method allows a serializable object to be removed from the file bag. To do this it adds the object to the removedElements vector and decrements the size of the file bag. If the number of removed elements exceeds the number of elements held in the cache then the file bag is re-cached. This involves calling the reCache() method.
- getSize() returns the size of the file bag.
- isEmpty() tests to see if the file bag is empty.

Note that a number of the methods are synchronized, such as addElement(), removeElement() and contents(). This ensures that if the FileBag class is being used within a multithreaded program there is no chance that the scheduler will pre-empt the thread, adding, removing or listing the elements in the file bag. This should ensure that no instance of the FileBag can end up in an inconsistent state.

8.7.4 Enumerating Over a `FileBag`

There are many situations in which we want to be able to enumerate over a collection of data elements. Indeed, the classes Vector and Hashtable provide methods which return objects whose class implements the enumeration interface for exactly this purpose. We therefore need the ability to enumerate over a FileBag. However, we do not wish to load all the elements held in the cache file into memory in order to achieve this enumeration, as this would defeat the purpose of the FileBag itself. Instead, we provide a set of methods that allow the start of an enumeration and subsequent processing of each element in turn. These methods are listed below. Note that if an attempt to add to or delete from the `FileBag` is made during an enumeration, the enumeration pointer is lost and the process must be restarted.

- `elements()` Sets the file bag up ready for enumeration. It pretends to return an enumeration object, but this is in fact the file bag that received the method.
- `nextElement()` Returns the next element in the enumeration sequence. The method throws the `FileBagEnumerationException` when an element has been added or deleted while the enumeration was in progress and the `NoSuchElementException` if no more elements exist.
- `hasMoreElements()` returns true if there are still elements to enumerate.

The `FileBagEnumerationException` class is presented in Listing 8.5. There is not much to note about this class except that it is a subclass of `NoSuchElementException`. This is because the exception(s) thrown by the `nextElement()` method are defined in the interface `java.util.Enumeration`. This interface specifies that this method only throws a `NoSuchElementException` (or by implication one of its subclasses). By making the `FileBagEnumerationException` a subclass of `NoSuchElementException` we can throw either exception out of the `nextElement()` method.

Listing 8.5 *FileBagEnumerationException.java*

```
package fbc;

public class FileBagEnumerationException extends
    Exception {
public FileBagEnumerationException () {
    super("Exception during file bag enumeration");
  }
}
```

An example of using the enumeration methods with a file bag is presented below:

```
Enumeration e = filebag.elements();
while (e.hasMoreElements()) {
  System.out.println(e.nextElement());
}
```

8.7.5 The `dispose` and `finalize` Methods

The `dispose()` method is used to free up file resources once the `FileBag` is no longer required. It closes the `ObjectOutputStream` and then deletes the serialization cache file. This method should be called whenever the file bag is no longer required.

As a safety check, the `finalize()` method (which is executed when the object is garbage collected) calls the dispose method if a reference is still held to the `ObjectOutputStream`. However, users should not rely on the `finalize` method to free up resources, as the `finalize` method may never be run (for example if the program terminates before the garbage collector runs).

8.7.6 Using the `FileBag` Class

As an example of using the `FileBag` class try out the code in Listing 8.6.

Listing 8.6 *An example of using a* `FileBag`

```
public static void main (String args []) {

  // Test harness for FileBag class
  FileBag f = new FileBag();
  f.addElement("John");
  f.addElement("Paul");
  f.addElement("Denise");
  System.out.println("\nContents of file bag:");

  Enumeration e = f.elements();
  while (e.hasMoreElements()) {
    System.out.println(e.nextElement());
  }
  f.addElement("Phoebe");
  f.addElement("Andrew");
  f.removeElement("Paul");

  System.out.println("\nNew contents file bag:");

  e = f.elements();
  while (e.hasMoreElements()) {
    System.out.println(e.nextElement());
  }

  f.dispose();
}
```

8.8 Online Resources

A collection of Java data structure classes that provide `Bags`, `Sets` and `Ordered-Collections` can be obtained from

   `http://www.gamelan.com/`

Note that the JDK 1.2 includes many data structure collection classes.

9   *Frameworks*

9.1 Introduction

Designing complex software systems is hard. It is a great deal easier to reuse an existing software system, merely modifying it where necessary, than to build it from scratch. These two facts have led to a great deal of interest in what have become termed "software frameworks" in the object-oriented community. A software framework has been described as "the reusable design of a system or a part of a system expressed as a set of abstract classes [and concrete classes] and the way instances of (subclasses of) those classes collaborate". For example the Model–View–Controller (MVC) framework is a very powerful way of creating graphical user interface applications.

9.2 What is a Framework?

A framework is a reusable design of a program or a part of a program expressed as a set of classes. That is, a framework is a set of prefabricated software building blocks that programmers can use, extend or customize for specific computing solutions. With frameworks, software developers don't have to start from scratch each time they write an application. Frameworks are built from a collection of objects, so both the design and code of a framework may be reused. However, frameworks are not necessarily easy to design or implement. Questions such as "How much will it cost?" to produce a framework and "How much will we benefit?" from the framework are difficult to answer. In addition, reusing frameworks instead of libraries can cause subtle architectural changes in an application, calling for innovative management.

Frameworks can provide solutions to different types of problem domain. These include application frameworks, domain frameworks and support frameworks:

- *Application frameworks* encapsulate expertise applicable to a wide variety of programs. These frameworks encompass a horizontal slice of functionality that can be applied across client domains. An application framework might provide the basic facilities of a payroll system or a geographic information system. These facilities could then be used to construct a concrete payroll (or GIS) system with the features required by a specific organization.

- *Domain frameworks* encapsulate expertise in a particular problem domain. These frameworks encompass a vertical slice of functionality for a particular client domain. Examples of domain frameworks include a control systems framework for developing control applications for manufacturing systems or drawing frameworks such as HotDraw, Unidraw for C++/X-Windows and DRAW_Master for C++/OS/2 and Windows environments.

● *Support frameworks* provide system-level services, such as file access, distributed computing support or device drivers. Application developers typically use support frameworks directly or use modifications produced by system providers. However, even support frameworks can be customized – for example when developing a new file system or device driver.

Since frameworks are reusable designs, not just code, they are more abstract than most software, which makes documenting them more difficult. Documentation for a framework has three purposes. Documentation must provide:

1. the purpose of the framework
2. how to use the framework
3. the detailed design of the framework

The second and thirds points are the difficult issues for those developing frameworks. It is one thing to document a concrete system; it is quite another to document a partially abstract structure which may be used in a diverse set of ways. This is the primary challenge facing those documenting frameworks (see Chapter 10 for a discussion of the use of patterns as a way to document frameworks).

9.3 MVC: An Example Framework

The intention of the MVC framework is the separation of the user display from the control of user input and from the underlying information model, as illustrated in Figure 9.1. There are a number of reasons why this is useful:

● reusability of application and/or user interface components
● ability to develop the application and user interface separately
● ability to inherit from different parts of the class hierarchy
● ability to define control style classes which provide common features separately from how these features may be displayed

This means that different interfaces can be used with the same application, without the application knowing about it. It also means that any part of the system can be changed without affecting the operation of the other. For example, the way that the

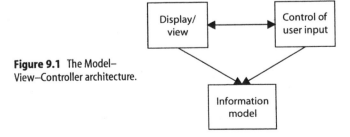

Figure 9.1 The Model–
View–Controller architecture.

graphical interface (the look) displays the information could be changed without modifying the actual application or how input is handled (the feel). Indeed the application need not know what type of interface is currently connected to it at all.

9.3.1 What Java Facilities Support the MVC

Java provides two facilities that together allow the separation of the application, interface and control elements. These are:

- The observer/observable model. This allows application programs and user interfaces to be loosely coupled.
- The delegation event model. This provides listeners which act as controllers handling various events which may occur.

In JDK 1.0 and 1.0.2 Java could only really support the Model–View relationship. This relationship used the dependency mechanism implemented by the `Observable` class and the `Observer` interface. However, in JDK 1.1 a delegation event mechanism was introduced which allows the controller to be separated out from the user interface. Thus it is now possible to have separate model, view and controller objects. Below we will look at these two mechanisms before considering how they are used to implement Java's MVC framework.

9.3.2 Observers and Observables

In Java, dependency is a relationship that can be used to relate two objects such that, as the state of one changes, the state of another automatically changes in an appropriate manner. In such a relationship we say that one object is dependent upon another. The dependency mechanism is implemented in the class `Observable` within the `java.util` package. This class is a direct subclass of `Object`. This means that any class can inherit from `Observable` and thus take part in a dependency relationship. In Java terminology the object which is the head of the dependent relationship (i.e. the object on which other objects depend) is referred to as the `Observable` object, while the dependent object is referred to as the observer object. This is because the observable object allows other objects to observe its current state. An observable object can have zero or more observers all of which are notified of changes to its state via the `notifyObservers()` method.

The basic implementation, inherited from `Observable`, provides a `Vector` of objects. These objects will observe the observable object (collectively these objects are known as the object's observers). For example, in Figure 9.2 the object `Account` has two observers: `Manager` and `Debt Collector`. The links to the dependent objects are held by `Account` in a `Vector` of observers called `obs`. The `addObserver()` message is used to add an object to another object's dependency `Vector`. Now when an account goes into the red (overdrawn) the manager and the debt collector can both be informed.

We can use this mechanism to tell one object that another object has changed in some way. To do this we use two sets of methods. One set is used to state that something has changed. These are called "changed" methods. The other set are used

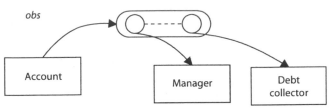

Figure 9.2 An object and its observers.

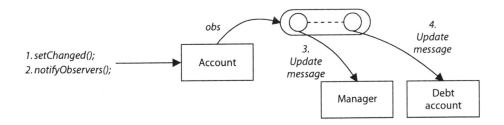

Figure 9.3 The dependency mechanism in action.

to state what type of update is required. These are called "update" methods. They work as illustrated in Figure 9.3, which illustrates the sequence of messages that are sent in response to the changed messages being sent to an object. That is, when `Account` is sent the `setChanged()` and `notifyObservers()` messages (usually by itself) all its observers are sent an `update()` message. Again from the point of view of `Account` much of this behaviour is hidden.

The other end of this relationship is the `Observer` object. The `Observer` interface defines the abstract update method, which must be implemented by objects that wish to take part in a dependency relationship. The actual `Observer` interface definitions is essentially:

```
public interface Observer {
    void update(Observable observable, Object arg);
}
```

As with all interfaces, any concrete class implementing this interface must provide the body of the update method. Thus any class implementing this interface can be guaranteed to work with the notification methods used in an observer object.

9.3.3 The Delegation Event Model

The Java delegation event model introduced the concept of listeners. Listeners are effectively objects which "listen" for a particular event to occur. When it does they react to it. For example, the event associated with the button might be that it has been "pressed". The listener would then be notified that the button had been pressed and would decide what action to take. This approach involves delegation because the responsibility for handling an event generated by one object may belong to another objects.

9.4 The MVC Framework in Java

This section describes how the MVC framework can be implemented using the core Java language features. Note that the JFC in JDK 1.2 also uses a framework based on the MVC. However, you may wish to use the MVC explictly in your own code, or you may not have access to JDK 1.2. We therefore present this description.

9.4.1 The Model Class

Figure 9.6 illustrates that there is no direct link from the account object to the interface. However, the dependency mechanism defined by Java can be used to inform any object, interested in the state of the account object, that a change has occurred. Thus it is possible to use the observer/observable mechanism to provide a Model class which informs observers of changes in its state. The Model class of our MVC framework is illustrated below:

```
import java.util.Observable;
/**
 * Base abstract class of all Models in the MVC.
 * <p>
 * Provides the notifyChange() method to notify
 * registered observers of changes
 */
public abstract class Model extends Observable {
  // Method used to notify observers
  public void notifyChanged() {
    setChanged();
    notifyObservers();
  }
}
```

Thus an interface object can register itself as an observer of the model object. Then, when a change is made to the state of the model, it can inform its observers that a change has occurred and that they should update themselves. In this way the interface object can be told when to update its display, without the model object having to know that it even exists.

9.4.2 The Controller Classes

The root of the Controller class hierarchy is the abstract Controller class. This class defines all the basic facilities required to implement a controller. That is, it allows a view and model to be linked to the controller. The source code for this class is presented below.

```
/**
 * The Controller class is an abstract class for the
 * control element of the MVC.
 */
public abstract class Controller {
  protected View view;
  protected Model model;

  public Controller (View view) {
    setView(view);
    setModel(view.getModel());
  }

  public void setView(View view) { this.view = view; }
  public View getView() { return view; }
  public void setModel(Model model) { this.model =
    model; }
  public Model getModel() { return model; }
}
```

A convenience controller class for controllers handling button action events is also provided. This is the `ActionController` class. This class is also an abstract class that extends the `Controller` class and implements the `ActionListener`. This means that any subclass of `ActionController` must implement the `actionPerformed()` method.

```
import java.awt.event.*;
/**
 * The ActionController class is an abstract
 * convenience class for button controllers
 */
public abstract class ActionController extends
Controller implements ActionListener {
  public ActionController (View view) {
    super(view);
  }
}
```

`ActionControllers` are controllers that are registered as event listeners for the various input elements on the interface (view). For example, the `ActionController` class would be subclassed to provide a controller for a panel containing a set of buttons.

9.4.3 The View Class

The `View` class is the root class of the view class hierarchy. It allows a controller and a model to be registered and can register itself with a model as an observer of that model. In this case it also acts as the top-level frame of an application (however, if necessary a `ViewFrame` and a `ViewPanel` class could be provided). It this extends the frame class and implements the `WindowListener` interface. It provides null implementations for most of the `WindowListener` methods. For the `windowClosing()` method it provides a basic application "exit" implementation.

```java
import java.awt.*;
import java.awt.event.*;
import java.util.*;

/**
 * The abstract View class of the MVC framework.
 * Requires the implementation of the
 * update(Observable o, Object arg) method.
 */
public abstract class View extends Frame implements
WindowListener, Observer {
  protected Controller controller;
  protected Model model;

  public View () {
    /* Add the listener for the view */
    addWindowListener(this);
  }

  public View(Controller controller) {
    this();
    this.controller = controller;
  }

  public void setController(Controller controller) {
    this.controller = controller;
  }

  public Controller getController () { return
    controller; }

  public void setModel(Model model) { this.model =
    model; }

public Model getModel() { return model; }

  public void registerWithModel() {
    model.addObserver(this); }

  public void windowClosed(WindowEvent event) {}
  public void windowOpened(WindowEvent event) {}
  public void windowDeiconified(WindowEvent event) {}
```

```
public void windowIconified(WindowEvent event) {}
public void windowActivated(WindowEvent event) {}
public void windowDeactivated(WindowEvent event) {}
public void windowClosing(WindowEvent event) {
  System.exit(0);
}
}
```

As a view is a subclass of a `Frame` it can, of course, be made up of a number of objects, such as a subpanels panels and canvasses, as well as graphical components, such as buttons and text fields. In turn, layout managers can be used to control the way in which these objects are arranged within the window frame.

9.5 The Balance Application

The application we shall construct using the MVC framework described above is illustrated in Figure 9.4. This application allows users to keep track of their current balance. This is done using two buttons that indicate whether the amount input should be treated as a deposit or a withdrawal. The amount to be used in the current transaction is input by the user in the first of the text fields, while the current balance is displayed in the second text field.

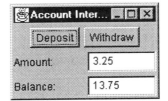

Figure 9.4 The GUI for the Account application.

The overall structure of the application is that illustrated in Figure 9.5. Note that the view object (`AccountInterface`) and the controller objects have direct links between them. However, although the interface and the controller objects have links to the application (`anAccount`), the application knows nothing directly about the interface or the controllers. This means that the application is independent of the interface and its controllers and may actually have various different interfaces associated with it. One of the advantages of this approach is that any one of the three elements can be modified without the need to change the others.

The system interaction is illustrated in Figure 9.6. This figure illustrates the various messages sent once a user clicks on the Deposit button. There are a number of points you should note about this example:

1. Neither the display nor the controllers hold onto the balance. It is obtained from the account whenever it is needed.
2. The controller relies on the delegation event model to determine that it should do something.

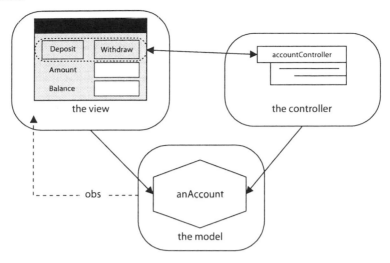

Figure 9.5 The MVC architecture as it is implemented by the Account application.

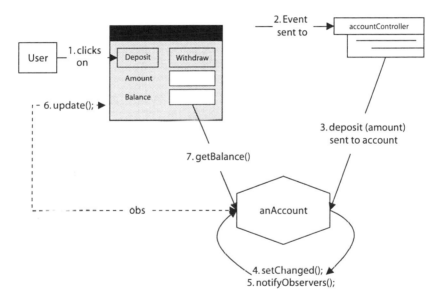

Figure 9.6 Interaction in the Account application.

3. When the controller asks the model to change it doesn't tell the display – the display finds out about the change through the observer/observable mechanism.

4. The account is unaware that the message deposit(amount); came from the controller. Thus any object could send a deposit message and the account would still inform its dependents about the change.

9.6 The Application Code

The class hierarchy, illustrating the inheritance relationships between the application classes and the framework classes, is presented in Figure 9.7. This illustrates that the `AccountInterface` is the view (of the MVC architecture), that the `Account` class is the `Model` and the various controllers provide the last element of the MVC. Each of these classes is presented below.

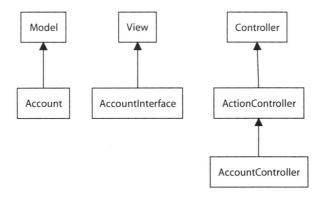

Figure 9.7 The class hierarchies for the `Account` application.

9.6.1 The `Account` class

The `Account` class extends the `Model` class by providing an implementation of the `withdraw()` and `deposit()` methods. Note that these methods must call the `notifyChanged()` method (inherited from `Model`) in case the `account` is involved in an MVC implementation.

```
public class Account extends Model {
  private double balance = 0.0;

  public Account (double initialBalance) {
    setBalance(initialBalance);
  }

  private void setBalance (double anAmount) {
    balance = 0.0;
    deposit(anAmount);
  }

  public void deposit (double anAmount) {
    balance += anAmount;
    notifyChanged();
```

```
    }

    public void withdraw (double anAmount) {
      balance -= anAmount;
      notifyChanged();
    }

    public String stringBalance () {
      return String.valueOf(balance);
    }
  }
```

9.6.2 The `AccountInterface` class

This class provides the concrete implementation of the abstract `View` class. It extends `View` and thus can act as a frame and as an observer, and can handle window events. The core elements which allow the `AccountInterface` to fit into the MVC are the setting of the model and setting the controller (both operations inherited from `View`) and the implementation of the `update()` method (mandated by the `View` class implementing the `Observer` interface). The remainder of this class is implementation-specific. This involves the creation of a button subpanel and a text subpanel. These are described below.

```
import java.awt.*;
import java.util.Observable;
import java.util.Observer;

/**
  * Purpose: to define an example AccountInterface
  * which extends View.
  */
public class AccountInterface extends View {
  protected TextPanel textPanel;

  public static void main (String args []) {
    new AccountInterface();
  }

  public AccountInterface () {
    setTitle("Account Interface");

    // Create the model and register the view
    setModel (new Account(0.0));
    registerWithModel();

    // Create and store controller
    setController(new AccountController(this));
```

```
    // Create the Button panel
    ButtonPanel buttonPanel = new ButtonPanel(this);
    add("North", buttonPanel);

    // Next set up the text panel
    textPanel = new TextPanel(this);
    add("Center", textPanel);

    /* Now pack the window and make it visible */
    pack();
    setVisible(true);
  }

  // The update method is called whenever the models
  // state changes
  // Note we need to cast the model to Account to call
  // StringBalance()
  public void update (Observable o, Object arg) {
    textPanel.balanceField.setText(
        ((Account)(getModel())).stringBalance());
  }
}
```

The `ButtonPanel` subpanel merely displays two buttons. These buttons are labelled" Deposit" and "Withdraw". The action events generated by these buttons are handled by the `AccountController`, which is a subclass of the `ActionController`.

```
class ButtonPanel extends Panel {
  public ButtonPanel (View view, Controller cont) {

    Button button = new Button("Deposit");
    button.addActionListener(cont);
    add(button);

    button = new Button("Withdraw");
    button.addActionListener(cont);
    add(button);
  }
}
```

The `TextPanel` subpanel defines the two textual fields displayed. One is used to read in an amount, the other to print out the balance.

```
class TextPanel extends Panel {
  protected TextField inputField, balanceField;

  public TextPanel (AccountInterface view) {
    setLayout(new GridLayout(2, 2, 5, 5));
```

```
        add(new Label("Amount: "));
        inputField = new TextField(8);
        add(inputField);
        add(new Label("Balance: "));
        balanceField = new TextField(8);
        add(balanceField);
    }
}
```

9.6.3 The Controllers

The AccountController is a concrete subclass of ActionController that defines how the events generated by the view (or its subpanels) should be handled. In this particular case it deals with events generated by the buttons in the button panel. That is what should happen when the Withdraw and Deposit buttons are pressed.

```
class AccountController extends ActionController {
    public AccountController(View view) {
        super(view);
    }
    public void actionPerformed(ActionEvent event) {
        String action = event.getActionCommand();
        double amount;
        // Converts the numerical strings in the text
        // input field to a double
        amount = (Double.valueOf(((AccountInterface)
            (getView())).textPanel.inputField.getText()))
                                                .doubleValue();
        // Depending on which button is pressed, the
        // amount is either deposited or withdrawn. Note
        // need to cast model to Account
        if (action.equals("Withdraw"))
            ((Account)(getModel())).withdraw(amount);
        else if (action.equals("Deposit")) {
            ((Account)(getModel())).deposit(amount);
        }
    }
}
```

9.6.4 The Instance Structure

The instance diagram that reflects the instantiation of the application is presented in Figure 9.8. The dashed boxes indicate the relationship between the source code and concepts such as model, view and controller. Note that this application (like many applications) has a view made up of other views, each with their own controller. Of course, if this was a real application we might well have very many classes representing the application rather than just the single class presented.

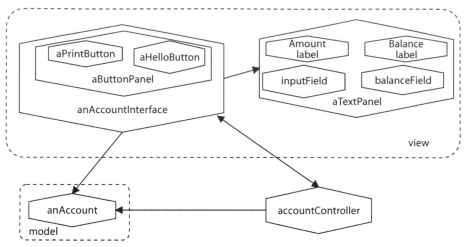

Figure 9.8 The instance structure of the application.

9.6.5 Discussion

The MVC allows a developer to adopt a particular style of GUI construction based around a set of cooperating classes. Of course this architecture is more complex than using a single class containing the whole system. That is, this class would hold the application code, the window definition and the event handling code. However, we would have lost the following advantages:

- reusability of parts of the system
- the ability to inherit from different parts of the class hierarchy
- modularity of system code
- resilience to change
- encapsulation of the application

Although these issues might not be a problem for an application as simple as that presented here, for real-world systems they would certainly be significant. It is hoped that you are now aware of the benefits of adopting the MVC architecture and will try to adopt this approach in your own systems.

9.7 Designing Object-Oriented Frameworks

The process of designing and implementing frameworks is not trivial and is, in many ways, harder than designing and implementing a one-off application. This is because the framework needs to be complete, robust, generic, easy to use, extensible and flexible if it is to be effective:

- *Complete* A framework must provide all the infrastructure required to construct applications. This includes documentation and concrete examples, as well as the underlying skeleton of the framework. If any of these are missing (in particular the underlying skeleton), this will act as an impediment to the adoption of the framework.

- *Robust* A framework that is not robust will soon be ignored, as users will not want to have to debug the framework as well as their own code.
- *Generic* A framework that is not generic (relative to its application area) will be difficult to apply except in very specific ways. This can reduce the incentive for organizations to adopt a framework.
- *Easy to use* A framework which is difficult to use will not be adopted, as few developers have the time to gain the necessary understanding to take advantage of such a framework.
- *Extensible* Users of the framework should find it easy to add and modify default functionality. That is, the framework should provide hooks so that users can apply the framework in different ways.
- *Flexible* One of the claimed benefits of frameworks is that they can be applied and used in ways that were not envisaged by their creators. They therefore need to be flexible.

The first step in developing a framework is to analyze the application problem domain such that you know the requirements of any frameworks, the types of frameworks that would be useful and how they might be used. For example, look for the types of subsystems that are built repeatedly. A pseudo-natural language parser might be a common subsystem within a range of diagnostic tools.

The next step involves identifying what is common about these systems and what is different. This allows the identification of the primary abstractions for the framework. These are the components that are constant across applications (even though they may have different names in these different applications). Note that it is often easiest to work bottom-up in identifying these abstractions (in some cases the designs of the system might be the best starting points and in others the source code).

The third step involves taking these abstractions and constructing a skeleton for the framework. This skeleton should provide the basic infrastructure (comprised of the abstract concepts) for the framework. This is a bit like attempting to produce a set of abstract classes and their interactions for some application, without filling out all (or most) of the concrete classes.

As the framework takes shape you should be continually attempting to refine it by adding more default behaviour and more hooks into it, as well as additional ways for users to interact with it. You will also need to produce concrete instantiations of the framework to test its functionality and to customizability. These example instantiations should be included with the framework as part of the delivered product (whether it is delivered internally or externally to your organization).

The whole development process is extremely iterative but is by necessity subject to the strictest of software engineering practice. In addition, suitable documentation of the framework is essential (and this is where design patterns come into their own) from design, implementation and user perspectives. The next chapter discusses the use of design patterns for documenting frameworks.

9.8 General Guidance for Framework Development

The following list provides some useful general comments about framework development:

- Develop frameworks by examining existing applications.
- Develop small focused frameworks (breaking down larger frameworks when the opportunity to do so is identified).
- Build frameworks using an iterative process, prototyping how the frameworks will be used all the time.
- Always look out for additional functionality for the framework. For such functionality, determine whether it should be a default behaviour of the framework or whether a hook should be provided to allow a user to implement it.
- Good documentation is essential and should include sample instantiations of the framework, descriptions of the framework architecture, descriptions of the framework and its intent, guidelines on using the framework and cookbook examples for particular operations.

9.9 Further Reading

For further information on the Model–View–Controller architecture see:

Krasner G.E. and Pope S.T. (1988) A cookbook for using the Model–View–Controller user interface paradigm in Smalltalk-80. *Journal of Object-Oriented Programming*; 1(3): 26–49.

10 *Patterns for Documenting Frameworks*

10.1 Introduction

There is a growing interest in what have become known generically as patterns – to be more precise, in design patterns. Historically, design patterns have their basis in the work of an architect, C. Alexander, who designed a language for encoding knowledge of the design and construction of buildings. The knowledge is described in terms of patterns that capture both a recurring architectural arrangement and a rule for how and when to apply this knowledge. That is, they incorporate knowledge about the design as well as the basic design relations.

This work was picked up by a number of researchers working within the object-oriented field. This then led to the exploration of how software frameworks can be documented using (software) design patterns. In particular, the work of Johnson provided the form that these design patterns take and the problems encountered in applying them. This was published by K. Beck and R. Johnson in a paper entitled "Patterns generate architectures" in the proceedings of the European Conference on Object-Oriented Programming in 1994.

Since 1995 and the publication of the "Patterns" book by the *Gang of Four* (E. Gamma, R. Helm, R. Johnson and J. Vlissades), interest in patterns has mushroomed. Patterns are now seen as a way of capturing expert and design knowledge associated with a system architecture to support design as well as software reuse. In addition, as interest in patterns has grown their use, and representational expressiveness has grown.

The remainder of the chapter is structured in the following manner: Section 10.2 considers the motivation behind the patterns movement, Section 10.3 considers what a pattern is and is not. Section 10.4 describes how patterns are documented. Section 10.5 briefly considers when patterns should be used, and Section 10.6 discusses the strengths and limitations of patterns. Section 10.7 then presents an example pattern using Java. This pattern considers how you can use a mediator along with a set of associated objects to communicate in a loosely coupled manner.

10.2 Motivation Behind Patterns

There are a number of motivations behind design patterns. These include:

1. Designing reusable software is difficult. Finding appropriate objects and abstractions is not trivial. Having identified such objects, building flexible, modular, reliable code for general reuse is not easy, particularly when dealing with more than one class. In general, such reusable "frameworks" emerge over time rather than being designed from scratch.

2. Software components support reuse of code but not the reuse of knowledge.

3. Frameworks support reuse of design and code but not knowledge of how to use that framework. That is, design trade-offs and expert knowledge are lost.

4. Experienced programmers do not start from first principles every time; thus, successful reusable conceptual designs must exist.

5. Communication of such "architectural" knowledge can be difficult, as it is in the designer's head and is poorly expressed as a program instance.

6. A particular program instance fails to convey constraints, trade-offs and other non-functional forces applied to the "architecture".

7. Since frameworks are reusable designs, not just code, they are more abstract than most software, which makes documenting them more difficult. Documentation for a framework has three purposes and patterns can help to fulfil each of them. Documentation must provide:
   - the purpose of the framework
   - how to use the framework
   - the detailed design of the framework

8. The problem with cookbooks is that they describe a single way in which the framework will be used. A good framework will be used in ways that its designers never conceived. Thus, a cookbook is insufficient on its own to describe every use of the framework. Of course, a developer's first use of a framework usually fits the stereotypes in the cookbook. However, once they go beyond the examples in the cookbook, they need to understand the details of the framework. However, cookbooks tend not to describe the framework itself. But in order to understand a framework, you need to have knowledge of both its design and its use.

9. In order to achieve high-level reuse (i.e. above the level of reusing the class set) it is necessary to design with reuse in mind. This requires knowledge of the reusable components available.

The design patterns movement wished to address some (or all) of the above in order to facilitate successful architectural reuse. The intention was thus to address many of the problems which reduce the reusability of software components and frameworks.

10.3 Design Patterns

10.3.1 What are Design Patterns?

A design pattern captures expertise, describing an architectural design for a recurring design problem in a particular context. It also contains information on the applicability of a pattern, the trade-offs which must be made, and any consequences of the solution. Books are now appearing which present such design patterns for a range of applications. For example, the *Gang of Four* book is a widely cited book that presents a catalogue of 23 design patterns.

Design patterns are extremely useful for both novice and experienced object-oriented designers. This is because they encapsulate extensive design knowledge and proven design solutions with guidance on how to use them. Reusing common patterns opens up an additional level of design reuse, where the implementations vary, but the micro-architectures represented by the patterns still apply.

Thus, patterns allow designers and programmers to share knowledge about the design of a software architecture. They capture the static and dynamic structures and collaborations of previous successful solutions to problems that arise when building applications in a particular domain (but not a particular language).

10.3.2 What They are Not

Patterns are not concrete designs for particular implementations. This is because a pattern must be instantiated in a particular domain to be used. This involves evaluating various trade-offs or constraints as well as detailed consideration of the consequences. It also does not mean that creativity or human judgment has been removed, as it is still necessary to make the design and implementation decisions required. Having done that, the developer must then implement the pattern and combine the implementation with other code (which may or may not have been derived from a pattern).

Patterns are also not frameworks (although they do seem to be exceptionally well suited for documenting frameworks). This is because frameworks present an instance of a design for solving a family of problems in a specific domain (and often for a particular language). In terms of languages such as Java, a framework is a set of abstract cooperating classes. To apply such a framework to a particular problem it is often necessary to customize it by providing user-defined subclasses and to compose objects in the appropriate manner (e.g. the MVC framework). That is, a framework is a semi-complete application. As a result any given framework may contain one or more instances of multiple patterns and in turn a pattern can be used in many different frameworks.

10.4 Documenting Patterns

The actual form used to document individual patterns varies, but in general the documentation covers:

1. The motivation or context that the pattern applies to.
2. Prerequisites that should be satisfied before deciding to use a pattern.
3. A description of the program structure that the pattern will define.
4. A list of the participants needed to complete a pattern.
5. Consequences of using the pattern, both positive and negative.
6. Examples of the pattern's usage.

Table 10.1 The design pattern template

Heading	Usage
Name	The name of the pattern.
Intent	This is a short statement indicating the purpose of the pattern. It includes information on its rationale, intent, the problem it addresses etc.
Also known as	Any other names by which the pattern is known.
Motivation	Illustrates how the pattern can be used to solve a particular problem.
Applicability	This describes the situation in which the pattern is applicable. It may also say when the pattern is not applicable.
Structure	This is a (graphical) description of the classes in the pattern.
Participants	The classes and objects involved in the design and their responsibilities.
Collaborations	This describes how the classes and objects work together.
Consequences	How does the pattern achieve its objective? What are the trade-offs and results of using the pattern? What aspect of the system structure does it let you vary independently?
Implementation	What issues are there in implementing the design pattern?
Sample code	Code illustrating how a pattern might be implemented.
Known uses	How the pattern has been used in the past. Each pattern has at least two such examples.
Related patterns	Closely related design patterns are listed here.

The pattern template used in the *Gang of Four* book provides a standard structure for the information that comprises a design pattern. This makes it easier to comprehend a design pattern as well as providing a concrete structure for those defining new patterns. A summary of this template is presented in Table 10.1.

A pattern language is a structured collection of patterns that build on each other to transform needs and constraints into architecture. For example, the patterns associated with the HotDraw framework provide a pattern language for HotDraw. What is HotDraw? HotDraw is a drawing framework developed by Ralph Johnson at the University of Illinois at Urbana-Champaign. It is a reusable design for a drawing tool expressed as a set of classes. However, it is more than just a set of classes; it possesses the whole structure of a drawing tool, which only needs to be parameterized to create a new drawing tool. It can therefore be viewed as a basic drawing tool and a set of examples that can be used to help you develop your own drawing editor!

Essentially HotDraw is a skeleton DrawingEditor waiting for you to fill out the specific details. That is, all the elements of a drawing editor are provided, including a basic working editor, which you, as a developer, customize as required. What this means to you is that you get a working system much, much sooner and with a great deal less effort.

HotDraw was first presented at the OOPSLA'92 conference in a paper entitled "Documenting Frameworks using Patterns" by Ralph Johnson. This paper considered the problems associated with documenting complex reusable software systems using HotDraw as a concrete example. Included with the paper are a set of appendices which act as very useful guides on how to change the default drawing editor. The appendices represent HotDraw's pattern language and comprise 10 different patterns. These 10 patterns explain how to define drawing elements, change drawing elements, add constraints between graphic objects, add lines etc.

We first used HotDraw in mid-1993, knowing nothing about patterns, and didn't really understand the paper. However, we found the appendices helped us to customize the drawing editor quickly and painlessly. We read only those patterns we needed to understand what we wanted to do and ignored other patterns. Over time we found that we read those other patterns as and when we needed them.

10.5 When to Use Patterns

Patterns can be useful in situations where solutions to problems recur, but in slightly different ways. Thus, the solution needs to be instantiated as appropriate for different problems. The solutions should not be so simple that a simple linear series of instructions will suffice. In such situations patterns are overkill. They are particularly relevant when several steps are involved in the pattern which may not be required for all problems. Finally, patterns are really intended for solutions where the developer is more interested in the existence of the solution rather than how it was derived (as patterns still leave out too much detail).

10.6 Strengths and Limitations of Design Patterns

Design patterns have a number of strengths, including:

- providing a common vocabulary
- explicitly capturing expert knowledge and trade-offs
- helping to improve developer communication
- promoting ease of maintenance
- providing a structure for change

However, they are not without their limitations. These include:

- not leading to direct code reuse
- being deceptively simple
- easy to get pattern overload (i.e. difficulty in finding the right pattern)
- they are validated by experience rather than testing
- no methodological support

In general, patterns provide opportunities for describing both the design and the use of the framework as well as including examples, all within a coherent whole. In some ways, patterns act like a hyper-graph with links between parts of patterns.

However, there are potentially very many design patterns available to designers. A number of these patterns may superficially appear to suit their requirements. Even if the design patterns are available online (via some hypertext-style browser) it is still necessary for designers to search through them manually, attempting to identify the design which best matches their requirements.

In addition, once they have found the design that they feel best matches their needs, they must then consider how to apply it to their application. This is because a design pattern describes a solution to a particular design problem. This solution may include multiple trade-offs which are contradictory and which the designer must choose between, although some aspects of the system structure can be varied independently (some attempts have been made to automate this process).

To illustrate the ideas behind frameworks and patterns the next section will present the mediator pattern taken from the *Gang of Four* book.

10.7 An Example Pattern: Mediator

This pattern is based on that present in the *Gang of Four* book on pages 273–282. The Java code was written specifically for this chapter.

Pattern name: Mediator

Intent: To define an object that encapsulates how a set of objects interact. Mediator promotes loose coupling by keeping objects from referring to each other explicitly.

Motivation: Object-oriented design encourages the distribution of behaviour among objects. However, this can lead to a multiplicity of links between objects. In the worst case every object needs to know about/link to every other object. This can be a problem for maintenance and for the reusability of the individual classes.

These problems can be overcome by using a mediator object. In this scheme other objects are connected together via a central mediator object in a star-like structure. The mediator is then responsible for controlling and coordinating the interactions of the group of objects.

Applicability: The mediator pattern should be used where:

- A set of objects communicate in well-defined but complex ways. The resulting interdependencies are unstructured and difficult to understand.
- Reusing an object is difficult because it refers to, and uses, many other objects.
- A particular behaviour is distributed among a number of classes and we wish to customize that behaviour with the minimum of subclassing.

Structure: The class diagram for a mediator is illustrated in Figure 10.1.
A typical object diagram for a mediator is illustrated in Figure 10.2.

Participants:
- **Mediator** handles communication between colleague objects.
- **ConcreteMediator** defines how the mediator should coordinate the colleagues' interactions. It knows and maintains its colleagues.

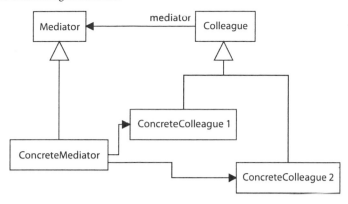

Figure 10.1 Mediator class diagram.

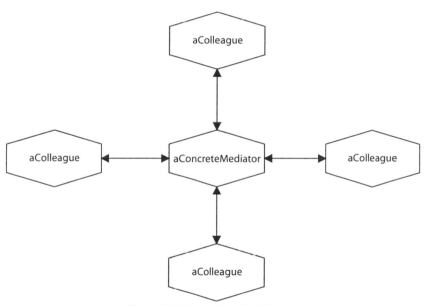

Figure 10.2 A mediator object diagram.

● **Colleague classes** Each colleague knows its mediator object. It communicates with this mediator object in order to communicate with other colleagues.

Collaborations: The mediator object receives messages from colleagues and relays them to other colleagues as appropriate.

Consequences: The mediator pattern has the following benefits and drawbacks:

1. It limits subclassing to the mediator (e.g. by changing the routing algorithm in the mediator you can change the system's behaviour).
2. It de-couples colleagues.

3. It simplifies object protocols from many-to-many down to one-to-many.

4. It abstracts how objects cooperate.

5. It centralizes control.

Implementation: The following implementation issues are relevant to the mediator pattern:

1. Omitting the abstract `Mediator` class. If there is only to be one mediator class there is no reason to define an abstract class.

2. Colleague–mediator communication. The colleagues need to tell the mediator that when something interesting happens to them they wish to relay that to their colleagues. This could be handled via a dependency mechanism (see the Observer pattern) or by direct communication by the object. For example, the colleague could tell the mediator that something has changed and then allow the mediator to interrogate it to find out what. This is the approach taken in the sample code example.

Sample code: The following illustrates the basic structure for the classes used in a simple mediator-based system. The assumption used is that when colleagues need to communicate with the mediator, a colleague passes itself as an argument, allowing the mediator to identify the sender. The `Mediator` class (in Java) is:

```
import java.util.*;
public abstract class Mediator {
   private Vector colleagues = new Vector();
   public void addColleague(Colleague col) {
      colleagues.addElement(col);
   }
   public abstract void changed (Colleague col);
}
```

Concrete subclasses of `Mediator` (such as `CommunicationManager`) implement the `changed()` method to affect the appropriate behaviour. The colleague passes a reference to itself as an argument to the `changed()` method to let the mediator identify the colleague that changed.

`Colleague` is the abstract class for all colleagues. A `Colleague` knows its mediator.

```
public abstract class Colleague {
   private Mediator mediator;
   public void addMediator(Mediator med) {
      mediator = med;
   }
   private void changed() {
      mediator.changed(this);
   }
}
```

As an example, consider an application in which we wish to inform members of a software team whenever a meeting has been arranged (we will ignore the issue of checking that all the team members can make that meeting). Rather than construct a rigid set of links between the members we will use the Mediator pattern. We can then define a CommunicationsManager class (which inherits from Mediator) as follows:

```java
import java.util.Enumeration;
public class CommunicationsManager extends Mediator {
  public static void main (String args []) {
    CommunicationsManager c = new
      CommunicationsManager();
    c.setup();
    c.sampleMeeting();
  }

  public void setup () {
  int i;
  String teamMembers [] = {"John", "Denise",
    "Phoebe", "Isobel"};
  for (i = 0; i teamMembers.length; ++i) {
    addColleague(new TeamMember(teamMembers[i]));
    }
  }

  public void sampleMeeting () {
    // This is just an example; the manager would
    // not normally initiate this.
    TeamMember aPerson;
    aPerson = (TeamMember)colleagues.firstElement());
    aPerson.meeting("9:00am 10/3/97");
  }

  public void changed (Colleague person) {
    TeamMember item;
    String theMeeting =
      ((TeamMember)person).currentMeeting();
    for (Enumeration e = colleagues.elements();
        e.hasMoreElements(); ) {
      item = (TeamMember)e.nextElement();
      if (item != person) item.newMeeting(theMeeting);
      }
    }
  }
```

This class sets up the colleagues to be linked to the CommunicationsManager. In this case the colleagues are all instances of a class TeamMember (see below). It then uses an example method to trigger off communications between the teamMember objects. To achieve this the CommunicationsManager implements its own changed() method. This method merely passes on details of the current meeting to the other team members.

The `TeamMember` class extends the `Colleague` class and (for this simple example) can be defined as:

```
import java.util.Vector;
public class TeamMember extends Colleague {
  // Instance variables
  String name, meeting;
  Vector meetings = new Vector();
  // A Constructor
  public TeamMember (String aName) {
    name = aName;
  }
  public void meeting(String aTimeAndDate) {
    meeting = aTimeAndDate;
    System.out.println("Generating a meeting " +
      aTimeAndDate + " for " + name);
    changed();
  }
  public String currentMeeting () {
    return meeting;
  }
  public void newMeeting (String aTimeAndDate) {
    meetings.addElement(aTimeAndDate);
    System.out.println("Adding " + aTimeAndDate +
      " for " + name);
  }
}
```

This class defines the functionality of the `TeamMember` objects. It inherits all the functionality it needs to work with any form of mediator. The only detail that needs to be incorporated is a call to the `changed()` method when appropriate (in this case in method `meeting()`). An example of this application running is presented in Figure 10.3.

Known uses: ET++ and the THINK C class library use director-like objects in dialogs as mediators between widgets. Smalltalk/V from Digitalk used it as the basis of its application architecture.

Related patterns: Facade differs from Mediator in that it abstracts a subsystem of objects to provide a more convenient interface. However, its protocol is unidirectional whereas mediator is multidirectional. Colleagues can communicate with a mediator using the Observer pattern.

10.8 Summary

In this chapter we have explored the concepts of patterns as a method of documenting the design of reusable software architectures. Such patterns have a great deal of potential. However, online support for browsing and applying patterns

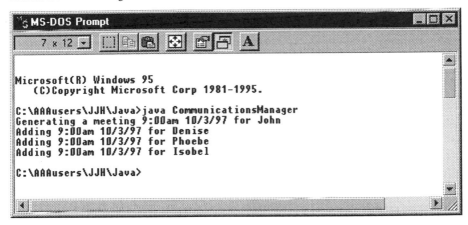

Figure 10.3 The CommunicationsManager application.

is required. In addition, work on methodologies which consider how to define and apply patterns is required.

10.9 Further Reading

The original patterns work for architectural design was published as:

Alexander C., Ishikawa S. and Silverstein M. with Jacobson M., Fiksdahl-King I. and Angel S. (1977) *A Pattern Language.* Oxford University Press, Oxford.
Alexander C. (1979) *The Timeless Way of Building.* Oxford University Press, Oxford.

A number of books and a great many papers have been written about patterns in recent years. The most influential of these is book by the so called *Gang of Four*: Erich Gamma, Richard Helm, Ralph Johnson and John Vlissides.

Gamma E., Helm R., Johnson R. and Vlissades J. (1995) *Design Patterns: Elements of Reusable Object-Oriented Software.* Addison-Wesley, Reading.

Two further patterns books are:

Buschmann F., Meunier R., Rohnert H., Sommerlad P. and Stal M. (1996) *Pattern-Oriented Software Architecture – A System of Patterns.* John Wiley and Sons, Chichester.
Fowler M. (1997) *Analysis Patterns: Reusable Object Models.* Addison-Wesley, Reading.

10.10 Online References

A Web page dedicated to the patterns movement (which includes many papers as well as tutorials and example patterns) can be found at:

```
http://st-www.cs.uiuc.edu/users/patterns/patterns
```

Part 2
Java Testing

11   *Testing Object-Oriented Systems*

11.1 Introduction

Testing object-oriented systems is a very important issue as more and more organizations are starting to develop Java-based applications. Many such organizations have been forced to come up with their own solutions for assuring the quality of their product. However, little attention has been focused on this subject at Java-centred conferences or in Java literature. There is a particular scarcity of literature on "how to" test Java systems as well as tools to support such testing. For organizations just starting to use Java for major projects this is a very worrying situation.

Object-oriented techniques do not (and cannot) guarantee correct programs. They may well help to produce a better system architecture, and an object-oriented language may promote a suitable coding style, but these features do not stop a programmer making mistakes. Although this should be self-evident, for a long time there was a feeling that object-oriented systems required less testing than systems constructed with traditional procedural languages.

Where the testing of object-oriented systems has been considered it is often the user interface of the system that has actually been tested in a principled or systematic manner. These tests usually concentrate on overall system functionality, usability issues (such as the ability of the user to use the system or the speed of response) and stress or exception testing. Stress or exception testing relates to attempting to break the operation of the system by inputting unacceptable data or crashing part of the system (e.g. an associated relational database system) to ensure that the system can recover from such catastrophic failures.

However, this chapter aims to show you that if anything, object-oriented systems require more, not less, testing than traditional programming languages. In the remainder of this chapter we shall consider what effects inheritance, encapsulation, polymorphism and dynamic typing have on testing as well as approaches to method and class (unit) testing, object integration and system testing.

11.2 Why is Testing Object-Oriented Systems Hard?

11.2.1 An Example

To illustrate the point, consider the following (somewhat pathological) Java. In this method the message sent to the last element in the vector held in v is either `drive()` or `fire()`. This depends on the value of the first element in the vector and the object held by the variable o. If they are "equal" then the last element receives the request to `drive()`; otherwise it receives the request to `fire()`:

```
public void foo(Vector v, Object o) {
  if (o.equals((Button)v.firstElement())) {
    ((Car)v.lastElement()).drive();
  } else {
    ((Tank)v.lastElement()).fire();
  }
}
```

In this case it is very difficult to determine statically what is going to happen in this method. This is because until the method is executed, we do not know the content (let alone the type (class) of the objects) in the vector v or the object o. This means that we cannot be sure that the first element of the vector can be cast to a `Button` or that the last is castable to a `Car` or a `Tank`. Indeed we cannot determine whether the last element of the vector will respond to the methods `drive()` and `fire()`. Indeed, we cannot even be sure of which version of the methods `equals()`, `fire()` and `drive()` we might execute. For example, methods `drive()` and `fire()` may be defined anywhere within the class hierarchies from which `Car` and `Tank` inherit (as well as `Car` and `Tank` themselves). We therefore do not know:

1. What the contents of the vector v will be.
2. What the contents of o will be (remember: any object could be held in o as all classes inherit from `Object`).
3. Which implementation of `equals()` will be used.
4. Whether the last element of the vector will be castable to a `Car` or a `Tank`.
5. Which versions of the methods `drive()` or `fire()` we will execute.

It could be argued that this is true, but irrelevant. However, the point is that the compiler would resolve a number of the above issues at compile time in other languages, such as Ada or Pascal. These static compile-time checks can identify what type of object will be held in the vector, which version of `drive()` will be executed etc., whereas in Java it is left up to the developer to ensure that no problems are likely to occur.

As you can see from this very simple (although slightly contrived) example, traditional static test generation techniques, although of use in object-oriented languages such as Java, do not provide the whole answer. In the example above, the problems are due to the late binding and polymorphism of object-oriented languages.

11.2.2 What Makes it Hard?

Part of the problem for object orientation is that the space of possibilities is so much greater. For example, not only are we concerned about objects sending messages requesting that other objects run specified methods correctly, we are also concerned with which class of object will receive the message and which class of object sent the message, as this will therefore have an effect on which method will be used. These issues are related to the polymorphic[1] nature of object-oriented languages and the use of abstraction and inheritance as a basic system construction tool.

In addition, encapsulation leads to a fundamental problem of observability, as the only way to observe the state of an object is through its operations. This is fine for black box testing, but makes white box testing extremely difficult. Black box testing relates to the testing of a program against its specification, while white box testing relates to the testing of a program based on its implementation.

Traditional control flow analysis techniques are also not directly applicable, as there is no definite sequential order in which methods will be invoked. That is, another object may request that a method is executed at a point that cannot be statically determined (see example in introduction). Indeed, as the state of the object may affect what the method does, it may not even be possible to determine how the method will behave. Of course this does introduce the issue of "what is correct behaviour?". However, we will leave the issue of "correctness" until a later section.

In traditional programming languages the basic unit of test is usually taken to be a procedure or function. However, it should be seen from this brief discussion that the object-oriented equivalent, i.e. the method, cannot be taken as the basic unit of test. It is affected by the state of the object, possibly and by the state of the class (if the class has class variables), may interact in unforeseen ways with other methods and may rely on methods defined elsewhere in the class's superclass hierarchy.

Inheritance also affects testing and introduces the following question "after a change, to what extent should the code currently in the system be re-tested?". In a traditional programming language it is usually quite straightforward to identify what parts of the system code are affected by some change. In an object-oriented system it is far less obvious.

The implication of the above is that in object-oriented programs, such as those implemented in Java, the basic unit of test must be considered to be the class. That is not to say that care is not given to exercising individual methods within a class, merely that the individual methods should not be treated in isolation.

11.2.3 Why a Lack of Emphasis?

Part of the reason for the lack of Java testing literature or tools is probably due to the background of Java. In the past it was often used as a single (or at most a few) developer's language. These developers would then use Java to implement "exciting" applets on Web pages. However, with the advent of release 1.2 of JDK and the introduction of Enterprise JavaBeans, intended to allow developers to integrate Java applications with legacy code relational databases, CORBA-compliant ORBs etc. this situation has changed drastically.

Java programs (whether applets or applications) require testing just as any other software requires testing. Indeed, the type of testing normally applied to traditional programming languages is also required by object-oriented systems. However,

---

1   Polymorphism is the ability to send the same message to different instances that appear to perform the same operation. However, the way in which the message is handled depends on the instance's class.

object orientation imposes unique requirements on the testing process. Why these requirements exist and how they can be handled is the subject of the remainder of this chapter.

11.3 Inheritance

Inheritance is a fundamental feature of object-oriented programming languages. However, it is both a blessing and a curse. For example, many programmers believe that they can inherit many of the features they require in their new classes from existing classes (and often they can). However, they also tend to feel that it is not necessary to test those features they have inherited because they have been tested very many times before (both by the system developers and by the many thousands of users). However, this is misleading because in defining a new subclass they have changed the context within which the methods will execute – at least in the subclass. The problem is that each new subclass may not require any re-testing and may very well function acceptably, but you are relying on a continuing hypothesis. Of course, this hypothesis may have held many times before, but there is no guarantee that it will hold this time. Interestingly, the same problem also occurs with Ada generics and C++ templates. For example, with Ada generics each instantiation of the generic package may work as intended, but equally this time it may fail.

11.3.1 The Effects of Inheritance

There are a number of ways in which inheritance can affect the testing required in a subclass. The following list summarizes these and lists the type of testing required:

- *Adding functionality.* For example, by adding new methods. In these situations, the tests should concentrate first on the new functionality, to ensure that the class works correctly (relative to its specification). If the new functionality calls on existing methods, then tests should be performed to ensure that these methods continue to function correctly. If the new methods, or the methods they call, modify any existing instance variables, then the effects of these changes should be determined. This may result in re-testing the whole class.
- *Overriding methods.* In these situations, the newly defined methods must of course be tested. This should test the new definition to ensure that it handles the same range of values as the original and produces the same results. If this is not what was desired, then overriding was not the correct approach.

   Next, all the methods which invoke the overridden operation must be re-tested. This can be done by using the tools provided with the Java system to identify all the senders of the messages associated with the changed methods (see the discussion on profiling later in this book). This will provide the initial test list. If the behaviour of inherited methods is changed in any way then this should be treated as adding functionality and tested as above.
- *Superclass references.* If the subclass changes anything used by the superclass, for example by referencing a protected static (class) variable, then the superclass

must also be subjected to incremental testing. Again, the process needs to identify the elements of the class which have been affected and to test those elements. In the case of a pool variable, it may also involve testing other classes that reference the pool variable.

11.3.2 Incremental Testing

Incremental testing is one obvious answer, i.e. we don't want to re-test the whole class if we don't need to; only those elements which have been affected by the additions in the subclass need to be tested. Of course, this is the key issue here: determining whether or not we "need" to re-test a subclass. One answer is that it is the properties of the class which are affected by the subclass, including which instance variables may be altered and which methods may be directly or indirectly affected, which determine what should be re-tested. For example, a directly affected method may be one which is called by a (re)defined method in the subclass or which directly references an instance variable which is modified by (re)defined methods. Indirectly affected methods are much harder to identify. They are methods that may be affected due to a chain of interactions. For example, suppose that a method "a" references an altered instance variable and modifies another instance variable. This results in a second method operating in a different way generating a different result that is used by a third method. The third method is indirectly affected by the original change in the instance variable. In the worst case, every element of a class may be affected in such a way. In such cases, either the whole class must be re-tested or the developers must use their own intuition and experience to decide how much testing is required.

A subtlety that can often be missed is that although an inherited method has not been changed, a method that it calls may have been redefined in the subclass. Thus the inherited method is directly affected by the subclass and must be re-tested. For example, consider the very simple case presented below:

```
public class Collection {
  Vector contents = new vector(10,10);
  public void add(Object o) {contents.addElement(o);}
  public void addAll(Object [] items) {
    for (int i = 0; i items.length; i++)
                  add(items[i]);
  }
}


public class Set extends Collection {
  // Only add an object if it is not already
  // a member of the set
  public void add(Object o) {
    if (!contents.contains(o))
      super.add(o);
  }
}
```

In the above code the method addAll() (defined in the class Collection) is inherited as is in the subclass Set. No change has directly been made to it. However, the addAll() method calls the add() method. This method has been overridden in the subclass. Thus although the addAll() method was not directly modified, its behaviour is dependent on a method which has been modified. In turn, note that the add() method in Set extends rather than completely replacing the parent method.

In testing the subclass Set as well as testing the implementation of add() we must consider the method addAll(). We want to be sure that any inherited functionality (i.e. addAll()) has not been adversely affected in an unanticipated way (note that this implies that we have some sort of specification against which we can compare the functionality of the class). We must therefore also consider some form of regression testing. This can be achieved by defining an appropriate set of regression tests on the class side of the root superclass. A regression test is a test designed to prove that modifications made do not alter the overall behaviour of some method (or methods). These tests are usually provided by the originator of the code to allow those updating the updating the code to run the original tests without the need for detailed analysis of what the tests should contain.

The regression tests can therefore be performed whenever the root class or one of its subclasses is changed in any way. Ideally these tests should include their own evaluation so that a report can be generated (to the standard output or to a file) stating the result of the tests. If appropriate, additional tests can be defined (in subclasses of the root superclass) to test the added functionality. If new tests are defined each time the functionality is extended or modified, then the tests on the class side also act as a repository of testing knowledge which can be exploited by future users of the classes without the need to understand their full functionality.

Regression tests can be provided on the static side of a class. They can be used to instantiate an object appropriately and then to test the operation of inherited methods. This can be done by requesting that the current class be passed to the test method. This class can then be used to instantiate the test object. For example:

```java
import java.util.Vector;
import java.lang.reflect.*;
public class Collection {
  Vector contents = new Vector(10,10);
  public static void main (String args []) {
    Collection.test(returnClass());
  }
  /**
   * Used to specify the name of the current class
   */
  public static Class returnClass() {
  Class cls = null;
    try {
      cls = Class.forName("Collection");
    } catch (Exception e) {System.exit(1);}
    return cls;
  }
```

```
/**
 * Defines a static test method which will create an
 * instance of the class named by getName() -
 * ideally the current class - and present it with a
 * test set of data
 */
public static void test(Class cls) {
  // Set up test data
  String [] data = {"John", "Paul", "Denise",
    "Phoebe", "John"};
  // Use reflection to create an instance of the
  // appropriate class
  System.out.println("Instantiating : " +
    cls.toString());
  Collection col = null;
  try {
    // Obtain an array of the set of constructors
    Constructor [] cons = cls.getConstructors();
    Constructor con = null;
    Object [] consArgs = null;
    Class [] params;
    // Get hold of the null constructor
    for (int i = 0; i cons.length; i++) {
      params = cons[i].getParameterTypes();
      if (params.length == 0)
        con = cons[i];
    }
    // Create an instance using the null constructor
    col = (Collection)con.newInstance(consArgs);
  } catch (Exception e) {System.exit(1);}
  // Run the test
  col.addAll(data);
  System.out.println("The original data was:");
  for (int i = 0; i data.length; i++)
    System.out.print(data[i] + "   ");
  System.out.println("\nThe stored data is: ");
  col.print();
}
// Instance side definitions
public void add(Object o) {contents.addElement(o);}
public void addAll(Object [] items) {
  for (int i = 0; i items.length; i++)
    add(items[i]);
}

public void print() {
  for (int i = 0; i contents.size(); i++)
```

```
      System.out.println(contents.elementAt(i));
   }
}
```

In this `test` method a simple data set is created which can be used to test the operation of the `addAll()` method defined earlier. Note that the test method is written in such a manner that it will create an instance of whichever class is passed to it. It also provides a simple element of self-testing by printing both the original data and the data held by the `collection` to the standard output. The class `Set` can then be defined to use the regression test in the following manner:

```
public class Set extends Collection {
   public static String returnClass() {
     Class cls = null;
     try {
       cls = Class.forName("Set");
     } catch (Exception e) {System.exit(1);}
     return cls;
   }
   // Only add an object if it is not already
   // a member of the set
   public void add(Object o) {
     if (!contents.contains(o))
       super.add(o);
   }
   public static void main (String args []) {
     Set.test(returnClass());
   }
}
```

The result of executing the test method on the `Set` and `Collection` classes is illustrated in Figure 11.1.

Note that regression tests only test the inherited behaviour of an object. They do not test the additional behaviour that is beyond the scope of the parent class. Such behaviour should be tested by static methods defined in the new class.

11.4 Abstract Superclasses

Abstract superclasses bring together common features which are to be used in many subclasses. However, from a testing point of view they are a difficult problem. The definition of an abstract superclass is a class which is never intended to be instantiated and which does not provide, in its own right, enough functionality to be useful. Given these two features, it is extremely important to test abstract superclasses thoroughly. However, as they do not provide enough information to create an instance of the class, it is impossible to test the class directly. The tester should provide a subclass that acts as a test harness for the facilities defined in the abstract class (such a class can be easily removed from the delivered Java system).

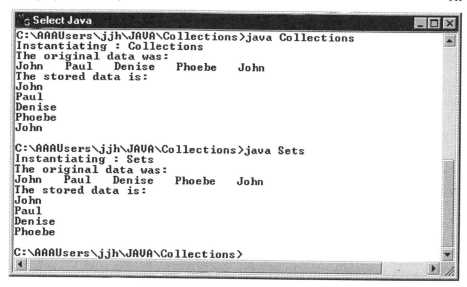

Figure 11.1 Running tests on Collection and Set.

The test subclass might provide a wide range of facilities. For example, a method may be defined which sets the state of the instance such that a particular method can be called and then sends a message causing the method (inherited from the parent class) to be executed.

Note that testing the abstract superclass does not mean that exhaustive testing of the methods in the subclasses, which inherit from it, is not required. As each subclass has changed the context within which the method will be run, the same approach to testing, as discussed in Section 11.3 must be performed.

11.5 Encapsulation

Encapsulation is a great bonus from the point of view of the users of an object – they do not need to know anything about the object's implementation, only what its published protocols are. This also means that the developer of the class knows that any potential users will have to come through the front door etc. However, for the tester of the class it is both a benefit and a drawback. It is a benefit because the encapsulated object is clearly designated for unit testing. That is, it is clear what the boundaries of the class are, and anything that is not in the class is in another class and thus does not come into the picture (from the point of view of unit testing). It is therefore possible to test the unit in isolation.

11.5.1 Black Box Testing

Encapsulation therefore promotes black box testing. Black box testing can be carried out in the normal way with the addition that the state of the object (and possibly the class) must be taken into account. Black box testing (also called specification-based testing) is aimed at testing a program against its specification only. That is, the class should be tested regardless of the way in which it has been coded. It is usually accomplished, even in object-oriented systems, by identifying a set of messages to send to the object and the parameters to use with these messages. The results of sending these messages are then compared with the original specification (assuming one exists). The product of this comparison is then used to determine whether the class has passed the test or not. In general, if some results were not as expected further testing would be used to determine the actual behaviour of the class. A decision would then be taken to determine what action was required (e.g. modification of the source code or, if appropriate, modification of the specification).

11.5.2 White Box Testing

Although encapsulation promotes black box testing, it can make white box testing much harder. White box testing (also known as program-based testing) is complementary to black box testing. It consists of examining the internal structure of a piece of code to select test data which will exercise that code thoroughly, either because that piece of code is critical or to gain confidence in the code to eliminate it from suspicion (for example if you are attempting to track down the source of some undesired behaviour).

A problem with encapsulation is that while it is entirely possible to view the source code and identify the tests to perform, it is not possible to access the instance variables of the object directly, nor is it usually possible to monitor the execution of the methods externally to the object.

Of course, in most Java environments you could use the debugger and the inspector to examine the source code during execution (and indeed this is the intention of these tools). However, using such tools presents problems for both traceability and accountability. Thus it is not possible to trace the tests that have been performed during a project nor is it possible to record these tests and their results for later quality audits. Of course, you can require developers to note what they are doing, but this is nowhere near as good as having the system do it for you automatically. This approach also fails to support repeatability of tests. That is, once you have completed your testing, it is not possible to re-run the tests and check the results following some change to the class.

11.5.3 Overcoming Encapsulation During Testing

In Java it is possible to work around the problems imposed by encapsulation in a number of ways. For example, one relatively object-oriented approach is to define a test subclass for the class being tested (this approach has already been mentioned above). The tester can then define an appropriate set of test harness methods that exercise the class in the desired manner. As the test harness methods have the same ability to access the state of the object (unless they are private) as the methods under test, it is possible to determine the object's state before and after a method is executed. The results of these tests can then be written to the standard output and/or to a file. If the results are written to a file, the tests can be re-run at a later date and the new results compared with the previous results. This is cleaner than writing print statements within the source code of the methods to be tested; however, it does not allow the internal operation of the methods to be monitored as closely.

To monitor the actual execution of the desired methods, it is possible to place print statements before and after the invocation of the super method. For example:

```
void age() {
  System.out.println("Current age " + age);
  super.age();
  System.out.println("New age " + age);
}
```

11.6 Polymorphism

Polymorphism is the ability of objects to send the same message to instances of different classes that have a common superclass. It is made possible by the dynamic binding of messages to objects. That is, it is only at runtime that it is possible to determine to which object the messages will be sent. From the point of view of testing, there are a number of problems associated with polymorphism. Each of these is discussed separately below.

11.6.1 Undecidability

Polymorphism allows the programmer to specify which message will be sent to an object, but not which object will receive that message. This will only be determined at runtime. It is therefore not possible to provide any form of static check to see that the message will be "understood" by the object (other than checking that at least one class somewhere in the system will respond to that message). In addition, even when it is known that the object receiving the message will understand the message (e.g. all objects in Java understand printString), it is not possible to identify which version or implementation of the method will be executed. That is, the tester will know that the object will understand the message toString, but which version of toString will be used will depend on the class of the receiver. It might be that defined in class Object, or that defined in class Vector etc.

It is therefore impossible for testers to know what would be an appropriate range of tests for a polymorphic message expression. They therefore have to make assumptions about the range of objects that are likely to be sent the message. In some cases this range may be very large indeed. In such situations it is necessary to produce one or more class hierarchies for different implementations of the method. These trees can then be used to identify those classes in which new definitions of the method are provided. The assumptions being used in the tests should, of course, be made explicit in the test report, so that they can be challenged if it is felt that they were inappropriate.

11.6.2 Extensibility of Hierarchies

Another problem associated with polymorphism is presented when an operation, which possesses one or more parameters which are polymorphic, is being tested. That is, the operation can be called with a range of different types of object as a parameter. For example, a parameter may be assumed to be a graphical `Component`; however, it could be a `Component`, a `Button`, a `Panel`, a `Frame`, a `ScrollPane` or an `Applet`. Each of these has specific features which may or may not affect the operation of the method. They may also contain elements that are of any type, which in turn may or may not affect the method's behaviour. Another example is the `paint(Graphics)` method. In this case the graphics object passed to the paint method of a `Canvas` or `Panel` may be a graphics context displayed on the screen or it may be a print job, to allow the current `Canvas` or `Panel` to be printed. If it is a print job object then it will not understand the BLiT operations and may thus case a problem.

As testing a method consists of checking its effects when executed for various combinations of actual parameters, a test suite must ensure that all possible input types are covered. This of course implies that some form of specification exists which specifies the acceptable range of input types. However, it is impossible to plan a set of tests in which you check all possible parameter values for a method. This is because the range of different types of objects that could be presented to a method is huge in Java.

Remember that the hierarchy of classes is very large (e.g. every class under `Object`) and is freely extensible. For example, we can define our own stack and queue classes. However, even if the method we are testing (which takes a parameter of type `Object`) includes a test to see if it has been presented with an instance of such a data structure class, it could easily encounter a type of class for which it was never designed. If the method is part of a class that is to be provided as part of a set of "highly" reusable classes, either within a single project or for external use, this is a significant issue.

11.6.3 Heterogeneous Containers

As has been briefly mentioned above, there are many classes that are designed to hold elements which may be any instance in the system. In Java, this means that they can hold instances, classes or interfaces. If the tester is considering a method that will be applied to, or will consume, the members of such a heterogeneous container (e.g. a data structure such as `Vector`, `Hashtable` or `Stack`), it is almost impossible to ensure that a complete range of tests has been performed. For example, it may be assumed that all the members of such a container are conventional instances of user-defined classes; however, there is nothing to stop the member of one of these containers being a class etc.

In such situations care must be taken to ensure that reasonable usage of the method has been tested. In other words, with reference to the class's specification, assumptions must again be made, this time about the use of the method. Again, these assumptions should be documented so that they can be challenged if necessary at a later date.

11.7 Additional Java-Specific Features

11.7.1 Anonymous Classes

Anonymous classes introduce another complexity to the testing process that is particular to Java. Not only are they more difficult to test physically (it is difficult to get hold of them to make an instance of them), they also only exist for the duration of some method. Combined with this is the fact that, in general, they only make sense within the context they are defined in.

One typical use of anonymous classes is in the creation of an object on the fly, as a parameter to a method. Again, care must be taken to test the receiving method against its specification and not the assumptions that this led to.

11.7.2 Inner Classes

Inner classes were adding as part of release 1.1 of the JDK. They are classes defined within the context of an enclosing class or method. They are special in that they can access methods and instance variables of the enclosing class. This means that they are subject to all the issues previously discussed above for method inheritance. That is, they may be dependent on the state of the enclosing class's instance variables or the behaviour of the enclosing class's methods for their correct operation. Thus if the state of an instance variable of implementation of a method is redefined in a subclass, the behaviour of an inner class may be altered.

11.7.3 Reflection

The reflection API allows a programmer to call any constructor on a class, and any method or instance variable (known as a field in reflection terms) on an object or class using a string. As the string can be stored in a variable, it is impossible to determine all the possible string values that will be passed to the appropriate reflection methods. It is therefore advisable not to use the reflection API unless it is absolutely necessary (as it is for tool builders) or unless the developer makes appropriate use of exception handlers. However, if the developer has used reflection, then a reasonable set of tests should be identified. Once again, the assumptions used to generate this set should be made explicit.

11.8 Summary

In this chapter we have considered some of the special problems which face a developer when testing an object-oriented system (with special consideration for

Java implementations). As has been discussed, inheritance, abstraction, polymorphism and encapsulation all play a major part in determining the best practice in testing Java systems. A number of recurring themes have been:

- The importance of specifying what a class or object is intended to do.
- The use of typical examples of usage to aid in the adequate testing of methods and classes.
- The adequacy of testing and the importance of deciding what is sufficient.
- Examples and assumptions need explanation (including their context).

A final comment is that this chapter should not put you off constructing large complex systems in Java. Rather it should make you aware of the difficulties you will face in testing such a system.

11.9 Further Reading

Little has been written about the special problems of testing object-oriented systems. However, see the following papers:

Barbey S. and Strohmeier A. (1994) The problematics of testing object-oriented software. In *SQM'94 Second Conference on Software Quality Management*, Vol. 2 (eds. M. Ross, C.A. Brebbia, G. Staples and J. Stapleton), pp. 411–426.
Barbey S., Ammann M.M. and Strohmeier A. (1994) Open issues in testing object-oriented software. In *ECSQ'94, European Conference on Software Quality*, Basle, Switzerland, pp. 17–20.

These papers are an exception and provide an excellent introduction to the subject of testing object-oriented systems. For a discussion of the effects of inheritance on object-oriented testing see:

Perry D.E. and Kaiser G.E. (1990) Adequate testing and object-oriented programming. *Journal of Object-oriented Programming*; 2(5): 13–19.

The next chapter in this book also provides further reading on the subject of object-oriented testing.

12 Testing Java Code

12.1 Introduction

In the last chapter we discussed the problems facing the tester of an object-oriented system (and in particular a Java system). We also briefly considered some approaches that overcome these problems. In this chapter we will consider the current best practice in testing object-oriented systems.

12.2 Class and Instance Sides

As was stated in the last chapter, the basic unit of test in Java is the class. However, there are two sides to a class: one is referred to as the *class side* and the other the *instance side*. The class side can be tested directly by sending messages to the class. However, the instance side can only be tested by creating instances of the class. That is, although you define the instance's methods in the class, you must test them using an instance. An important point to remember is that it may be necessary to use both the class and instances of the class together to adequately test both the class side and the instance side. For example, let us assume we have a class such as that illustrated in Listing 12.1.

Listing 12.1 *Instance and class method interaction*

```
public class Database {
static String Driver = "sun.jdbc.odbc.JdbcOdbcDriver";
static void setDriver(String s) {
  Driver = s;
}
public void databaseConnect(String url,
                            String userid,
                            String password) {
    Class.forName(Driver);
    Connection con =DriverManager.getConnection(url,
      userid, password);
    ...
  }
}
```

In this situation, it is possible to test the class side method setDriver() directly by sending a message to the class in isolation. However, it is not possible to test the instance method databaseConnect() without considering the range of values which may be returned by Driver. In this case, it is the string "sun.jdbc.odbc.JdbcOdbcDriver" which is returned; however, any subclass could redefine this static variable, thus allowing any one of a range of strings specifying different database drivers to be returned. As the databaseConnect() method may be inherited by other classes, we cannot guarantee which class will receive the getConnection() message.

12.2.1 Testing Methods in a Class

Each method in a class should first be tested in isolation. However, once all the individual methods in the class have been tested, threads through the methods in the class should be identified. Postulating scenarios of normal and exceptional usage (which may have been produced when the class was being designed) can do this. By tracing the results of these scenarios through the class it is possible to identify threads of execution among the methods in the class. An example of a thread of execution is illustrated in Figure 12.1. This thread was obtained by considering a scenario in which a person object has a birthday. This leads to the person object being sent the message birthday. The associated method birthday is presented below:

```
public void birthday() {
   System.out.println("A happy birthday to " + name);
   this.incrementAge();
   System.out.println("I am now " + age);
}
```

From the scenario that a person might have a birthday and therefore receive the message birthday, and from examining the source code of birthday (and incrementAge) we might draw the thread of execution presented in Figure 12.1.

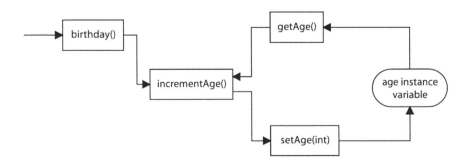

Figure 12.1 A thread of execution through an object.

12.2.2 Object State

Another point to bear in mind when testing a class is that both instances and classes have state. For example, a class may have a class instance variable which is used to keep a record of the number of instances which have been created of that class. This information may be used purely for bookkeeping or may be used to limit the number of instances created. In the latter case, a test needs to be performed which sets the counter to its limit, and then a new instance should be requested. This could be done either by creating the required number of instances or by manually setting the counter to the appropriate value (e.g. by using the debugger or inspector within your development environment).

It is also important to remember that although a method has been tested in the context of an instance's state, it is possible that some unintended sequence of message sends could result in the method being executed with the object in an unintended state. It is therefore not possible to test individual methods in isolation thoroughly, nor is it sensible to ignore the state of the object when performing these tests. It is of course quite possible to ignore the state; however, testers do so at their peril.

12.2.3 Private Methods

Some methods are defined such that the user of the class is never expected to see them. This may be because they do some housekeeping which is local to the object (for example an initialization method) or because they provide facilities which are relevant to the internals of the object and not to the external interface to the object. In Java, this method hiding is enforced via the access modifier `private`. This can make it difficult for the tester, as it is not possible to access these methods from outside the class. In such situations it is necessary to define test methods *inside* the class that will be removed from the runtime system before it is deployed. This is useful from a testing point of view, as the tester can test the individual execution of these methods in a black box fashion.

12.2.4 Class (Static) Variables

An additional problem with testing classes (as opposed to unit testing in other languages) is the presence of class (or static) variables. These are rather like global variables. If such variables are public then any Java code can change them. If they are default or protected then they have limited scope, but those objects within their scope can still change their values. It is therefore possible for one class (or its instances) to have a profound effect on the operation of a completely different class or its instances elsewhere in the system. This is something that requires careful thought.

12.2.5 Tracing a class's operation

In order to trace a class's operation it is possible to create a subclass that mirrors the parent class's methods exactly. The subclass's methods can then print the value of any parameters into the method before calling the (parent) method. Subsequently the test method can then print any results returned by the (parent) method before returning the result. If necessary, tests can be performed to ensure that the parameters or the returned value are within anticipated ranges. The advantage of testing the class method calls in this way is that all test information is encapsulated into a test subclass that can be removed from the Java program for the delivered system.

It should be noted that Java does provide two types of trace in the class `Runtime`. These are `traceInstructions()` and `traceMethodCalls()`. These operations can be used to turn on two levels of trace:

- `traceInstructions(boolean)` This method sets the tracing of Java byte code instructions. When tracing is set to *true*, each byte code instruction that is executed, as well as all entries and exits from method calls, are printed to the standard error output. This can result in a huge amount of information being generated, which can make it very hard to see what is happening (a case of severe information overload).

- `traceMethodCalls(boolean)` This method sets the tracing of method calls. When tracing is set to *true*, each time a method is entered or exited the method name is printed to the standard error output. This is a less detailed trace than that produced by `traceInstructions()`.

`traceMethodCalls()` can be a particularly useful way of automatically printing the methods involved in an operation. It does, however, print all the method entries and exits once it is switched on, whereas you may only want to know about one single method.

A useful technique is to use a subclass to switch on `traceMethodCalls()` before calling a parent class's methods and switch it off before leaving the subclass. For example:

```
public void print() {
  Runtime rt = Runtime.getRuntime();
  rt.traceMethodCalls(true);
  super.print();
  rt.traceMethodCalls(false;
}
```

12.3 Sources of Test Information

The concept of use cases is an important source of test cases. A use case is a particular interaction, between the system and a user of that system (an actor), for a particular purpose (or function). The users of the system may be human or machine. A complete set of use cases therefore describes a system's functionality based around what actors should be able to do with the system. Opportunities for the merging of the use case specifications into test specifications abound.

A style issue, rather than a testing issue, is that it is good style to provide a set of test examples, often on the class side, which exercise some behaviour of the objects of the class. These can be used to illustrate how to use the objects of the class. They can also act as a form of regression testing either when the class is modified or when a subclass is defined. If these test methods are placed in appropriate protocols, then the whole protocol can be filed out in one go, thus creating a test file. For classes which will not act as the root of the system, the `public static void main(String args [])` method is a good place to put calls to such test methods.

12.4 Object Integration Testing

The above section deliberately only deals with the issue of testing a class in isolation. This involves individual method testing followed by testing combinations of methods. Object integration testing involves testing instances of the same or different classes when they are collaborating in some operation. This is different from traditional procedural integration testing, as the structure of traditional programming languages is fairly rigid and is unlikely to vary while the system is executing. It is also different from statically bound procedural programs, because when a language such as Pascal is used the compiler is able to test to see whether the called procedure or function definition matches the calling definition. For example, if a procedure expects an integer as a parameter the compiler checks that an integer is being presented to it.

In Java, neither the structure of the objects is fixed nor are the actual types of parameters etc. likely to be known. It is therefore necessary to perform object integration testing in a methodological and principled manner. If the specification of two classes indicates that they are intended to collaborate to achieve some behaviour, then those two classes should be tested together. Again the specification should be used to generate scenarios which exercise normal and abnormal interactions. These scenarios can then be used to define tests to perform. Having tested the two classes, other cooperations may be identified involving these and other classes. Each of these collaborations also needs to be tested.

Integration testing (like multiple method testing in a single class) relies on the identification of scenarios that will be used to define appropriate test suites. However, consideration should also be given to identifying anticipated message paths. The differences between these two tests are akin to black box and white box testing for a single method. The scenario-based testing relies on testing the specification of the behaviour of the collaborating objects, while the white box testing is intended to test particular message paths through the classes. Again, the two approaches to testing are intended to be used together.

12.5 System Testing

System testing of Java systems should be carried out in essentially the same way as system testing of any computer system. This is because a system implemented in Java should be subject to the same types of requirements as a system written in any other language. There are some special situations which you might wish to test for, such as ensuring that the system does not run out of memory before a garbage collection is forced or that the system will still work once the image has been "stripped" of those classes not required by the production system (e.g. the compiler classes). However, in general the system should be subject to the same range of tests as any other.

12.6 Summary

Throughout the chapter, guidance has been given to ways to overcome the problems inherent in testing object-oriented systems. In the next chapter we shall consider a simple way of providing built-in self-testing for classes in Java.

12.7 Further Reading

In 1994 a special issue of the *Communications of the ACM* was published which focused on testing object-oriented systems. In this special issue a number of papers cover topics related to object-oriented testing. For example, design for testability in object-oriented systems is discussed. This is a particularly important issue given the effects of inheritance, polymorphism and particularly encapsulation on testing.

Binder R.V. (Guest Editor) (1994) *Special Issue of Communications of the ACM, Object-oriented Software Testing*; 37(9).

A good discussion of incremental testing for C++ (much of which is also relevant to Java) can be found in:

Harrold M.J., McGregor J.D. and Fitzpatrick K.J. (1992) Incremental testing of object-oriented class structures. In *Proc. 14th International Conference on Software Engineering*, pp. 68–79. ACM Press.

13 *Assertions in Java*[1]

13.1 Introduction

Any software system, whether object-oriented or not, relies on the state of the system being "correct" at certain stages of its execution. To take a very simple example, when a numerical division operation is performed the divisor must be non-zero. If this is not the case, the system may crash in an unpredictable and uncontrolled manner.

One way of indicating such requirements is to state that the system must be in some state either before or after an operation. Such a statement about the state of a software system is called an *assertion*.

Assertions often form the basis for software specification. In some systems, the assertions are embedded in the software as *annotations* or formal comments. However, it can be useful to make the assertions executable so that the correctness of the system is checked at runtime.

A simple technique is to make the code do its own self-testing using a method call and a programming language exception mechanism. The code checks that the statement passed to it is true, thus allowing it to test that the code is behaving as expected. If the statement is false the method uses an exception to stop processing, thereby enabling debugging.

In the remainder of this chapter we introduce the concept of assertions, how they can be used and how they can be implemented. In particular we introduce two types of assertion: one that generates a runtime exception if it fails and one that generates a checked exception (which must be handled by the programmer) if it fails. We then provide a brief analysis of the facilities provided by this approach.

13.2 Assertions and Their Uses

An assertion is a logical statement about the state of a software system. In formal methods, such as VDM, software is specified by making assertions about the pre- and post-conditions of functions and operations. These assertions may be used to prove properties of the system, such as consistency, formally. During the development process, the abstract specification is refined into code. The problem with this approach is that the assertions used in the specification are very often lost during the

---

1   This chapter is based on a paper originally written in collaboration with Dr F.W. Long, of the Department of Computer Science, University of Wales, Aberystwyth.

refinement process and, indeed, it may not be possible to express the assertions in the final implementation language.

Programming languages have been developed which enable assertions to be embedded into the code itself. Tools available with these language systems enable the assertions to be checked and, in some cases, proved.

Another approach is to introduce assertions into existing programming languages by using formal comments, called annotations, or by pre-processing. The C programming language has been extended with annotations by Flater, Yesha and Park, and Ada has been similarly extended into. Annotation pre-processors for C have also been produced. In these systems, tool support enables the assertions to be checked against the program code. However, extra-language syntax is required and, in the case of annotations, the assertions are lost when the program is compiled.

It may be better to have assertions as part of the code so that they provide a permanent defensive programming mechanism for detecting faults at runtime. The exception mechanism of a programming language can be used for this. In the following sections we show how this can be done for Java.

13.3 Using Assertions in Java

Assertions can be implemented in Java as part of an `assertion` package. This package can provide assertion classes that take an assertion and throw an exception if the assertion is false. The package could also define its own exceptions, thereby allowing a programmer to catch assertion exceptions. The assertion package we have defined provides two separate assertion classes and two different types of exception:

- `Assertion` The class `Assertion` allows programmers to use assertions within their code.
- `CheckedAssertion` The class `CheckedAssertion` allows programmers to use assertions within their code but forces them to catch a `CheckedAssertionException` explicitly.
- `AssertionException` The `AssertionException` class extends the `RuntimeException` class so that programmers do not have to handle the exception raised.
- `CheckedAssertionException` The `CheckedAssertionException` class extends the `Exception` class in order that programmers are forced to handle the exception raised.

The difference between the checked and the non-checked assertions for the developer is that they must explicitly handle any exceptions raised by the `CheckedAssertion` class, whereas they can chose to ignore the fact that an exception may be raised by the `Assertion` class (see Section 13.3.1).

We have defined a new package, `assertion`, which holds the four classes listed above. Other classes can then use these four by importing the `assertion` package. An example of how these classes are used is presented below:

```
import assertion.*;
public class Example {
  public static void main (String args []) {
    Example e = new Example();
    e.test(1, 2);
    e.test(2, 1);
  }

  // Uses the static method assert in class
  // Assertion to test truth of statement
  public void test(int a, int b) {
    System.out.println(
      "In test with " + a + " and " + b);
        Assertion.assert(a < b);
  }
}
```

This example creates a simple class `Example` which uses the `Assertion` class to handle the result of checking the relationship between a and b. The result of running this application is presented below:

```
>java Example
In test with 1 and 2
In test with 2 and 1
assertion.AssertionException: Failed assertion
  at assertion.Assertion.assert(Assertion.java:41)
  at Example.test(Example.java:11)
  at Example.main(Example.java:7)
```

We could have caught the `AssertionException` within a `try{}..` `catch{}` block. For example:

```
try {
  e.test(1, 2);
  e.test(2, 1);
} catch (AssertionException e) {
  System.out.println("First parameter larger than
second");
}
```

This would have allowed us to respond in an appropriate manner. Below we examine the implementation of the `Assertion` and `AssertionException` classes and their checked counterparts.

13.3.1 Exceptions in Java

In Java all exceptions must extend the class `Throwable` or one of its subclasses (Figure 13.1). The class `Throwable` has two subclasses, `Error` and `Exception`.

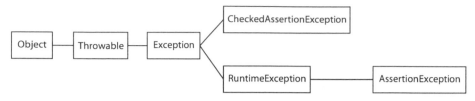

Figure 13.1 The assertion exception hierarchy.

Errors are unchecked exceptions. These are exceptions which your methods are not expected to deal with. The compiler therefore does not check that the methods can deal with them. In contrast, most exceptions (but not RuntimeException and its subclasses) below the class Exception are checked exceptions.

13.4 Assertions in Java

13.4.1 The Assertion Class

The Assertion class (a direct subclass of Object) makes two methods publicly available for handling boolean expressions. These are:

- assert(boolean bool) This determines the effect of the boolean result passed to it.
- assert(boolean bools[]) This determines the effect of the array of expressions passed to it.

The second method is really a convenience method that repeatedly calls the first method on each element in the array.

The implementation of the assert(boolean bool) method is relatively straightforward. The method checks whether the boolean value is false or not. If it is false an exception is raised:

```
public class Assertion {
  /** Don't make assertion instances */
  Assertion () {};
  /**
  * Checks the truth of the boolean value passed to it
  * if false, raises an exception.
  */
  public static void assert (boolean bool)
      throws AssertionException {
    if (!bool)
      throw new AssertionException(
        "Failed assertion");
```

```
    }

    /**
     * Checks the truth of an array of boolean values
     */
    public static void assert (boolean bools [])
        throws AssertionException {
      for (int i = 0; i bools.length; i++) {
        assert(bools[i]);
      }
    }
}
```

13.4.2 Switching Assertion Checking Off

In the released version of the system, the assertion checks may waste processing time. They could therefore be replaced by a null version of the method:

```
/**
 * Turns off assertion testing
 */
public static void assert (boolean bool)
    throws AssertionException {
  return true;
}
```

As Java dynamically loads the appropriate `.class` file at runtime, we could distribute the final version of the system with an `Assertion.class` file based on the above implementation of assert. We would therefore not even need to recompile the system being released.

Another approach would be to have a system property (called `assertion. status`). This property could then be referenced to see whether assertion checking should be turned on or not. If the system property was true then the assertion could be tested, if it was false then the value true would automatically be returned. For example:

```
public static void assert (Boolean bool)
      throws AssertionException {
  if (System.getProperty(assertionStatus))
    if (!bool) throw new AssertionException(
        "Failed assertion");
    else
      return true;
}
```

With either approach the overhead of the extra method dispatch is relatively small; of course, if it is still significant we could write a utility to find the senders of the assert method and to comment out the assertion statements.

13.4.3 The `AssertionException` class

The `AssertionException` class is a subclass of the `RuntimeException` class, as illustrated in Figure 13.1. The definition of the `AssertionException` class is provided below. Note that it provides two constructors, which are used to initialize the string displayed to the user.

```
/**
 * Provides a new class of Exception for assertion
 * handling
 */
public class AssertionException extends
      RuntimeException {
  AssertionException () {
    this("Assertion exception");
  }
  AssertionException (String information) {
    super(information);
  }
}
```

13.5 `CheckedAssertion` and `CheckedAssertionException`

These classes are essentially the same as the `Assertion` and `Assertion-Exception` classes, except that the `CheckedAssertion` class throws the `CheckedAssertionException` and the `CheckedAssertionException` extends the `Exception` class (as shown in Figure 13.1).

The advantage of providing the two types of assertion is that developers can decide how much control to give to the user of a component. If they wish they can force the users to handle the exception and thereby allow them to take charge of any problems which occur. This can result in code that is more resilient to erroneous situations.

For completeness the two classes are presented below. First the `Checked-Assertion` class:

```
public class CheckedAssertion {
/* Don't make checked assertion instances */
CheckedAssertion () {};

public static void assert (boolean bool)
throws CheckedAssertionException {
    if (!bool)
      throw new CheckedAssertionException(
        "Failed assertion");
  }
```

```
public static void assert (boolean bools [])
throws CheckedAssertionException {
    for (int i = 0; i bools.length; i++) {
      assert(bools[i]);
    }
  }
}
```

The CheckedAssertionException class is presented below:

```
public class CheckedAssertionException
    extends Exception {
  CheckedAssertionException () {
    this("CheckedAssertion exception");
  }
  CheckedAssertionException
      (String information) {
    super(information);
  }
}
```

13.6 Analysis

13.6.1 Design Methods Using Assertions

Assertions are particularly useful for testing pre-conditions, post-conditions and class invariants (values which are not expected to change within a class). The Syntropy design method makes extensive use of such assertions. It would therefore be possible to use the assertions identified during the design as the basis of the assertions to place in the Java code.

13.6.2 JavaBeans

The use of assertions could be extremely useful when working with JavaBeans (the Java component model). In such situations developers produce reusable components which developers will use in many different ways. By using assertions, developers can ensure that the state of the bean at any time is correct. If the state is not correct then they can take appropriate action. The assertions can therefore be used as guards against inappropriate states, parameters etc.

13.6.3 Shortcomings

The simple approach to inserting assertions into Java code that has been described in this chapter cannot provide the following, more sophisticated, type of assertion:

1. Assertions that relate output values of methods to their input values. For example, suppose one defined a method that swapped the values of its two parameters.

```
void swap (SomeType x, SomeType y) {
  SomeType z;
  z = x;
  x = y;
  y = z;
}
```

One might want to assert, just before the method returns, that the new value of x is equal to the old value of y, and that the new value of y is equal to the old value of x. This is not possible with our assertion mechanism. Assertion mechanisms for which this is possible have additional syntax which allows the "before and after" values of variables to be distinguished.

2. Assertions that involve quantified expressions. Formal methods allow expressions to be quantified by "for all", "exists" or "not exists". So the fact that a natural number N was prime could be asserted by saying that there did not exist numbers P and Q with $1 < P, Q < N$ and $P*Q = N$. Again, this is not possible with our assertion mechanism. Mechanisms that can handle the full power of the predicate logic must have additional syntax and be provided with sophisticated theorem-proving tools.

13.7 Summary

Recent commentators have suggested that assertions provide a valuable defensive programming technique. Indeed, it has been stated that one of the nine ways advocated for making code more reliable is to "use assertions liberally".

We have demonstrated a simple mechanism for introducing assertions into Java programs. Two classes have been defined, Assertion and CheckedAssertion. The former allows assertions to be used very simply. Any exceptions thrown as a result of the assertions failing may be caught, or propagated out of the program. The CheckedAssertion class requires the exceptions to be caught or explicitly listed in a throws clause for the methods involved. This provides greater control and "self-documentation" of the assertion mechanism.

Our assertion mechanism is particularly valuable when Java is used in larger, critical applications, where developers are implementing classes for general use, and for JavaBeans components.

13.8 Further Reading

For further information on the provision of assertions within programming languages the following are recommended:

Flater D.W., Yesha Y. and Park E.K. (1993) Extensions to the C programming language for enhanced fault detection. *Software – Practice and Experience*; **23**(6): 617–628.

Gaution P. (1992) An assertion mechanism based on exceptions. In *Proc. 4th C++ Tech. Conf.*, pp. 245–262. USENIX Association.

Joch A. (1995) How software doesn't work. *Byte*; 49–60, December.

Luckham D.C., von Henke F.W., Krieg-Brückner B. and Owe O. (1987) *Anna – A Language for Annotating Ada Programs*. Lecture Notes in Computer Science, vol. 260. Springer-Verlag, Berlin.

For discussions on how to use assertions within a program and its design see:

Rosenblum D.S. (1995) A practical approach to programming with assertions. *IEEE Transactions on Software Engineering*; **21**(1): 19–31.

Cook S. and Daniels J. (1994) *Designing Object-Oriented Systems: Object-Oriented modelling with Syntropy*. Prentice Hall, New York.

Part 3
Java Performance

14 *Performance: Tooling Up*

14.1 Introduction

The momentum behind Java has swept the world, first with Java applets embedded in Web pages, and more recently as a language for serious applications. It has a lot to offer – a well thought out language, a good class library, locale independence and platform independence to name but a few. If you have heard of Java being rejected as a serious application language, the chances are it was on the grounds of poor performance.

Clearly, algorithmic complexity has the greatest effect on performance, whatever the language. The sorting demonstration applet that comes with the Java Development Kit (JDK) provides a graphic example of this, comparing the performance of various sorting algorithms. Nevertheless, having chosen the most appropriate algorithm, you can still make a surprising improvement in performance by applying some of the techniques described here.

In this part of this book, we take a look at optimizing the performance of Java, in terms of faster code and of reduced memory overhead. In this chapter, we start by exploring the reasons for Java's relatively poor performance, and how the standard Java tools that you use (the virtual machine and compiler) can affect this. Java is very different from languages such as C/C++, and an understanding of its strengths and weaknesses is essential to getting the most out of Java code. As a prelude to looking at how we can write optimized Java code, we stress the importance of targeting optimization and take a look at profiling code.

14.2 The Java Language

Comparing the performance of Java with a language such as C++[1] is rather unfair – they are not competing on a level playing field. When a language like C++ is compiled, the compiler takes the source code and produces machine code that can be directly understood by the processor it is aimed at (native code). On the other hand, Java is compiled into machine code for an abstract processor (known as Java byte code). This is platform-independent – each system provides a Java Virtual Machine (JVM) that interprets the byte code. Clearly, interpreting byte code will always be

---

1 We use C++ as a comparison, as it shares a similar syntax with Java and would be familiar to most readers. Most of the points made are equally valid for other languages, such as C, Pascal or Fortran.

slower than executing machine code directly, but this is the trade-off we make for platform independence.

Java is also a much more constrained language than C++ – for example, it checks that typecasts are valid and that array indices are not out of bounds. If you coded these checks into your C++ code, it could slow it down significantly.

C++ is also a statically linked language – when the compiler produces the executable program, it links together all of the class references to the actual class code. Java classes are dynamically linked. When the JVM first encounters a reference to a class, it searches the class-path for the corresponding class file and loads it into memory. The class-path is defined either by the CLASSPATH environment variable or by the -classpath flag when the JVM is started. The JVM searches for a class in each directory in the class-path, in the order that they are defined. Simply by putting the most frequently needed libraries first in the class-path, you can improve the performance of a JVM. The speed-up can be dramatic on some systems, particularly if the libraries are on networked drives.

Finally, Java uses an automatic Garbage Collector (GC) to manage memory. In a language like C++, you must explicitly allocate and deallocate memory for new object instances. With Java you still explicitly allocate memory (with the new keyword), but the GC reclaims the memory automatically when there are no more references to an object. This has implications both for speed and for memory overhead. Although most implementations of garbage collection are quite efficient, it is still slower than trusting the programmer to deallocate memory explicitly. In addition, the GC can kick in at inappropriate times, which can seriously affect the perceived speed of an application. As memory becomes scarce, the GC must be performed more often, again slowing down the application.

Because the programmer does not have direct control over memory deallocation, it becomes more difficult to manage memory efficiently. Garbage collection is discussed in more detail in Chapter 16.

Don't be downhearted by all of this doom and gloom – being aware of the problems is half the battle, and these chapters will show how you can make a significant difference.

14.3 Virtual Machines

Clearly, the tool that has the most impact on performance is the Java Virtual Machine. While the Java Virtual Machine Specification says what a JVM must provide, it does not specify how it should be implemented. For example, it says that a JVM must perform automatic garbage collection, but it does not say which algorithm should be used. Because of this, there are significant variations between different JVMs, both in terms of performance and memory overhead.

Here, we are concentrating on the standard JVM, that is, the one provided free of charge by Sun. Many of the virtual machines available are only licensed for use within a development environment and cannot be distributed. Because it is free, the standard JVM (or the cut-down Java Runtime Environment, JRE) is the one most widely used for distribution. In addition, most of the features described here are available in one form or the other in the other JVMs.

14.3.1 The Standard Virtual Machine

The standard Java virtual machine works within strict memory constraints. When it starts, it takes 1 Mbyte of memory from the underlying OS. During the life of the program, it can request up to a maximum of 16 Mbyte (versions of Java before 1.1 used values much less than this). The startup and maximum heap sizes can be configured using the -ms and -mx flags (the heap is the block of memory that your Java program can use for new object instances). For example, the following command starts the virtual machine with 4 Mbyte out of a maximum of 24 Mbyte:

```
java -ms4m -mx24m MyClass
```

If you find that you are getting out-of-memory errors, or that the application as a whole slows down when large amounts of data are in memory (causing the GC to be called more often), try increasing the maximum size of the heap. Note that, once the virtual machine has requested memory from the operating system, it will not return it (even when it doesn't need that much memory any more).

Java also lets you specify the amount of memory available for the stack (the stack is the block of memory available for local variables). The stack is only used for the primitive types (e.g int, long, object references), and unless you have a very large number of local variables or very deeply nested method calls, you shouldn't need to worry about it.

The standard JVM runs the garbage collector asynchronously. This means that the GC will be called when explicitly requested by the application; when memory is very low; and every now and then in a background thread. It provides a number of flags to help control the garbage collector.

The -verbosegc flag instructs the JVM to write a message to the console every time the garbage collection is run. This is useful for seeing exactly when the GC is running.

The JVM can be instructed to stop running garbage collection asynchronously with the -noasyncgc flag. In this case, garbage collections will only be run when the JVM runs out of memory or when explicitly called.

As well as storing object instances in memory, Java must store information about each class being used. By default, when a class is no longer being used it is removed from memory. If it is needed at a later stage, it must be loaded back in. The -noclassgc flag prevents classes being garbage-collected. In some situations, this can improve the speed of code (at the expense of the memory overhead).

As already mentioned, the -classpath flag allows you to specify the directories to search for the Java classes. For example:

```
java -classpath c:\jdk\lib;c:\myLib MyClass
```

The semicolon used to separate the paths is platform-dependent – under Unix this would be a colon. There are a couple of other points worth noting. Firstly, if the -classpath flag is used, the JVM completely ignores the CLASSPATH environment variable – this means that you must specify every library explicitly. Secondly, if you are using the Java Runtime Environment, you can also use the -cp flag to prepend the value to CLASSPATH.

14.3.2 Just-In-Time Compilers

Just-In-Time (JIT) compilers are now widely available, and make a very significant improvement to the speed of Java code. Most browsers use a JIT to speed up Java applets. Note that JITs are part of the virtual machine, and are not to be confused with the Java source code compilers, such as javac.

When a method is called for the first time, the Java byte code is compiled (just in time for its first use), and executed as native code. The compiled code is stored for any subsequent calls to the method. The compilation phase is very fast and does not introduce a noticeable delay. The improvement in execution speed can be dramatic, particularly with processor-intensive code.

JavaSoft have now made available Symantec's JIT virtual machine as part of their Performance Pack for Windows. This is freely available for download at the JavaSoft Web site. It integrates transparently with the Java Development Kit (JDK) or the Java Runtime Environment (JRE).

14.3.3 Native Code

So why not compile the Java byte code into native code once, and store it as a native application? The reason JIT compilers were developed for Java is that they allow the classes to remain as byte code, which is platform-independent – this is necessary for applets on the Web. The case for retaining byte code in Java applications is less clear. One reason is that native compilation means that you need to make separate distributions of the application for each platform. Another is that keeping Java packages as byte code makes it easier to update them as new versions become available. For example, if your application uses the Internet Foundation Classes (IFC) from Netscape, when a new version becomes available you just need to replace the IFC library. If the application was compiled, it would need recompiling with the new library.

Nevertheless, if you are intending to deploy an application on a specific platform, then you can indeed choose to compile it into a native executable. Bear in mind, though, that the speed of the executable is only as good as the compiler and its runtime library – in some situations you may find that there is little improvement in performance over a good JIT.

Beware also that some tools for turning Java code into a native executable simply package the classes into a file and call on the original virtual machine (Microsoft's JEXEGEN does this).

As more applications are written in Java, it looks likely that native Java compilers will become part of the operating system. This would enable applications to be distributed as byte code and compiled as part of the installation procedure. If such a compiler could separate packages into dynamically linked libraries (most OSes support this), it could overcome the need to recompile applications for new library versions.

14.3.4 The HotSpot Virtual Machine

Despite being shrouded in secrecy, details are starting to emerge of an exciting new development in Java virtual machine technology. The new JVM, called HotSpot, promises a faster garbage collector and faster synchronized methods. But most importantly, it has a dynamically optimizing JIT compiler. As the program runs, it collects statistics on what is happening, helping it identify the "hot-spots", or critical areas of code. Using this information, it can perform dynamic optimizations, which include in-lining Java methods.

In-lining is a technique used by compilers to optimize for speed, whereby a call to a method is replaced by the actual method code. A source-code compiler can do very little in-lining in a Java program because of its polymorphic[2] nature – it cannot determine which method will be executed because it doesn't know the actual class of an instance. However, because HotSpot is optimizing dynamically as the program executes, it can determine the class of the instances and in-line accordingly.

This technology could potentially help Java outperform C/C++, which can only optimize using static information. There is little solid information about HotSpot available from Sun yet, but they claim the development is "pretty far along".

Furthermore, a number of companies (including Sun) are developing processors whose native code *is* Java byte code.

14.4 Java Compilers

The other tool that has a great effect on the performance of your code is the compiler that you use. Again, we are concentrating on the standard Java compiler distributed with Sun's JDK, `javac`.

You may have noticed the optimize flag -O. What optimizing does it actually do? The answer, in fact, is very little. It strips out all debugging information, which can make the class size smaller, it removes some (but not all) redundant code, and it attempts to in-line some method calls. And that's it as far as `javac` is concerned! C/C++ gurus looking for the compiler to eliminate common sub-expressions, or expand loops, or remove loop invariants are going to be disappointed. The story does not get any better with most of the commercial Java compilers either – the state of Java compiler technology is still relatively primitive.

By default, the `javac` compiler creates class files containing line number information (this is used for debugging, and by the exception mechanism to indicate which line of code generated the exception). If the code was compiled with the `-g` option, then the class files will also contain variable debugging information. This

---

2 Polymorphism in Java is the ability to send a message to an unknown object and have that object respond appropriately, as determined by its class. For example, we can send a `toString()` message to any object, and each one will respond differently.

extra data swells the size of the class files. By compiling with the −O flag, you can force `javac` to remove this extraneous data.

If the compiler can statically determine the value of a variable, it will also remove any redundant code. This means that the variable must be defined as `static` and `final`. For example, the following class contains an `if` statement that can be safely removed.

```java
public class MyClass {
  protected static final boolean debug = false;

  public void myMethod( ) {
    // This if statement should be removed by
    // the compiler.
    if( debug )
      System.err.println( "In myMethod" );
  }
}
```

Removing redundant code reduces the size of the class files and should slightly improve the speed of the code. In-lining may also be performed by the compiler. This can improve the speed of the code, but will swell the size of the classes (we look at in-lining in Chapter 15).

14.5 Targeting Optimization

The next two chapters look at how to write optimized code. Before considering this, it's worth making a few important points:

● Get your code working first
● Make optimization a well-targeted technique
● Assess the effects of your optimizations

It is important to get your code working before you start optimizing. Optimization usually requires the programmer to make compromises with good structure, encapsulation, flexibility, readability and maintainability, to name but a few! Because of this, optimized code is generally harder to understand and debug. It often pays to make a backup copy of your source code before you start optimizing!

Secondly, optimization should be a well-targeted technique. As noted above, optimized code usually involves compromises with good coding practice, and so should be kept to a minimum. In addition, you can waste a lot of time optimizing code that didn't need it in the first place. Java does use memory reasonably efficiently, and even the slowest Java operations take only nanoseconds. The benefits of optimization only become apparent for methods that are called a great number of times, or for classes that store a large amount of data.

In most programs you can find areas of performance-critical code. In terms of speed, this might be a method that is called a great many times, or a method that is inherently slow, for example.

Take a look at the source code (Listing 14.1) of java.io.RandomAccessFile. The read() method is a good example of a critical method – it is called frequently (once for every byte read from the file), and it is called by nearly all of the other reading methods (so speeding it up will speed up all of the methods that call it). The Java programmers recognized this, because they defined the method as native and linked it to some native code.

Listing 14.1

```java
public class RandomAccessFile
implements DataOutput, DataInput {
  ...
  public native int read() throws IOException;
  ...
  public final boolean readBoolean()
  throws IOException {
    int ch = this.read();
    if (ch < 0)
      throw new EOFException();
    return (ch != 0);
  }
  ...
  public final short readShort()
  throws IOException {
    int ch1 = this.read();
    int ch2 = this.read();
    if ((ch1 | ch2) < 0)
      throw new EOFException();
    return (short)((ch1 << 8) + (ch2 << 0));
  }
  ...
  public final int readInt() throws IOException {
    int ch1 = this.read();
    int ch2 = this.read();
    int ch3 = this.read();
    int ch4 = this.read();
    if ((ch1 | ch2 | ch3 | ch4) < 0)
      throw new EOFException();
    return ((ch1 << 24) + (ch2 << 16) +
      (ch3 << 8) + (ch4 << 0));
  }
  ...
  public final String readLine()
  throws IOException {
    StringBuffer input = new StringBuffer();
    int c;
```

```
    while (((c = read()) != -1) && (c != '\n')) {
      input.append((char)c);
    }
    if ((c == -1) && (input.length() == 0)) {
      return null;
    }
      return input.toString();
  }
}
```

Finally, you must assess the effects of your optimizations. This helps ensure that you are only optimizing code that needs it, and it also helps to give you a feel for which optimizations are the most effective in certain situations. The following chapters include some ideas for writing speed and memory test harnesses.

14.6 Profiling

The standard Java Virtual Machine can help you to identify the speed-critical areas in your code. If you run your application with the -prof:MyClass.prof flag, it will write profiling information to the file MyClass.prof. The format of this (large) file is, as yet, undocumented. However, the most useful information is at the beginning, where it lists all of the methods that were called during the life of the application, the calling method, the number of times the method was called, and the time spent in the method. The list is ordered by the number of times a method is called.

For example, consider the first line from an application profile that reads from a buffered random-access file:

```
count callee caller time
146903 cis/io/BufferedRandomAccessFile.read()I
cis/io/BufferedRandomAccessFile.readByte()B 2121
```

The read() method is called over 146 000 times (from the readByte() method), and the application spends a total of 2 seconds in this method alone. Clearly, any improvements in the speed of this method will have a dramatic effect on the performance of the application.

The profiling information also contains some information about the memory usage of the program, but this is less useful as it only refers to memory allocations of primitive types. The volume of profile information can be a little daunting, but there are a number of tools available that help you interpret the information. HyperProf is a good example of this, written entirely in Java. It also includes a nifty graphical display of the profile results, which, while not being terribly useful, is definitely worth a look!

Most of the time, you should be able to use the profiling ability of the JVM without problems, but there are a number of bugs in all of the Java versions from 1.02

inclusive! If you are not using any 1.1 features, you may decide to return to version
1.01 for profiling. The profiling fixes are promised with the release of Java 1.2,
although JavaSoft may apply the fixes to the current version of Java before this.

Windows users should note that the optimized version of the Java JVM (i.e. `java`)
does not profile correctly (it misses most of the method calls in the results). Instead
you must use the unoptimized version (`java_g`).

14.7 Summary

Java is a multi-platform, well-constrained language, but these features come at a
price in terms of performance. Nevertheless, the following tips can make a
significant difference, without needing any modifications to your code:

- Order the class-path so that the most frequently accessed libraries come first
- Use a Just-In-Time compiler, or possibly a native compiler.
- Use the optimize flag when compiling the release version of an application, but
  don't expect too much.
- If the application uses large amounts of data, make sure the JVM has enough
  memory to run efficiently.

Before you start optimizing your code, bear in mind the following points:
- Get your code working first.
- Make optimization a well-targeted technique – profiling will help you find the
  speed-critical code.
- Assess the effects of your optimizations.

Following on from this, we address the issue of writing faster Java code in Chapter
15, and in Chapter 16 we consider ways to minimize the size of Java class files and
reduce the runtime memory required for Java applications.

14.8 Online References

The Java Virtual Machine Specification is available from Sun at

```
http://java.sun.com/docs/books/JVMspec/index.html
```

A useful source of information on Java optimization can be found at

```
http://www.cs.cmu.edu/~jch/java/
```

The Win95 Performance pack JIT is available from Sun at

```
http://java.sun.com/products/jdk/1.1/
```

HyperProf, a useful Java profiling tool, can be freely downloaded from

```
http://www.physics.orst.edu/~bulatov/
```

15   *Optimizing for Speed*

15.1 Introduction

The programming community seems to believe that choosing Java as a language inevitably means poor performance. In reality, as you might expect, the speed of a Java application depends very much on the quality of the code. Indeed, improvements in performance from good coding can far outweigh those achieved from using a faster virtual machine.

In Chapter 14 we looked at how the Java compiler and the Java Virtual Machine (JVM) can affect performance. We also noted the importance of targeting optimization. In this chapter, we start by looking at writing a timing harness, an essential tool for assessing the effectiveness of optimization techniques. Following this, we consider how the standard Java library classes can be put to best effect, and how traditional optimization techniques can be applied to Java. Finally, by being aware of the relative speeds of various Java operations, we can come up with some strategies for writing the fastest code.

In the Chapter 17, we take a look at techniques that can be very effective in improving the perceived speed of an application – in particular that of future evaluation.

15.2 Timing Harnesses

A timing harness is a program that calculates the execution time of a piece of code. Timing harnesses are invaluable tools for both determining the slow areas of code and assessing the effects of optimization techniques. In the previous chapter, we discussed how profiling can help you identify the slow methods in your application. So why do we need to write test harnesses?

The problem with profiling is that it is intrusive – the virtual machine is checking the time of every method call, resulting in the whole application running slower. The results of profiling are still useful, but the times given must be taken as relative. A timing harness "sandwiches" the code that is of interest, so that it runs at normal speed. Profiling doesn't allow you to measure absolute time, and it doesn't allow you to assess the speed of code on different virtual machines.

In addition, profiling doesn't distinguish between separate calls to a method, so that you cannot time a single call to a method (perhaps operating on a particular set of data) in an application that calls the method elsewhere.

15.2.1 Difficulties

The biggest obstacle to writing timing harness in Java is the inconsistent speed of Java. Most Java VMs perform garbage collection (GC) asynchronously, so the GC can strike at any time to slow the application down. As discussed in the previous chapter, it is possible to configure the GC behaviour for the standard Java VM – we recommend running timing harnesses with the -noasyncgc -noclassgc flags to minimize any interference. In addition, it is a good idea to call garbage collection explicitly (with System.gc()) before the timing harness starts, to minimize the possibility of GC being called due to a lack of memory during the test.

Another problem is that there is no facility for measuring CPU time rather than elapsed time. This means that the timings will be affected by whatever else happens to be running at the same time – a significant problem on multi-user machines.

Turning off a Just-In-Time (JIT) compiler helps improve the consistency a little, although the timings will be significantly slower. Another tip for improving the consistency is to make sure that you put the timing harness's print statements after the timed code (printing is a relatively slow operation, and usually involves creating new StringBuffer instances as a by-product).

Because of these problems, timings are always going to be a little inconsistent. We recommend that you repeat the test in a loop (if possible), and also take an average over several runs of the test harness.

15.2.2 The System Clock

The simplest method of timing is to read the system clock before and after the test code has run. The current time (in milliseconds) is given by System.currentTimeMillis(). Listing 15.1 shows how this can be used to compare the time taken by two implementations of a method. There are two classes (each of which should be in a separate file). TimeMe is a class that provides a fast and slow implementation of a (nonsense) method. These methods are timed in a loop in the main() method of the Millis class, to give an average time.

Listing 15.1

```
public class TimeMe extends Object {

   public static double fast( ) {
      double result = 0.0;
      double temp = 12.3 * Math.PI;
      for( int i = 0; i < 5000; i++ ) {
         result += temp - i;
         result = (result < 0) ? -result : result;
      }
      return result;
```

```
      }

   public static double slow( ) {
      double result = 0.0;
      for( int i = 0; i 5000; i++ )
         result = Math.abs( result + 12.3 * Math.PI - i
            );
      return result;
   }

}

public class Millis extends Object {

   public static void main( String argv[] ) {
      double count = 200.0;

      System.gc( );
      long fastTime = System.currentTimeMillis( );
      for( int i = 0; i < count; i++ )
         TimeMe.fast( );
      fastTime = System.currentTimeMillis( ) - fastTime;

      System.gc( );
      long slowTime = System.currentTimeMillis( );
      for( int i = 0; i count; i++ )
         TimeMe.slow( );
      slowTime = System.currentTimeMillis( ) - slowTime;

      System.err.println( "Fast time=" + (fastTime /
         count) + " ms" );
      System.err.println( "Slow time=" + (slowTime /
         count) + " ms" );
   }
}
```

If you wanted as accurate a timing as possible, you would have to subtract the time taken by the loop itself.

15.2.3 Thread-Based Timing

Another approach to timing uses threads, and is only really suitable for timing small frequently called methods. The idea is to start a thread that calls the test method repeatedly in a loop. After each iteration of the loop, a counter is incremented. The thread is allowed to run for a set time, and is then stopped. By checking the counter, we can determine how many method calls were completed in the allotted time. The advantage this approach gives is that it allows you to set the time it takes for the test to run, irrespective of the JVM or platform the code is running on. This makes it particularly useful for benchmarking tests.

Listing 15.2 shows the thread-based equivalent of the previous test. The main() method in the Threads class creates a thread for each test, sleeps for a set time, and then counts the number of complete method calls. Each test has a separate Runnable class that can be started in a thread. Note that most of the test code is enclosed in a try-catch construct, as many of the thread methods can throw exceptions.

Listing 15.2

```
public class Threads extends Object {

  public static void main( String argv[] ) {
    long delay = 2500;

    try {
      TestSlow slow = new TestSlow( );
      Thread slowThread = new Thread( slow );
      TestFast fast = new TestFast( );
      Thread fastThread = new Thread( fast );

      System.gc( );
      fastThread.start( );
      Thread.currentThread( ).sleep( delay );
      fastThread.stop( );

      System.gc( );
      slowThread.start( );
      Thread.currentThread( ).sleep( delay );
      slowThread.stop( );

      System.err.println( "Fast time=" +
        ((double)delay / fast.count) + " ms" );
      System.err.println( "Slow time=" +
        ((double)delay / slow.count) + " ms" );
      System.exit( 0 );

    } catch( Exception e ) {
      System.err.println( e );
    }
  }
}
```

```
class TestSlow extends Object
implements Runnable {

  public int count = 0;

  public void run( ) {
    while( true ) {
      TimeMe.slow( );
      count++;
    }
  }
}

class TestFast extends Object
implements Runnable {

  public int count = 0;

  public void run( ) {
    while( true ) {
      TimeMe.fast( );
      count++;
    }
  }
}
```

Again, if the most accurate timings are required, you must take into account the time taken by the loops. Also, beware of using a timing period that is long enough for the counter to wrap around!

15.3 System Library Classes

Now we'll look at how we can use the Java class library to best effect. It's worth spending some time studying the source code to the classes (this is included in the JDK). As well as being a good example of Java coding, gaining a thorough knowledge of the library classes will help you get the most out of them.

15.3.1 Efficient Use of Storage

Most applications manipulate data of some sort, and using the storage classes efficiently can pay dividends. Take the humble Vector, for example. The Vector contains an Object array with room for a certain number of elements (its capacity). Every time this capacity is exceeded, the Vector creates a new Object array with a larger capacity (by default the capacity is doubled), and copies the elements across from the old array. The larger the Vector gets, the more expensive this operation becomes. However, the Vector class allows you to set the capacity (and the capacity increment) in the constructor. If you know roughly how many elements you need to store, you can avoid the need to expand the Vector. When the number of elements changes during the life of the Vector and you know in advance what capacity you need, the ensureCapacity() method can be used. There are similar methods in the Hashtable class.

15.3.2 File Operations

The speed of unbuffered file IO in Java (or any language) is terrible. Luckily, Java provides buffered stream classes that can be used in most situations. They should even be used with small files, as the increase in speed can be several orders of magnitude. However, if you are working with streams created in other people's code, you should try to establish whether the stream will already be buffered or not. Wrapping a buffered stream around an input stream that is already buffered will decrease its speed slightly. If you are using a buffered stream to write data, you should note that the data may not actually be written until the stream is closed, or its flush() method is called.

Unfortunately, Java does not provide a buffered version of the RandomAccess-File class. The effort it takes to write a BufferedRandomAccessFile class (Listing 15.3) is well worth it, as it has can have a massive effect in boosting performance. To copy a 1 Mbyte file, the BufferedRandomAccessFile is more than 9 times faster than RandomAccessFile. This difference in performance is accentuated under a Just-In-Time compiler (JIT), where the buffered version is more than 40 times faster.

Listing 15.3

```
public class BufferedRandomAccessFile extends Object
implements DataInput, DataOutput {
  ...
  public final void seek( long pos )
  throws IOException {

    // If the seek is into the buffer, just update the
    // file pointer.
    if( pos >= bufferStart && pos < dataEnd ) {
      filePosition = pos;
      return;
    }

    // If the current buffer is modified, write it to
    // disk.
    if( bufferModified ) {
      flush( );
    }
```

```
    // Move to the position on the disk.
    file.seek( pos );
    filePosition = file.getFilePointer( );
    bufferStart = filePosition;

    // Fill the buffer from the disk.
    dataSize = file.read( buffer );
    if( dataSize < 0 ) {
      dataSize = 0;
      endOfFile = true;
    } else {
      endOfFile = false;
    }

    // Cache the position of the buffer end.
    dataEnd = bufferStart + dataSize;
  }

  public final int read()
  throws IOException {

    // If the file position is within the data, return
    // the byte...
    if( filePosition < dataEnd ) {
      return (int)(buffer[(int)(filePosition++ -
        bufferStart)] & 0xff);

    // ...or should we indicate EOF...
    } else if( endOfFile ) {
      return -1;

    // ...or seek to fill the buffer, and try again.
    } else {
      seek( filePosition );
      return read( );
    }
  }

  ...
}
```

With Java 1.1 came object serialization – a very flexible and convenient way of making data persistent. It can save any class that implements the Serializable interface, and preserves all links between objects. However, if you don't need this functionality, it can be a significant overhead. When you are storing large amounts of data, you should consider writing the data directly.

15.3.3 Java Language Efficiencies

As well as having a good understanding of the library classes, knowing how the language itself works can lead to some simple optimizations. Consider the following code snippet, which returns a string representation of the contents of a (non-empty) Vector.

```
String result = "[" + elementAt( 0 );
for( int i = 1; i < size( ); i++ )
   result += ", " + elementAt( i );
return result + "]";
```

String concatenation in Java is performed by converting the string into a StringBuffer and using the append() method. Each time the for loop executes, Java converts result into a StringBuffer, appends the string literal and the element string, converts the whole lot back into a string and assigns it to result. If you use a StringBuffer explicitly, as in the next code example, there is only one conversion between the StringBuffer and the String, resulting in a threefold increase in speed:

```
StringBuffer result = new StringBuffer( "[" );
result.append( elementAt( 0 ) );
for( int i = 1; i < size( ); i++ ) {
   result.append( ", " );
   result.append( elementAt( i ).toString( ) );
}
result.append( "]" );
return result.toString( );
```

As we mentioned earlier, the virtual machine performs checks on things like array bounds and casting types. If these checks are already being performed, don't duplicate them! For example, if a method accepts a parameter that is an index into an array, don't explicitly check that the index is valid. Instead, trap the ArrayOutOfBoundsException – it may be slower to deal with an exception than to check the index, but this overhead only exists under exceptional circumstances. You can see this technique in the Vector.elementAt() method in Listing 15.4. Here the exception is only used to check for negative indices, as the object array (its capacity) may be larger than the size of the Vector.

Listing 15.4

```
public class Vector implements Cloneable,
   java.io.Serializable {
...
   public final synchronized Object elementAt(
      int index) {
      if (index >= elementCount) {
```

```
        throw new ArrayIndexOutOfBoundsException(index +
          " >= " + elementCount);
      }
      /* Since try/catch is free, except when the
         exception is thrown,
         put in this extra try/catch to catch negative
         indexes and display a more informative error
         message. */
      try {
        return elementData[index];
      } catch (ArrayIndexOutOfBoundsException e) {
        throw new ArrayIndexOutOfBoundsException(index
          + " < 0");
      }
    }
  }
  ...
}
```

As noted previously, most JVMs run garbage collection (GC) asynchronously in a background thread. If the garbage collector runs at an inappropriate time, it can badly affect perceived speed. The risk of this can be minimized by giving the virtual machine an appropriate amount of memory (see Chapter 14), and by calling the garbage collector explicitly when things are quiet (System.gc()). In the listings throughout this chapter, you can see that the garbage collector has been called before a test begins, so that the test is not disrupted by garbage collection due to the preceding test. However, you should note that calling gc() is only a request, and there is no guarantee that garbage collection will run at that time.

Finally, Java has inherited C's short-circuit evaluation of expressions. This means that when Java evaluates an expression, it works from left to right through the terms, and stops evaluating the terms when the outcome can be determined. This is in contrast to languages such as Ada, where every term in the expression is evaluated. Consider the following code snippet:

```
if( customer.isReady( ) || customer.isAngry( ) ) {
```

If the first term (customer.isReady()) evaluates to true, the expression will always be true, regardless of the remaining term. In this case, Java will not evaluate customer.isAngry(). You can use this to your advantage by placing the faster methods calls towards the left of an expression, so that the slower method calls are only made when necessary. For example,

```
if( obj.fastMethod( ) || obj.slowMethod( ) ) {
```

will generally be faster than

```
if( obj.slowMethod( ) || obj.fastMethod( ) ) {
```

We have only shown expressions containing logical ORs (||), but the principle holds for all of the logical operators.

15.4 Traditional Optimizations

Although this chapter concentrates on optimizations specific to Java, it may be useful to review some general techniques. Programmers moving to Java from a language like C++ may not be familiar with some of these techniques, as C++ compilers are much more sophisticated and many perform them automatically.

15.4.1 Elimination of Common Subexpressions

In a given block of code, there may appear a calculation or a method call that is performed several times unnecessarily. For example, in the following piece of code, the `calcAverage()` method is called no fewer than four times during each iteration of the loop, when only a single call would suffice.

```
for( int i = 0; i < 1000; i++ ) {
   top = calcAverage(i) * 1.67;
   bottom = calcAverage(i) * 3.21;
   max = Math.pow( calcAverage(i), calcAverage(i) );
   . . .
}
```

If `calcAverage()` is slow (or if it is inside a large loop), we can speed the code up significantly by calling the method only once, and storing the result in a temporary variable. This is known as eliminating common sub-expressions.

```
for( int i = 0; i < 1000; i++ ) {
   double avg = calcAverage(i);
   top = avg * 1.67;
   bottom = avg * 3.21;
   max = Math.pow( avg, avg );
   . . .
}
```

15.4.2 Eliminating Loop Invariants

Eliminating loop invariants is similar to eliminating common sub-expressions. This time we are looking for calculations (or method calls) that occur inside a loop, but that are not actually modified by the loop (they are loop-invariants). For example, in the following piece of code, the `((2.0 / Math.PI) / 360.0)` calculation is performed during every iteration of the loop, despite the fact that it does not change.

```
for( int n = 0; n < getSize(); n++ ) {
   double radians = getDegrees() *
      ((2.0 / Math.PI) / 360.0);
   . . .
}
```

A faster implementation would be to perform the calculation once outside the loop, and store it in a temporary variable.

```
double deg2rad = ((2.0 / Math.PI) / 360.0);
for( int n = 0; n < getSize(); n++ ) {
  double radians = getDegrees() * deg2rad;
  ...
}
```

There is one loop invariant that is very common in Java, but not immediately apparent. The termination condition in a for loop (n < getSize() in this case) is evaluated after every iteration of the loop. The same points apply here – if the loop is large, or if the calculation involves a slow method, it should be performed outside the loop.

```
double deg2rad = ((2.0 / Math.PI) / 360.0);
int size = getSize();
for( int n = 0; n < size; n++ ) {
  double radians = getDegrees() * deg2rad;
  ...
}
```

15.4.3 Expanding Loops

If you have a loop whose size can be determined in advance, it is possible to expand it into a series of commands. For example:

```
// In a loop
for( int n = 0; n < 4; n++ )
  total += data[n];

// Expanded
total += data[0] + data[1] + data[2] + data[3];
```

This type of optimization can have a particularly bad effect on the readability of your code, and so should be used sparingly. It is most often useful when the loop to be expanded is nested inside another (large) loop.

15.5 The Cost of Java Operations

Take a look at Table 15.1. It shows the time taken (in nanoseconds) to perform various operations in Java, for the standard Java VM (version 1.1.3), for Java with a JIT compiler (Java Performance Pack version 1.1.3), and for a native code compiler (SuperCede Java V1.0 – a Java 1.1 version is not yet available). The values themselves are not important (and are not intended to provide a balanced comparison between different JVMs) – we are interested in the relative cost of the different operations.

Table 15.1 Timings of some Java operations (in nanoseconds)

Operation	`java`	`java + JIT`	Native code
Local variable assignment	67	10	5
Instance variable assignment	280	14	5
Method call	541	40	40
Synchronous method call	1767	1215	2053
Object creation	2189	2250	1701
Array creation	178	14	13

Armed with this information, we can come up with some general rules for optimizing Java.

15.5.1 Use Shorthand Operators

Java has inherited the shorthand arithmetic operators from C/C++ (++, --, +=, -=, *=, /=, |=, &=). As well as being faster to type, they actually produce faster code, so use them whenever possible. For example, x++ or x += 1 are faster than x = x + 1, and x[i * j] *= pi is faster than x[i + j] = x[i + j] * pi (the latter example also benefits because the index expression is only evaluated once).

15.5.2 Accessor Methods and In-lining

You can see that accessing a local variable is (usually) faster than accessing an instance variable, and that accessing an instance variable is significantly faster than calling a method. This observation leads to the following tips:

1. For values that need to be accessed in performance-critical code, use public instance variables rather than accessor[1] methods.
2. If an instance variable or a value from a method is to be used many times in performance-critical code, store the value once in a local variable, and use that instead. This is particularly important if getting the value involves a slow calculation.
3. Given the relative expense of calling methods, it is sometimes useful to take advantage of in-lining.

There is a certain overhead associated with calling a method –parameters must be pushed on the stack, the method located, any return value pushed back on the stack, etc. In-lining code involves replacing a call to a method with the actual code contained in the method. This removes the overhead associated with calling a

---

1 An accessor method is one that gets or sets the value of an instance variable. It is generally considered good programming practice to use accessor methods rather than using the instance variables directly, because they provide a buffer between the specification and the implementation of the class.

method, at the expense of increasing the size of the code. Java as a language has limited scope for in-lining, as object variables in Java are polymorphic – sending a message to an object may result in different implementations of the method being called, depending on the class of the object. This makes it impossible for a compiler trying to in-line a method to determine which implementation of the method will actually be called.

The compiler can only determine that a particular method will be called if cannot be overridden: when the method is declared as private or final. This does not guarantee that the method will be in-lined – the standard Java compiler only in-lines small methods that do not contain local variables.

As always, the increase in speed comes at a cost. If you are forced into declaring your methods private or final, then you lose some of the flexibility of your class.

Listing 15.5 shows these tips in action, using a for loop referring to a local variable, an instance variable and a synchronized, in-lined and normal method (remember, the for loop evaluates its termination condition after every iteration). The times it gives are shown in Table 15.2. The difference in speed between an in-lined method and a local variable is slight, but if the method performed a calculation the difference would be significant.

Listing 15.5

```
public class Access extends Object {

  public int count = 1000000;

  public int getCount( ) {
    return count;
  }

  public final int getFinalCount( ) {
    return count;
  }

  public synchronized int getSynchronizedCount( ) {
    return count;
  }

  public static void main( String argv[] ) {

    Access access = new Access( );
    int count = access.getCount( );

    long syncTime = System.currentTimeMillis( );
    for( int i = 0; i < access.getSynchronizedCount(
      ); i++ ) {
    }
```

```
    syncTime = (System.currentTimeMillis( ) -
      syncTime);

    long methodTime = System.currentTimeMillis( );
    for( int i = 0; i < access.getCount( ); i++ ) {
    }
    methodTime = (System.currentTimeMillis( ) -
      methodTime);

    long inlineTime = System.currentTimeMillis( );
    for( int i = 0; i < access.getFinalCount( ); i++ ){
    }
    inlineTime = (System.currentTimeMillis( ) -
      inlineTime);

    long instanceTime = System.currentTimeMillis( );
    for( int i = 0; i < access.count; i++ ) {
    }
    instanceTime = (System.currentTimeMillis( ) -
      instanceTime);

    long localTime = System.currentTimeMillis( );
    for( int i = 0; i < count; i++ ) {
    }
    localTime = (System.currentTimeMillis( ) -
      localTime);
    System.out.println( "Synchronized Method call: " +
      syncTime + "ms" );
    System.out.println( "Method call: " + methodTime +
      "ms" );
    System.out.println( "In-lined method call: " +
      inlineTime + "ms" );
    System.out.println( "Instance variable: " +
      instanceTime + "ms" );
    System.out.println( "Local variable: " + localTime
      + "ms" );
  }
}
```

15.5.3 Synchronization

Table 15.2 also clearly demonstrates the effect that synchronization has on performance. A synchronized method is prefixed with the synchronized keyword, and is used to enforce atomic transactions on an instance of an object. That is, once a synchronized method is started, calls to other synchronized methods on that instance are queued until it finishes.

Table 15.2 Timing results produced by Listing 15.5

Type of access	Time for 1 000 000 iterations (ms)
Synchronized method call	1862
Method call	581
In-lined method call	230
Instance variable	230
Local variable	190

For this reason, if you know that your class will not be used in a multi-threaded environment, don't make the methods synchronized. If you are multi-threading, choose carefully which methods to synchronize. For the best performance, it is usually better to synchronize higher-level methods that are called infrequently rather than the lowest level, frequently called methods. For example, if you were writing the `RandomAccessFile` class, it would be better to synchronize the `readInt()` and `readLong()` methods rather than the low-level `read()` method that reads the individual bytes. The disadvantage of synchronizing at a higher level is that an instance may become locked for a longer time (and so for very interactive threads, performance could actually suffer). Nearly all of the Java standard classes use synchronized methods, to ensure they are "safe" in a multi-threaded environment.

15.5.4 Object Creation

We've left the most significant optimization for last. Referring back to Table 15.1, you can see that the overhead associated with creating an object is massive (which may seem rather sad in an object-oriented language). The timings given do not take into account any constructor code either. So, another rule for optimizing Java code is to minimize object creation.

If you are storing primitive types (e.g. `int`, `long`), then do not store them in a `Vector`. If you store a primitive type in a `Vector`, then you have to use one of the wrapper classes (e.g. `Integer`, `Long`) and create a new object every time you add an element. Instead, either use an array or define a primitive vector class (e.g. `IntVector`) that stores the values directly. If you are storing instances of classes that comprise only primitive types, consider splitting the class and storing the data in a group of primitive arrays (compromising encapsulation). For example, the array in the following code snippet contains a class storing an integer and a long integer:

```
class OnlyPrimitives {
   int recordNo;
   long offset;
}
OnlyPrimitives myArray[] = new OnlyPrimitives[1000];
```

The equivalent data could be stored in two arrays:

```
int recordNos[1000];
long offsets[1000];
```

By treating primitive types in this way, you also reduce the memory that they occupy.

The second way that you can minimize object creation is to reuse existing objects. A good example of this is reusing dialog boxes. Instead of destroying the dialog when it is closed, hide it instead. The next time it is needed, it can be shown without going through the slow construction process. This applies to non-GUI classes as well – design your classes with a `reset()` method. Some of the Java library classes provide methods for resetting the class – for example, `Vectors` can be reused (the `Vector` is reset with the `setSize()` or `removeAllElements()` methods). However, calling `removeAllElements()` on a large `Vector` is slower than creating a new one, as it sets every element in the underlying array to `null`. For most purposes, the method could simply set the `Vector` size to zero[2].

Listing 15.6 shows both types of optimization when storing values in a `Vector`. Because the `Vector`'s `removeAllElements()` method is slow, we have simulated the effect of a fast reset method by simply re-entering the data into the same `Vector`. Table 15.3 shows the results – not having to create a new `Vector` each time speeds things significantly, but the fastest approach by far is to use a primitive array (which also benefits from not having synchronized method calls).

Listing 15.6

```
import java.util.Vector;

public class Creation extends Object {

  public static void main( String argv[] ) {

    int storeCount = 10000;
    int count = 100;

    System.gc( );
    long newTime = System.currentTimeMillis( );
    for( int i = 0; i < storeCount; i++ ) {
      Vector v = new Vector( count );
      for( int j = 0; j < count; j++ )
        v.addElement( new Integer( i * storeCount + j
          ) );
    }
    newTime = System.currentTimeMillis( ) - newTime;
```

---

2 As usual, this is a compromise between memory and performance optimization. By setting each element in the array to `null`, `java.lang.Vector` ensures that there are no references left to the objects it contained. This allows the automatic garbage collector to reclaim the memory used by these objects. Clearly, if memory is tight, or the objects contained in the `Vector` are large, setting the elements to `null` will be important.

```
System.gc( );
long reuseTime = System.currentTimeMillis( );
Vector v = new Vector( count );
v.setSize( count );
for( int i = 0; i < storeCount; i++ ) {
  for( int j = 0; j < count; j++ )
    v.setElementAt( new Integer( i * storeCount +
      j ), j );
}
reuseTime = System.currentTimeMillis( ) -
  reuseTime;

System.gc( );
long arrayTime = System.currentTimeMillis( );
int array[] = new int[count];
for( int i = 0; i < storeCount; i++ ) {
  for( int j = 0; j < count; j++ )
    array[j] = i * storeCount + j;
}
arrayTime = System.currentTimeMillis( ) -
  arrayTime;

System.out.println( "New vector: " + newTime +
  "ms" );
System.out.println( "Reused vector: " + reuseTime
  + "ms" );
System.out.println( "Primitive array: " +
  arrayTime + "ms" );
  }
}
```

Table 15.3 The results from Listing 15.6

Type of creation	Time for storing 100 elements 10 000 times (ms)
New vector	8603
Reused vector	5237
Primitive array	741

15.6 Rewriting Library Classes

The Java class library is written for general-purpose use. If a class is not giving you the performance you require, then rewrite it, using the techniques described here (you have the original source code to refer to). Simply removing the synchronized keyword from most methods can speed them up significantly. Bear in mind though, that if a method is defined as `native`, then you are not likely to out-do it with a Java method.

Native methods are the last resort of a Java optimizer. Java allows you to link native code into your Java application. The disadvantage is that the application is now platform-dependent, although it is possible to write fallback Java methods for other platforms. Linking native methods is a subject in its own right, so we refer you to the Java Tutorial for a good introduction.

15.7 Summary

The following points provide some good rules of thumb for optimizing Java applications.

1. Use a Just-In-Time compiler or a native compiler if appropriate.
2. Use the optimize setting of your compiler, but don't expect it to do much more than in-line some methods. Keep a lookout for situations where you can eliminate common sub-expressions and remove loop-invariants.
3. Use a profiler to target your optimization effort.
4. Look at the class library API and source code to help you use the library classes efficiently.
5. If an accessor method is called frequently, store the value in a local variable, or use a public instance variable instead.
6. Avoid unnecessary synchronization, and keep synchronization to higher level methods.
7. Avoid unnecessary object creation – store primitive types in arrays and reuse existing objects.

15.8 Online References

The benchmarks were performed using Doug Bell's benchmark utility, available from

```
http://www.2nu.com/Doug/Benchmark/Benchmark.html
```

A useful source of information on Java optimization can be found at

```
http://www.cs.cmu.edu/~jch/java/
```

Source code for (among other things) `FastVector`, `FastStringBuffer` and `BufferedRandomAccessFile` are available at

```
http://www.aber.ac.uk/~agm/Java.html
```

The Win95 Performance pack JIT is available from Sun at

```
http://java.sun.com/products/jdk/1.1/
```

Native methods are introduced in the Java tutorial at

```
http://java.sun.com/docs/books/tutorial/index.html
```

15.9 References

The optimization examples were compiled by `javac` V1.1.3 with optimization turned on. They were run using `java` V1.1.3 without the performance pack JIT, on a 200 MHz Pentium Pro PC with 64 Mbyte of memory.

The classic book on compiler design is

Aho A.V. and Ullman J.D. *Principles of Compiler Design.* Addison-Wesley, Reading MA.

This contains some good material on optimization.

16 *Optimizing for Memory*

16.1 Introduction

When optimizing Java code, programmers naturally focus on improving performance. After all, the most common criticism levelled at Java is its relative lack of speed. There is, however, another side to optimization – that of optimizing for size (which is often in direct competition with performance). Optimizing for size manifests itself in two (related) forms: reducing the size of Java classes, and reducing the amount of memory used at runtime.

Java classes are already a very compact form of executable. However, when using applets the size of the classes (and hence the size of the class files) directly affects the start-up speed of the applet. The size of Java classes will also have an effect on the amount of runtime memory used by an application – the Java Virtual Machine (JVM) loads a description of every class used in an application. However, as there is only ever one of each class object in memory (compared with many instances of that class), the size of the class is much less important than the size of the instances.

The need to reduce the amount of runtime memory is less obvious than the need to reduce the size of class files for applets, especially as the standard amount of RAM in machines almost seems to double every few months. Nevertheless, Java is being used more and more for real applications. When large amounts of data are involved, memory optimization can become very important. It's also worth bearing in mind that any application that wastes memory will slow down as the memory becomes used up and the automatic garbage collection runs more often.

Chapter 14 looked at how the standard Java Compiler and JVM can affect the memory usage of Java. It also contains an important discussion of the need to target optimization. In this chapter, we consider some tools that can help reduce the size of classes. We explore how Java stores objects in memory, and how the garbage collector (GC) reclaims unused memory. Using this information, we discuss how to write memory test harnesses in Java (to help assess the effects of optimization), and how to write Java code that makes the best use of memory[1].

16.2 Reducing Class File Size

Before an applet can be executed via the Web, the class files must first be downloaded. The larger the class files, the longer the wait. This is a serious issue for commercial

---

1 Unless otherwise stated, the examples were run using the JDK V1.1.3 under Windows NT. The memory sizes quoted assume the same configuration.

Table 16.1 The possible sizes of `java.lang.Vector`

Compilation method	Class size (bytes)
`javac` with debugging	5330
`javac`	4163
`javac` with optimization	3398
`javac` with optimization and obfuscation	3107
`javac` with optimization in a JAR	2103
`javac` with optimization and obfuscation in a JAR	1934

systems as well as for more casual developers, as we are sure that we can't be the only ones to have given up waiting for an applet to load over a slow connection!

There are three main strategies for reducing the size of class files:

1. Using the optimize flag of the Java compiler
2. Compressing the classes in a Java archive (JAR)
3. Using a code obfuscator to reduce the space taken up by long identifiers

Table 16.1 shows how these strategies affect the `java.lang.Vector` class file. As you can see, the smallest class file is less than half the size of the largest file, which corresponds to halving the download time!

16.2.2 Compiler Optimization

As we discussed in Chapter 14, the compiler can directly affect the size of the class files. If a class is compiled with the debugging flag (-g), it will contain local variable information. By default, it will contain line number information (to help the exception mechanism). By compiling classes with the optimize flag (-O), the compiler removes both types of extraneous data. However, it is not possible to distinguish between speed and memory optimization – the compiler may in-line some methods to improve performance, which can increase the size of the class. Despite this, using the optimize flag nearly always decreases the size of a class.

16.2.2 Java Archives

Java 1.1 introduced the Java ARchive (JAR) file. This is a compressed file for Java classes (and resources), based on the ZIP compression format. This dramatically reduces the size of the class files – for example, the standard Java class library compresses from 8.63 Mbyte to 5.03 Mbyte. This is the easiest (and most effective) way of reducing the size of your class files. In addition, because the classes are packaged into one file, there is only one FTP transaction, which further speeds the downloading of an applet. Unfortunately, Java 1.1 has been slow at appearing in commercial Web browsers, although the latest versions (4.0) of Netscape and Internet Explorer support it.

JAR files are easy to create using the `jar` tool. For example,

```
jar -cf classes.jar *.*
```

will create a JAR file called "`classes.jar`" containing the contents of the current directory (the `-cf` means create a new file).

The `APPLET` tag in the HTML document now supports the `ARCHIVE` parameter. Assuming we wanted to run `MyApplet`, a class contained in the newly created "`classes.jar`", the `APPLET` tag would look like:

```
<applet code=MyApplet.class archive="classes.jar"
   width=200 height=200></applet>
```

If you are using a JAR file with an application, then you'll have to add the JAR file to the `CLASSPATH` environment variable.

16.2.3 Code Obfuscuators

Java links classes dynamically – that is, it doesn't attempt to find a class or a method until it first encounters that class referenced in some code. For this reason, each class file must contain the names of its identifiers. It follows, therefore, that using verbose identifier names can lead to larger class files. Luckily, this is not an excuse for using short and cryptic identifier names! There are a number of code obfuscators available whose primary purpose is to rename identifiers to make it difficult for other people to decode your classes. The identifiers are renamed to be short and cryptic, which also reduces the size of the class files.

Of course, there are some caveats. Firstly, you must obfuscate every class that is used in an applet – otherwise, the virtual machine (JVM) won't be able to match class and method identifiers. This means that you cannot obfuscate classes that you want to provide external access to (e.g. as part of a library).

In addition, any code that references an identifier by a string will fail (as the identifier has been renamed but the string has not been). An example of problem code would be `getClass( ).getMethod( "toString", null )`. However, this type of code is not found in many applications.

Most obfuscators work around these problems, but they do limit the obfuscators' effectiveness.

16.2.4 Exploiting Inheritance

It has long been considered good practice in object-oriented programming to create related classes by subclassing the same superclass (as discussed in Chapter 2). This allows you to move code that is common to both classes into the superclass, resulting in less code to write and maintain. Of course, this can also reduce the size of the classes as a whole, because there are no longer two copies of the same code.

This is not a fail-safe method of reducing the size of the classes – there is a certain size overhead associated with creating an extra class. Generally, this approach is worthwhile (from a class-size point of view) if there are lots of shared methods, or if the shared method is reasonably large.

Still on the subject of inheritance, your new classes will usually be smaller if you subclass a class that already exists. You can inherit most of the functionality that you need, and only have to define new code to modify its behaviour.

When creating applets, you should consider whether you actually need a new class, rather than using one of the library ones. The library classes are already on the client machine, and so do not need to be downloaded.

16.3 Memory Management

We can now take a look at how Java manages memory. The way in which Java reclaims unused memory, how this relates to the Abstract Windowing Toolkit (AWT), and how it stores objects in memory will help us determine the most effective ways of optimizing memory usage.

16.3.1 Java's Automatic Garbage Collection

Unlike most other languages, Java provides automatic garbage collection (GC) for freeing up memory. It makes sense to consider how this works before we take a look at how to minimize Java's runtime memory usage.

In a traditional language, you would create an object with a line of code like:

```
MyObject object = new MyObject( );
```

The program would reserve a chunk of memory from its heap (the name given to the memory available to the program), and use this to store the values of the object's instance variables. When the object was finished with, the memory would be returned to the heap with a line of code like:

```
free object;
```

Problems arise when the programmer forgets to free all of the redundant objects – the amount of free memory can gradually reduce over time. This is known as a memory leak, and is a common but difficult to find bug. Java allocates memory for new objects in this way, but does not require the programmer to explicitly free the object when it is finished with. Instead, a process called "automatic garbage collection" checks every object created on the heap. If there are no variables referring to that object, then there is no way that the object could be used in the future, and the memory can be reclaimed.

Exactly how the garbage collection works is left up to the virtual machine implementation. As a minimum, the garbage collection should be called when the JVM runs low on memory. It may also be called explicitly through a call to System.gc(), although this is only a request and may not be acted on immediately. Most JVMs run garbage collection asynchronously, which means that it runs periodically from a background thread. The actual method of tracking references to objects also varies. The algorithm may have to make a compromise between reclaiming all of the redundant memory and performance.

16.3.2 Freeing AWT Resources

The Java documentation only mentions in passing that the automatic garbage collection does not extend to parts of the AWT. Unfortunately, assuming that the GC will end all of your memory problems can lead to some serious memory leaks.

So why isn't the AWT garbage collected? Some of the AWT objects map directly to resources in the underlying operating system. For example, java.awt.Window is a Java class that maps to an operating system window. If the automatic garbage collector freed resources automatically, then you would need to maintain references to every resource until it was no longer needed. Consider Listing 16.1 – the Window variable is local to the method, and when the method ends, the variable is freed, leaving no references to the Window object. Nevertheless, we wouldn't want the window to disappear when the method ended.

Listing 16.1 *Local variable reference to* Window

```
public void showData( ) {
  Window window = new Window( );
  window.add( new DataPanel( ) );
  window.setVisible( true );
}
```

Classes that require you to free their memory explicitly usually provide a dispose() method. These include Frame, Graphics[2] and Window. The Image class has a flush() method for freeing its resources. When the instance is no longer required, you must explicitly free its memory by calling this method.

Let's consider a situation that frequently occurs in people's code. Listing 16.2 shows an ActionListener class (which could be responding to a menu selection, for example) that creates a modal dialog, and then returns when the dialog has been closed. The dialog is closed by a WindowListener that calls the Window.setVisible(false) method to hide the dialog.

Listing 16.2

```
public class Actions implements ActionListener {
  . . .
  public void actionPerformed( ActionEvent e ) {
    if( e.getActionCommand( ).equals( "showDialog" ) ) {
    MyDialog dialog = new MyDialog( frame, true );
    dialog.addWindowListener( new DialogCloser( ) );
    dialog.setVisible( true );
```

---

2 Note that you do not need to dispose of a Graphics object that comes as a parameter to paint().

```
    } else if( ... ) {
      ...
    }
  }
}

public DialogCloser extends WindowAdapter {
  public void windowClosing( WindowEvent e ) {
    e.getWindow( ).setVisible( false );
  }
}
```

The problem with this code is that every time the `actionPerformed()` method is called a new dialog is created. However, any previously created dialogs are still in memory – even though there are no references to them, the garbage collector does not free AWT windows. A well-written application would have either kept a reference to the dialog and reused it, or would have called `Window.dispose()` in the `WindowListener` class.

This is a very common mistake, even for experienced programmers. You could be forgiven for wondering why it doesn't cause more problems. Well, in reality, most applications only open a relatively small number of windows over their lifetime and the lost memory is not missed. However, if your application creates a large number of windows or images, or if it runs for long periods, then beware!

16.3.3 How Java Stores Objects in Memory

Before we go on to discuss ways of reducing the runtime memory overhead, let us consider exactly how the object instances are stored in memory. Object instances differ from data types in that they also contain methods that operate on the data. Objects in programs are generally stored in one of two ways. The simplest way is to store pointers to the methods' code inside each object (Figure 16.1). This is how C++ virtual methods are stored. This is fast, because calling a method only requires the virtual machine to follow a single pointer to the method code. The disadvantage is clear – the more methods, the larger the object instances become.

The other way is to make each instance of a class contain a reference to a class object which contains pointers to the methods for that class (Figure 16.2). This second approach (as used by Smalltalk) is clearly slower, as the virtual machine must follow two pointers (one to the method table, the other to the method). However, its significant advantage is that having lots of methods does not increase the size of an instance. Although the Java Specification does not define how objects should be stored in memory, the most popular JVMs available use a similar approach to this.

So, the point to note is that you can add methods to a class without having to worry about increasing the runtime memory overhead. In contrast to the first section, we assume that the size of the class object (of which there is only ever one in memory) is insignificant compared with the memory occupied by the class instances.

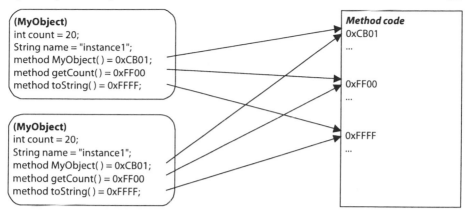

Figure 16.1 Instances store pointers to method code.

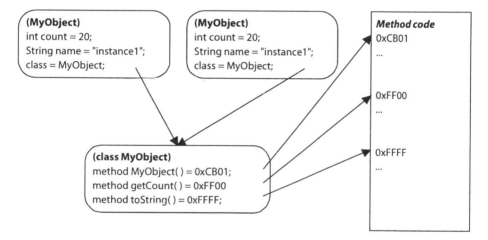

Figure 16.2 Class contains pointers to method code.

16.4 Strategies for Reducing Memory Overhead

16.4.1 Memory Test Harnesses

It's all very well pursuing strategies for optimizing memory, but unless we are aware of how much memory an object consumes, and thus how effective those strategies are, we are wasting our time. Luckily, the task of writing a memory test harness is relatively simple, providing we remember a few tips to avoid erroneous results.

Listing 16.3 shows a sample test harness to calculate the amount of memory used by an instance of `java.lang.Vector`. The test centres on the methods `freeMemory()` and `totalMemory()` in `java.lang.Runtime`, which return the amount of unused memory, and the total amount of memory available respectively. By combining the two, we can calculate the amount of memory used by Java, and see how this changes when we create a new instance of `Vector`.

Listing 16.3 *Memory test harness*

```
// Create all of the variables before the test starts.
Vector v = new Vector( );    // Load the class into
                             // memory.
Object o = null;
Runtime runtime = Runtime.getRuntime( );
long memoryOccupied = 0;

// Run the test.
System.gc( );
memoryOccupied = runtime.totalMemory( ) -
  runtime.freeMemory( );
o = new Vector( );
memoryOccupied = (runtime.totalMemory( ) -
  runtime.freeMemory( )) -memoryOccupied;

// Display the results.
System.out.println( memoryOccupied );
```

The Java VM is started with the −noclassgc −noasyncgc flags, to prevent the garbage collection kicking in unexpectedly and distorting the result. Most of the commercial Java IDEs do not give you this level of control over the JVM, so you may have to return to the JDK for these tests. The first thing that the code does is to create a new instance of Vector. The instance is not used, but it forces the Vector class to be loaded into memory so that it will not be accounted for later.

All of the variables are declared before the test starts, so that the memory occupied by the object reference is ignored. You can use the same format for checking primitive types, but you may need to include some reference to the variable after the memory test harness to prevent a compiler from concluding that it is not used and may be optimized away. The test can be adapted to find the size of the class objects in memory, but you can get a good idea of this simply by looking at the size of the class files.

Table 16.2 shows the size of some primitive types and some standard Java library classes using the JDK under MS Windows and Unix. The sizes of the primitive types are defined in the Java VM Specification. However, JVM implementations may align the data on different word boundaries, which can cause them to occupy more space. In this case, java is aligning objects on 8 byte boundaries, which explains why the Object and Integer instances are the same size.

16.4.2 Targeting Optimization

Optimization must be a well-targeted technique. It is all too easy to waste a lot of time optimizing code that doesn't actually need it – you must use the memory test harnesses to identify which parts of your code need the optimization. Apart from wasting your effort, optimization usually forces us to make compromises with good

Table 16.2 The sizes of some primitive types and objects

Data type	Bytes occupied
`int`	4
`long`	8
Empty array	16
Object reference	4
`java.lang.Object`	16
`java.lang.Integer`	16
`java.lang.Long`	24
`java.util.Vector`	80

design and coding practice, including encapsulation, abstraction and clear structure. This can affect the readability and maintainability of the code.

16.4.3 Setting References to Null

The simplest (and very effective) method of reducing memory overhead is to explicitly set object references to null when the instance is no longer required. This is particularly important if the instance is large. Once the reference to the instance has been removed, the GC can reclaim the memory that it occupies (you could also call the GC explicitly).

It can be easy to forget about object references that are no longer needed. For example, if you were storing a variable number of objects in an array, you might use an integer variable to count the actual number there. You could remove the last object simply by decrementing the count variable. However, the object reference will still be there unless you set it to null, and the memory cannot be reclaimed.

16.4.4 Making the Most of Storage Classes

Many of the standard storage classes provide methods that allow you to minimize the amount of memory that they use. For example, the Vector class can store a variable number of objects. It does this by creating an array of Object references with room for a certain number of elements (its capacity). By default, every time the capacity is exceeded, the Vector doubles the size of its Object array. Clearly, this can waste memory.

There are two ways of controlling this. First, when you have finished adding elements to the Vector, call its trimToSize() method, which will reduce the capacity to the smallest size possible. Alternatively, you can set the initial capacity and the amount the capacity may grow by in the constructor.

There are similar methods in the Hashtable class.

16.4.5 Primitive Types

Table 16.2 shows that the overhead of a basic object instance is 16 bytes. If any of your classes contain only primitive instance variables, you can split the class into its component parts (storing them in arrays). This can provide a very significant memory saving for large amounts of data, at the expense of losing encapsulation. For example, consider the following class:

```
class OnlyPrimitives {
    int recordNo;
    long offset;
}
```

If you stored 1000 of these in an array, it would take up 28 kbyte. However, the primitive int and long values could be stored separately:

```
int recordsNos[1000];
long offsets[1000];
```

In this case, only 12 kbyte would be used, which is a very significant saving.

For the same reason, using a Vector to store primitive values is inefficient, as the primitive values must be stored in wrapper classes (e.g. the java.lang.Integer class). 1000 int values consume 4 kbyte, whereas 1000 Integers use 16 kbyte – four times as much. The way to avoid this problem is either to store the values in an array, or to define storage classes that work directly with primitive types (e.g. IntVector).

These optimizations may also improve the performance of the code – this was discussed in Section 15.5.4.

16.4.6 File-Based Storage Classes

One solution to memory constraints is not to have the data in memory in the first place! If you have a large amount of data, you could store it in a file and only load the parts you need to work on. Of course, this would lead to extra complications in your program code, so we can resort to the OO solution of encapsulation and define some file-based storage classes.

These classes provide access to data, but the file access (or even database access) is hidden from the user. They may even be subclasses of the standard storage classes, such as Vector. They would include methods that allow the user of the class to free up a stored element. If the classes are general purpose (i.e. can store any Object subclass) and writing is allowed, the implementation of such a class can become complicated (for example, you wouldn't want the entire file to be rewritten whenever an element is modified). See Chapter 8 for a simple file-based Bag class.

16.5 Summary

To minimize the size of class files, you can:

1. Use JAR files if 1.1 compatibility is allowed.
2. Use the `javac` optimize flag to reduce the class size.
3. Use a code obfuscator to minimize overhead from verbose identifiers, bearing in mind its limitations.

   To reduce runtime overhead, you can:

1. Remember to free AWT resources.
2. Set object references to null when the instances are finished with.
3. Trim the capacity of storage classes to avoid wasted space.
4. Split classes into primitive arrays if you are storing lots of them.
5. Rewrite storage classes to work directly with primitive types.
6. Base the storage of data in a file, and only keep a small subset in memory.

Remember, these are strategies to be used selectively, and you must choose the most appropriate ones for each situation.

16.6 Further Reading

For an further example of file-based storage:

Howard R. (1997) StoreTable: a Java class for simple object persistence. *Java Report*; 2(5): 45.

16.7 Online References

The Java obfuscator used was Jobe, available from

    http://www.primenet.com/~ej/index.html

A useful source of information on Java optimization can be found at

    http://www.cs.cmu.edu/~jch/java/

The Java Virtual Machine Specification is available from Sun at

    http://java.sun.com/docs/books/vmspec/index.html

17 Future Evaluators

17.1 Exploiting Idle Processor Time

In many applications there are periods of time when the processor is effectively idle (for example, during user input or while waiting for a server to respond to a request). In these situations this idle resource could be exploited. For example, information (such as a processor-intensive calculation) that will be required in the future by the application could be generated. If the result has been calculated before it is needed, then the performance of the system will appear instantaneous to the user. If the calculation has not yet been completed, at least some of the work will already have been performed.

For example, consider the situation where a user is inputting information via a user interface. This system is part of an online helpdesk system that maintains records of customer configuration, histories etc. The user is first presented with a screen of input fields which allow them to input data on the current customer and any problems they may be facing. Once they have done that, a history screen is displayed, which presents the user with additional information about the customer they are dealing with. If the system waited until the user had entered the first screen of data before requesting the database information there would be a delay.

However, having filled in the fields relating to their name and address, the system has enough information to query the database for the current customer information. While the user completes the remainder of the first input screen the database can be queried for the customer's history file. This can then be presented to the user for confirmation/updating as soon as the first screen has been completed.

One way of handling such asynchronous processing is via a future evaluator. A future evaluator is an object that will provide a result at some point in the future, but in the meantime can either be used in place of that result or can provide an intermediate result. For example, in Figure 17.1, a processor-intensive calculation is being performed. The result of this process is to be displayed in the text field in the window. If this process were performed before the window was created, then a long delay would occur following the initiation of the program before the window was displayed. Instead, a future evaluator object has been used. This object will either return a string of three dots or the result of the numeric computation. Figure 17.1 illustrates the result of requesting the value of the future before the result has been completed. Figure 17.2 illustrates the result of performing this same request after the result has been generated. The program that generated this interface is illustrated in Listings 17.1, 17.2 and 17.3, given later in this chapter.

Figure 17.1 Displaying the
"early" value.

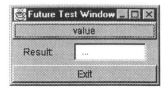

Figure 17.2 Displaying the
actual result of the future
evaluator.

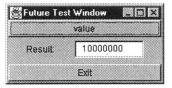

If you are still confused, think of the future evaluator as a proxy object that can be queried for a result. The querying thread will then:

● obtain the result held by the future, if one is available, or

● obtain an intermediate result, or

● be suspended until a value is forthcoming (if the future has not completed its task).

In effect, a future evaluator is a separate process which performs the required operations, but which abstracts this so that the programmer can treat the future as the required information.

In this chapter you will see how this can be achieved in Java. The basic concept of futures and lazy evaluators is not new; however, to the best of our knowledge this is the first time they have been introduced in Java. Before introducing the evaluators themselves we need to review the concept of a `Thread` and the use of `wait()` and `notifyAll()` for inter-thread communication. We will also introduce a (very simple) inner class.

17.2 Processes in Java

A Java process is a preemptive lightweight process termed a *thread*. A thread is a "lightweight" process because it does not possess its own address space and it is not treated as a separate entity by the host operating system. Instead, it exists within a single machine process using the same address space. However, these lightweight threads are called "green" threads in Java, as it is also possible to exploit native threads. This is discussed later in this chapter.

Every thread has an associated priority that, by default, is the same as the thread that spawned it. Threads with a higher priority are executed before threads with a lower priority. A thread with a higher priority may interrupt a thread with a lower priority. Depending on the Java Virtual Machine (JVM) implementation you are using, the scheduler may or may not perform time slicing between threads of the same priority.

A thread is considered to be alive unless it has been stopped (when it can be considered dead). A thread can be explicitly stopped or can stop by completing its run() method.

There are two ways in which to initiate a new thread of execution:

- Create a subclass of the Thread class and redefine the run() method to perform the set of actions that the thread is intended to do. For example, see the class Worker in Listing 17.1.

- Define a new class that implements the Runnable interface. It must define the run() method and can be started by passing an instance of the class to a new Thread instance. For example, see the class Test in the sample application in Listing 17.2.

In both cases, we define a class that specifies the operations or actions that the new thread (or execution) performs. Thus, the multi-threaded aspects of Java all conform to the object-oriented model.

It should be noted that a class Process also exists in the java.lang package. This class is used when executing a program on the host platform in a separate process to the JVM. It is not intended for Java applications nor for modules written in a language such as C which provide the implementation of a method. An instance of the Process class is returned in response to the exec() method being sent to the Runtime class.

17.3 Inter-process Communication

Processes can communicate in Java with each other in a number of ways. In particular the wait() and notify()/notifyAll() methods can be used with signals to synchronize threads. For example, one thread can wait on a signal object until another thread notifies that signal object that it should allow the first thread to continue. Such signals are often referred to as semaphores.

In Java any object can be used as a signal is this way, as the above methods are defined in the class Object. The wait() method causes the issuing thread to suspend itself until a notify() or notifyAll() method is sent to the signal object. The notify() method unblocks at most one thread (if no thread is waiting then the notify is lost). The notifyAll() method unblocks all threads waiting on the signal object.

Unfortunately things are not quiet as straightforward as implied by this description. In reality each object has an object lock flag. This lock flag is used with the keyword synchronized to ensure that while a thread has the lock flag it is not interrupted by the scheduler, and thus any operations within the synchronized block or method will be guaranteed to run to completion. The methods wait(), notify() and notifyAll() are operations which must not be interrupted. They must therefore be placed within a block synchronized on the receiving object. Thus in Listing 17.1 the code stating that the thread must wait on the signal is placed within a block synchronized on the signal object. Note that once a thread issues a `wait ()` it will be suspended until a notify is issued even though the wait is within a synchronized block.

17.4 Implementing Future Evaluators

Listing 17.1 presents the definition of the class `Future`. This class takes an object which implements the `Runnable` interface (thus ensuring that the object will respond to the `run()` method) and an object to be used as the early return value. This is used if the value of the future evaluator is requested before a result has been generated. In Listing 17.3 a string of three dots is returned as the early return value. If the early return value is not provided or it is set to `null`, then the thread issuing the call to the future will be suspended until a result is provided. Two constructors are therefore provided: the first takes one parameter (the object to be evaluated) and the second takes two parameters (the object to be evaluated and the early return value). The one parameter constructor is actually a convenience constructor for the two-parameter constructor, as all it does is call the latter constructor with a default second parameter (in this case `null`).

Listing 17.1 *The class* `Future`

```
package idle;

import java.util.*;

public class Future {
  private Runnable futureValue;
  private Object earlyReturnValue;
  private Thread thread;
  private Object signal = new Object();

  /**
    * Private inner class used to handle the evaluation
    * of the future value.
    */
  private class Worker extends Thread {
    public void run() {
      futureValue.run();
      synchronized (signal) {signal.notifyAll();}
    }
  }

  /**
    * Create a future evaluator for the supplied
    * runnable object
    */
```

```
      public Future (Runnable futureValue) {
        this(futureValue, null);
      }

      /**
       * Create a future evaluator for the supplied
       * runnable object with the specified early return
       * value.
       */
      public Future (Runnable futureValue, Object
            earlyReturnValue) {
        this.futureValue = futureValue;
        this.earlyReturnValue = earlyReturnValue;
        thread = new Worker();
        thread.setPriority(Thread.MIN_PRIORITY);
        thread.start();
      }

      /**
       * Returns either the value calculated by the future
       * or an early result object if one has been
       * provided.
       */
      public Object value () {
        if (thread.isAlive()) {
          if (earlyReturnValue == null) {
            // Then calling process will have to wait for
            // the signal to be set
            synchronized (signal) {
              try {signal.wait(); }
              catch (InterruptedException e) {}
            }
          } else { return earlyReturnValue; }
        }
        return futureValue;
      }
    }
```

The two-parameter constructor records the object to be evaluated and the early
return value. It then creates a separate thread (using the Worker inner class) which
will be used to generate the result of the operation to be performed. This thread is
given the minimum priority so that it only runs when the processor would otherwise
be idle. Note that, once a thread is created, it must be started before it can execute.
Communication between the worker thread and the future evaluator is achieved via
a signal object that can be used to synchronize them.

The `Worker` class is a private inner class used to handle the evaluation of the future value. It does this by calling the method `run()` on the object held in the future value instance variable. Once this method has run to completion the signal object is sent the message `notifyAll()`. This allows any threads waiting on this signal to proceed.

The `value()` method, defined in the `Future` class, is the method which determines whether the result is available, whether an early return value should be used or whether the current thread should be suspended. It does this by first checking to see whether the worker thread is alive. If the `run()` method of the worker thread has terminated then the thread will not be alive. If the `run()` method has terminated then a result should be available. If the thread is alive, then a check is made to see whether an early return value is available. If it is then it is returned. If not, the calling thread must `wait()` for the signal object to be set before returning the result of the evaluation.

17.5 Working with Future Evaluators

A future evaluator takes an instance of an object that implements the `Runnable` interface. This ensures that the object being passed to the future will define the method `run()`. Thus it is assumed that the method `run()` will implement the desired operation. For example, in Listing 17.2 the class `Test` implements the `Runnable` interface by defining a method `run()` which counts up to the number 10 000 000.

Listing 17.2 *The class* `Test`

```
import idle.*;

public class Test implements Runnable {
   long result;
   public void run() {
      for (int i = 0;  i < 10000000;  i++)  result++;
}
   public String toString () {return "" + result;}
}
```

To create a future evaluator that will perform this calculation in a separate (low-priority) thread, we can use one of the `Future` class constructors. For example:

```
Future f = new Future(new Test(), "...");
Future f = new Future(new Test());
```

The first constructor will result in a future evaluator which will either return "..." or the actual result (depending on whether the result is available or not). The second constructor will result in a future evaluator that will block the calling thread when it requests a result. The important issue here is that the execution of a separate thread, the handling of requests for a result and the suspension of the calling thread (if appropriate) are all handled *transparently* as far as the user of the future is concerned.

As an illustration of actually using a future evaluator within a simple application consider Listing 17.3. This listing presents a test harness class that creates a window into which the future value is to be displayed whenever the value button is selected. If the value has not yet been generated, a series of dots is displayed instead (as specified when instantiating the Future evaluator). Figure 17.1 illustrates such a situation. Figure 17.2 illustrates the same window displaying the actual result.

Listing 17.3 *Using a future evaluator*

```
import idle.*;
import java.awt.*;
import java.awt.event.*;
public class FutureWindow extends Frame implements
ActionListener{
  Future future;
  TextField text;

  public static void main (String args []) {
    Future f = new Future(new Test(), "...");
    new FutureWindow(f);
  }

  public FutureWindow (Future future) {
    super("Future Test Window");
    this.future = future;

    Button b = new Button("value") ;
    b.addActionListener(this);
    add("North", b);

    // Create a panel to display the result
    Panel p = new Panel();
    p.add(new Label("Result:    "));
    text = new TextField(10);
    text.setText((future.value()).toString());
    p.add(text);
    add("Center", p);

    b = new Button("Exit");
    b.addActionListener(this);
    add("South", b);

    pack();
```

```
      setVisible(true);
   }

   public void actionPerformed(ActionEvent e) {
      String label = e.getActionCommand();
      if (label.equals("Exit")) {System.exit(0);}
      else {text.setText((future.value()).toString());
      }
   }
}
```

17.6 Lazy Evaluators

A number of variations on the theme of future evaluators can be conceived: a particularly useful one being the lazy evaluator. This is an evaluator that only attempts to produce a result if one is requested. The advantage of this evaluator is that all the necessary data retrieval can be performed ahead of time, but the expensive data processing will only be performed if a value is actually required. For example, assume that some value in an interface is time-consuming to calculate and requires some database searches to acquire the data for the calculation, but is only required in a very few cases. One way this could be handled would be to use a lazy evaluator that retrieved the necessary data, but only performed the calculation on those few occasions. To do this, the Future class is modified such that the worker thread executes as a high-priority process but is only executed when a value is actually requested. Prior to that it provides a proxy result (such as the string of dots used above).

17.7 Native Threads

In the above example, the "green" threads all run within the JVM. This is fine for our simple example; however, in many situations we would be able to get much better performance if we could exploit the underlying hardware and run completely separate processes, potentially on different processors. This would provide real concurrency. The Java Native Threads pack provides facilities for doing exactly this.

This pack enables the JVM to use native threads when running Java code, relying on the (Solaris kernel) operating system to schedule the threads onto parallel processors.

17.8 Summary

With the increasing use of Java as a client–server tool, the use of evaluators such as those presented above is likely to grow. In the chapter we have illustrated how future and lazy evaluators can be implemented simply and effectively in Java. Little code was required to provide these operators, as the facilities provided by Java easily map onto the requirements of these operators. In turn, the users of such evaluators need not know anything about threads, thread interaction etc. to exploit future and lazy evaluators. The only thing they need to know is how to implement the interface `Runnable`.

17.9 Online References

For information on Java Native Threads see

```
http://java.sun.com/products/jdk/1.1/packs/
   native-threads/
```

18   Real-Time Java

18.1 Introduction

This chapter considers Java as a language for real-time computer systems. This may not be as absurd as it at first appears, as the language from which Java evolved (called Oak) was designed for "smart" consumer electronic devices (such as TV-top control boxes). Thus Oak was intended for embedded systems comprised of small, potentially low-performance, but varied devices. In this chapter we look at real-time systems, what they are, what the requirements are for their languages and how Java fares as a real-time language. We also consider ways of overcoming the limitations that Java's garbage collector imposes.

18.2 What are Real-Time Systems?

A real-time computer system, according to Cooling (1991), is one which "must produce correct responses within a definite time limit". The effect of not responding within this limit is either a performance degradation and/or a system malfunction. Notice that this definition does not define the time limit. Depending upon the system, this time limit could be microseconds, seconds, minutes or even hours. The point is that the computer system must be guaranteed to respond with (presumably) the correct response within the specified time limit.

The ability to respond within such a time limit is the key issue in real-time systems. However, this is often a point of confusion, as many people consider real-time to equate to "very fast response". This may well be necessary in order to ensure a response within the time limit, but is not an essential feature of a real-time system.

The need to respond in a timely manner is what sets real-time systems apart from both batch and online systems (this is not to say that an online system cannot be a real-time system). For example, the exact amount of time taken to display a file within a word processor is rarely considered to be critical to its performance (and certainly does not affect whether it will malfunction or not), although excessive time taken is likely to be a problem.

There are some myths associated with real-time systems that need to be dispelled. One has already been mentioned: that "real-time systems must be fast". Another is that real-time systems are embedded systems (systems operating as one element of a larger system). Again this is one (quite common) way of using a real-time system. In such systems the computer system may be performing a control or monitoring function. Another myth, following on from this, is that real-time systems must be compact and require the use of a minimum amount of memory. Again this may be a requirement of a particular system, but is not a defining feature of a real-time system.

To summarize, a real-time system is a system that must provide an appropriate response within a certain time period.

18.3 Language Requirements

The requirements made of a programming language used for real-time systems are the same as those for any other software system, with one or two additions. Firstly, the language used must be able to handle different events as they occur with predictable performance. Thus the designer of the system must be able to predict the delivered performance of the system under all situations. Secondly, the language must support the servicing of multiple events, where these events appear at random and asynchronously. In general this implies that it is possible to prioritize the processing of these events by separate, potentially asynchronous, processes. Once again these issues relate to the ability to ensure that the response time of the system is within prescribed limits.

Associated issues tend to relate to execution speed and memory requirements. This is because, as indicated above, some real-time systems need to be very fast or to be able to run within limited resources (such as memory). This last issue may relate both to the ability of the executable to fit into memory and to the amount of memory required during system execution.

However, the primary concern is the predictability of the performance of the system. The performance characteristics of any language used for a real-time system must be deterministic.

18.4 Java for Real-Time Systems

How does Java fare as a language for real-time systems, given the discussion presented above? Java is certainly a modern computing language that possesses all the elements required for well-engineered reliable code (for example, exception handling and data encapsulation.). Indeed, it has been shown that there is a one-to-one matching between the language features of Java and those of Ada 95 (a language which is often considered to be particularly suited to real-time systems).

One major advantage that Java has over many other languages is direct support for multiple threads (or lightweight processes) to execute at the same time. These processes are lightweight, as by default they run within the Java Virtual Machine (the JVM), and it is the virtual machine which schedules them and controls their execution. However, it is worth noting that the Java Solaris Native Threads Pack is already available, which, when installed, allows the JVM to use native threads when running Java code. That is, a native thread can execute a separate process on the same or other processors.

However, such language features only deal with the practicalities of implementing the logic of the system. It is still necessary to address the two most important aspects of real-time systems: predictability and (as indicated above to a lesser extent) performance. These are discussed below, and solutions to some of the issues raised are presented in the next section.

18.4.1 Predictable Performance in Java

The biggest obstacle to predictable performance in Java is the garbage collector. This issue has already been discussed in Chapter 15 when considering Java performance measurements. As has already been stated it is possible to control some aspects of the way in which the JVM performs garbage collection from the command line that alleviates some of the problems. Allied with control of the garbage collection process is the careful use of Java's features, allowing a developer to predict accurately the performance of a Java program. This thus ensures that a response can be delivered within specified time constraints (this will be discussed in more detail in the next section).

18.4.2 Java Performance

Java, as a language which compiles to byte codes which are then interpreted, is inherently slow! This is a widely held belief that is not necessarily correct. Chapters 15 and 16 described a variety of techniques that can be used to ensure that developers gain maximum performance from their JVM.

18.4.3 Caching Objects: Be Green and Recycle Objects

In addition to the guidance given in Chapters 15 and 16, the caching of objects can improve the predictability of a system's performance. This approach relies on never dereferencing an object. Instead, when it is no longer required an object is recycled. That is, a developer never throws an object away;, instead it is placed in a cache, from where it is recycled. This recycling process involves resetting the object to its initial state. Then, when another example of this class of object is required, rather than allocating more memory the previously cleaned object is used. Listing 18.1 illustrates the basics for such an object cache. The cache holds any type of object and uses a method clean() to reset that object[1]. Note that the methods add(Object) and get() are synchronized. A synchronized method is one that is guaranteed to run to completion even if another thread is trying to pre-empt the current thread. Although synchronizing methods has a performance overhead, this is necessary, as the cache may be operating in a multi-threaded program and care must be taken to ensure that an object is not retrieved from the cache during the process of adding an object. If this happened the system could find itself in an inconsistent state.

---

1   Assumes that a method clean() is added to the Object class.

Listing 18.1 *An object cache*

```
import java.util.*;

public class Cache {
  Vector contents = new Vector(10, 10);
  public synchronized void add(Object o) {
    o.clean();
    contents.addElement(o);
  }
  public synchronized Object get() {
    if (contents.size() != 0) {
      Object o = contents.lastElement();
      contents.removeElement(o);
      return o;
    } else {
      return null;
    }
  }
}
```

The class presented in Listing 18.1 defines a *very* simple object cache. This cache adds objects to a vector and removes them in a last in, first out manner. It assumes that any object added to the cache has a method `clean()` defined for it. This method will delete the state of the object. For example, if objects of the class `Employee` were to be added to the cache, and the class `Employee` defined a person's name, salary, department and age, then the resulting `clean()` method might resemble that presented below:

```
public class Employee {
  String name, department; double salary; int age;
  ...
  public void clean() {
    name = null; department = null;
    double = 0.0; age = 0;
  }
}
```

Note that any object which contains other objects must call the method `clean()` on these objects rather than setting that variable to null. This is because the contained object will be garbage-collected, rather than recycled, if all references to it are removed.

Once this is done, if an object of the type that is cached is required then the cache is queried for a recycled object. If the cache returns null then a new instance is created. Once the program finishes with this new instance it is returned to the cache. For example:

```
public static void main (String args []) {
  Employee e;
  e = (Employee)cache.get();
```

```
    if (e == null) {
        e = new Employee();
    }
    ...
    cache.add(e);
}
```

Note that in the cache a vector has been used to hold the objects available for recycling. This is an object in its own right. However, it is an object that can hold references to other objects and does not in itself take up much memory. Thus, it should not be a significant drain on the available memory. In addition, the two-parameter Vector constructor has been used to ensure that when a vector grows, it does so by 10, rather than doubling in size.

18.5 Summary

As has been shown in this chapter (and previous chapters), Java can be used as a language for real-time systems. However, care needs to be taken with such a development to minimize the effect of garbage collection on the predictability of the system's performance. It is interesting to note that following the suggestions made above, it is likely that the resulting systems will be significantly less object-oriented than would normally be the case with a well-engineered Java program. This of course may reduce its clarity and thus its comprehensibility, and might be considered by some to indicate a certain naïveté of program design. However, in this case it is not naïveté which has resulted in the program's lack of object-oriented features but rather a detailed understanding of the issues involved and how to ensure the required program response times.

The relevance of Java as a language for real-time systems is increasing with the development of the Java card API, dedicated chips for use in embedded systems and as a general-purpose programming language. This trend is likely to continue as Java is seen not only as a language for the Web, but also as the effective object-oriented language that it is.

Finally, the issue of performance has been considered to be secondary to that of predictability in this chapter. Part of the reason for this is the primary importance of predictability in real-time systems, but also because of the belief that the performance of Java environments is already improving and will continue to improve. This will therefore remove any doubts about Java's ability to perform to the required standard, and thus any performance obstacles will be removed.

18.6 Further Reading

Cooling J.E. (1991) *Software Design for Real-time Systems*. International Thomson Computer Press, London.

Part 4
Graphic Java

19 *Evolution of the Java User Interface*

19.1 Introduction

The Java environment is still evolving at a breakneck pace. The area of the language that has seen most of the changes is undoubtedly the Abstract Window Toolkit (AWT). The Java Foundation Classes (JFC), a much more sophisticated windowing system, have been released piecemeal, starting with Java 1.1, and have been released fully in Java 1.2. In the meantime, Netscape's Internet Foundation Classes (IFC) have appeared on the scene.

The air is thick with acronyms, and it's not surprising that many people are confused as to what is changing and what features they should be using to develop new applications. This part of the book aims to clear up that confusion. We are not providing a "how-to" guide, as there are a proliferation of these already.

This chapter explores the evolution of the Java user interface classes, explaining the shortcomings of the AWT and how the new systems attempt to overcome them.

The following two chapters examine the features provided by the IFC and the JFC in more detail. We then look at the new Java Media frameworks, and consider the issues in designing good user interfaces for Java.

19.2 The Abstract Window Toolkit

For applets to be able to run on any platform, the designers of Java needed to provide a platform-independent API for building graphical user interfaces (GUIs). This is an inherently difficult task – different operating systems provide significantly different facilities and styles. The designers wanted fast graphical components that were consistent with the operating system that was running the applet – this prevented the user from having to learn how to use a new style of interface. There were two main choices: give the components the ability to draw and manage themselves using the look and feel[1] of various operating systems, or to provide a uniform way of accessing the operating system's components.

---

1 Look and feel: the user interfaces of different operating systems are characterized by their look (the appearance of windows and buttons, etc.), and their feel (how the users are allowed to interact with the system).

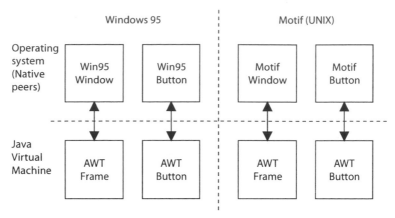

Figure 19.1 Java classes wrap native peers.

The Smalltalk language provides graphical components that have the ability to draw themselves in different styles. This is a very flexible system, but it does mean that the components have to be rewritten in order to simulate the appearance of components in a new operating system. In addition, at the time Java was first released, the performance of these components would have been pretty poor (without a Just-In-Time compiler).

Instead, the Abstract Window Toolkit (AWT) uses a native peer system (Figure 19.1). The AWT provides a set of graphical classes that act as wrappers to native components provided by the operating system. The native components manage the behaviour and repainting of the components, and the AWT classes provide a uniform, platform-independent interface to those components. All access to the native components is through the `Toolkit` class (and its associated peer classes, which comprises native methods that call the operating system). This localizes the platform-dependent code, making it easier to port the AWT to different platforms.

Because the components that appear on the screen are actually native, they are as fast as any other interface on the system, and they provide a familiar look and feel. Experienced programmers were quite shocked to be able write a user interface on one platform and to run it unchanged on many others!

However, the AWT honeymoon didn't last – as programmers tried to create more sophisticated interfaces, the shortcomings of the AWT become more apparent. Probably the most significant problem is that the AWT must pander to the lowest common denominator native peers. That is, if a feature of a component is not supported on one of the platforms, then it cannot be supported in the AWT. The effect of this is that the AWT interfaces have a relatively poor set of components compared with other toolkits. Programmers side-stepped this problem by writing new component classes in Java (indeed, many commercial Java systems include libraries of Java components). Unfortunately, the look and feel of these components is fixed and they look out of place under some operating systems.

Another significant problem is the limited scope for subclassing components. The Java classes simply pass messages to the native components, so that most of the code that controls the behaviour of a component is embedded in the operating system. When subclassing an AWT component, we can have very little effect on how the component works. For example, consider the `List` class, which allows the user to select an item from a list. If we wanted to present a list of icons instead of text strings, then we would have to write a new component from scratch, as the drawing code for `List` is embedded in its native peers.

The system used for event handling also had its problems. The components pass every message that they receive up through the container hierarchy, until one of the containers handles the event. This means that in order to handle the events, the programmer must subclass a component. If the lower level components are subclassed, this leads to a proliferation of classes and dispersed code that is hard to understand. If the higher-up containers are subclassed to handle the events, then there is a massive amount of message-passing for each event, which can be very slow.

There are other, not so important, problems. In particular, the underlying native components generally behave slightly differently between platforms, which can affect the platform independence of an interface. For example, changing directory using the `FileSelector` dialog on one platform might change the system's current directory on one platform, but not on other. Although these are largely problems with the implementation of the AWT Toolkit (and not the AWT itself), subtle platform dependencies have dogged the AWT since its introduction.

19.3 The Internet Foundation Classes

We have made some important criticisms of the AWT here, but it has made an important contribution to Java – it is possible to produce reasonable cross-platform GUI applications using the AWT. Nevertheless, there was a need for change, which resulted in the development of the Internet Foundation Classes (IFC) by Netscape. This is a class framework (see Chapter 9) available free from Netscape's Web site.

The most important contribution of the IFC was the lightweight component, in the form of the `View` class. Every IFC component is coded in pure Java (without a native peer), which means that it behaves exactly the same on every platform, and the components may be subclassed and their behaviour directly modified. Unfortunately, this forces the user to learn another look and feel (Figure 19.2).

The IFC also side-steps one of the most unpopular features of the AWT (particularly with beginners) – its layout managers. Because AWT components would appear with different sizes on different platforms, it made it difficult to specify their positions based on absolute coordinates. The layout managers provided a flexible solution to this problem by managing the layout of a container globally. In addition, they have the ability to react well to changes in the container's size. As usual, this flexibility comes at a price – many programmers found the layout managers counter-intuitive and unwieldy (particularly the `GridBagLayout`). We haven't cited the layout managers as a problem with the AWT though, as most experienced programmers acknowledge that they are a powerful solution to the problem.

With the IFC, the problem of components having different sizes on different platforms is much reduced, as the components are written in pure Java. Beginners are

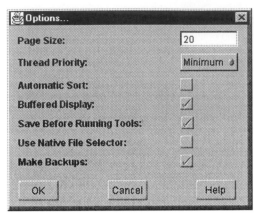

Figure 19.2 An interface using the Internet Foundation Classes.

much happier with the support the IFC provides for specifying the size and position of components directly, although it does also provide layout managers that are equivalent to the AWT ones. Netscape also provide a free GUI builder for the IFC, called the Constructor, which is regarded as one of the best available. The Constructor positions components using absolute coordinates. The IFC provides a precursor of the object serialization found in Java 1.1, which allows the Constructor tool to save complete dialogs in a file which can be restored by an application.

The method of reuse of the IFC components is different from that of the AWT. The AWT forces you to subclass a component in order to use it, whereas the IFC components provide a rich set of methods for customizing their behaviour and appearance. The event model is more efficient, and doesn't require subclassing. It comes in two forms –targets/commands and observers. Components such as buttons allow you to define a target class that should be sent a particular command when the button is pressed. Most components also support an observer that is informed when events occur. For example, the `Window` class allows you to set a `WindowObserver` that is notified when the window opens, closes, resizes etc.

The IFC is more than just a collection of component classes. It provides an application framework, with support for multiple internal windows (allowing complete applications to be embedded in a Web page), drag-and-drop, clipboard functions and more. It also simplifies a number of AWT features (for example, image loading is much easier).

It is worth remembering that the IFC is not a standard part of the Java class library, so it will need to be distributed with your code. This is not likely to be a problem for applications, but it could slow the downloading of applets that use it.

19.4 Other Contributions

Soon after the introduction of the IFC, Microsoft introduced the Application Foundation Classes (AFC), again available free from their Web site. This aimed to solve the problem of the limited features in the AWT by including Java classes that mapped to the very rich component set of MS Windows. Although the UI classes were written in pure Java, the look and feel were undoubtedly of MS Windows.

The AFC provided many of the same advantages as Netscape's IFC. It also provided access to MS Windows specific features, such as Dynamic Data Exchange (DDE) and ActiveX. If you need these platform-specific features, perhaps you should take a look (although maybe Java is not the best choice in this case).

However, many developers are wary of tying themselves to the AFC, as there is no "migration path" to the new Swing components in the Java Foundation Classes (JFC). In addition, Microsoft are replacing the AFC with the Windows Foundation Classes (WFC), a native code library which will only run under MS Windows.

19.5 The Java Foundation Classes

Meanwhile, Sun were taking a keen interest in the developments from other companies, and produced the Java Foundation Classes (JFC), with help from Netscape. These are based on the best ideas from the IFC, but go much further.

It is rather difficult to define the bounds of the JFC, as it has trickled out piecemeal since Java 1.1. The 1.1 release of Java introduced support for lightweight components (components without an underlying native peer), by modifying the `Component` and `Container` classes. Programmers could now define new components without the overhead of subclassing the `Canvas` class. In addition, components now used the delegation event model for event handling, which was a much more efficient and flexible system. Java 1.1 also introduced the JavaBeans mechanism, object persistence and basic clipboard support. All of these features were important for the development of the JFC.

The core part of the JFC is Swing, the name given to the new Java interface classes. These classes are included in Java 1.2. Swing provides a very rich and flexible lightweight component set, which is JavaBeans-compatible and written in pure Java. The components support double-buffering, which, combined with a good JIT, gives good performance. Most components are based on the Model–View–Controller (MVC) architecture which separates the data from the views of the data – this gives unparalleled flexibility. For example, it is quite trivial to subclass a `JList` (the Swing equivalent of a `List` component) to display pictures instead of text.

By defining components in Java, we are left with the problem of an unfamiliar look and feel. Luckily, one of the most exciting features of Swing components is their support for pluggable look and feels. Swing provides a set of factory classes that the components use to generate their appearance and behaviour. By providing a new set of factory classes, the interface can have a completely different look and feel. This makes it perfectly possible to use a Macintosh-style interface under Unix, for example – even to swap between styles in the program. In addition, it is easy to link most of the Swing components to database tables, allowing them to link to JDBC-compatible databases. At last, the features and flexibility we need!

Most of the useful features of the IFC appear in Swing, including support for drag-and-drop (except that this time it is integrated with the clipboard, allowing drag-and-drop operations from other native applications).

Swing doesn't stop at new graphical components – it also provides support for the application itself. The most significant of these features is the Undo mechanism. This framework makes it quite trivial to implement a sophisticated stackable undo system in your application.

The JFC also includes the Java 2D API, which provides a much richer graphics context, with support for scaling, line and fill styles etc. It is still backward-compatible with the AWT, and it is possible to build interfaces using components from both (although you should not mix components using the old event model with those using the Delegation Event Model). In addition, the JFC provides a "migration path" for IFC applications. This doesn't mean that IFC applications will work under the JFC – rather, that the JFC will support those features provided by the IFC and it will be possible to upgrade the applications without too much fuss. We examine the reality of this in Chapter 20.

19.6 Summary

The Abstract Window Toolkit (AWT) provided the first platform-independent user interface system for Java that was perfectly satisfactory for relatively simple interfaces. However, problems with subtle inconsistencies across platforms, inflexibility and inefficient event handling meant that its days were numbered.

The Internet Foundation Classes (IFC) made a number of important advances – in particular, lightweight, flexible components. In places, it is significantly easier to use than the AWT. Although its best features have been fed into the JFC, the JFC has not yet stabilized. In contrast, the IFC has been available long enough to be quite stable and robust.

The Java Foundation Classes (JFC) are definitely a giant leap for Java interfaces. The rich set of lightweight components with pluggable look and feel provides the best of all worlds.

19.7 Online References

Netscape's IFC is available from

```
http://developer.netscape.com/library/ifc/index.html
```

Microsoft's AFC can be found at

```
http://www.eu.microsoft.com/java/sdk/20/afc/default.htm
```

Java 1.2 is available through Sun's JavaSoft Web pages:

```
http://java.sun.com/
```

Also, check out the Swing home pages:

```
http://java.sun.com/products/jfc/swingdoc-current/
   index.html
```

The Java 2D pages:

```
http://java.sun.com/products/java-media/2D/index.html
```

20 *The Internet Foundation Classes*

20.1 Introduction

The Internet Foundation Classes (IFC), from Netscape, provide a sophisticated user interface framework that is available in a stable form today. It overcomes many of the problems with the Abstract Window Toolkit (AWT), and many of its features have formed the basis of the Java Foundation Classes (JFC), which form part of Java 1.2.

The Internet Foundation Classes are more than a set of GUI classes. The IFC provides an application framework. A framework is a set of cooperating classes that encapsulate a design. In terms of the IFC, this means that the IFC classes encapsulate the design of a generic application that may be extended to make application design and coding easier. At least, that's the theory! In practice, it depends on how well the requirements of your application map to the model used in the IFC. Nevertheless, even if you decide not to use all of the facilities of the IFC, it is still quite easy to take advantage of the superior GUI classes.

The previous chapter examined some of the problems with the AWT, and provided an overview of the IFC. In this chapter, we take a closer look at the features provided by the IFC, discuss porting IFC applications to the new JFC (in Java 1.2), and discuss which things you should consider before deciding to develop a new application with the IFC. We explore the important concepts behind the IFC rather than providing an application development guide.

20.2 Application Framework

All IFC applications must subclass the `Application` class. This class initializes the IFC, and also provides support for the clipboard and multiple documents[1]. `Application` provides an `init()` method, which should be overridden to initialize the

---

1 Multiple documents: the term "document" is used to describe the unit of data used by an application. Thus a document under a word processor might refer to a letter or to a chapter of a book, whereas a document under a graphics editor might refer to a picture. Many modern applications allow you to have more than one document open at one time, with each document usually stored in an internal window. Note that there is only one instance of the application open – this is different from having each document open in a separate instance of the application.

234   Key Java

application. IFC applications generally do not use the constructor, as the IFC itself
has not been initialized by this stage (the same situation holds true for AWT
applets).

The application is started by calling its `run()` method, and terminated when its
`stopRunning()` method is called. Listing 20.1 shows a simple "Hello World"
application under the IFC, as shown in Figure 20.1. We go on to look at windows and
views later.

Listing 20.1

```java
import netscape.application.*;

class HelloWindowOwner implements WindowOwner {

  public void windowDidHide( Window w ) {
    Application.application( ).stopRunning( );
  }

  public void windowDidBecomeMain( Window w ) { }
  public void windowDidResignMain( Window w ) { }
  public void windowDidShow( Window w ) { }
  public boolean windowWillHide( Window w ) { return
    true; }
  public boolean windowWillShow( Window w ) { return
    true; }
  public void windowWillSizeBy( Window w, Size s ) { }
}

public class HelloWorldApp extends Application {

  public void init( ) {

    Label label = new Label( "Hello World",
      new Font( "Helvetica", Font.ITALIC, 32 ) );
    label.moveTo( 8, 8 );

    ExternalWindow window = new ExternalWindow( );
    window.sizeTo( 192, 80 );
    window.addSubview( label );
    window.setOwner( new HelloWindowOwner( ) );
    window.show( );
  }

  public static void main( String argv[] ) {
    HelloWorldApp app = new HelloWorldApp( );
    app.run( );
```

```
        System.exit( 0 );
    }
}
```

Figure 20.1 "Hello World" using the IFC.

In the `init()` method of the application, we create a new window containing a label view (a view is the equivalent of an AWT component). We set the `WindowOwner` of the `Window`, so that when the window is closed the application is terminated.

20.2.1 Application Observers

The IFC handles events in no fewer than four different ways (depending on the type of event)!

1. By overriding methods. The `View` class provides methods that are called when the mouse is moved or a key is pressed, for example. You may override these methods when creating a new type of view.
2. By defining targets and commands. Most views allow you to set a target that will receive commands when something significant happens (for example, when a button is pressed).
3. Setting owners. Many classes allow you to set an owner class, which will be notified when the configuration of the view changes. For example, the `TextField` class allows you to set a `TextFieldOwner`, which is notified when the text has been modified, and when editing starts or stops.
4. Setting observers. Observers are similar to owners, except that you may add more than one observer.

The `Application` class allows you to add objects that implement the `ApplicationObserver` interface. These objects are notified when the application starts or stops, when the current document changes (see next section) and when the view containing the current input focus changes.

The ability to determine when the application stops can be very useful for different parts of the application to "tidy up". In particular, if your application starts up child processes, an `ApplicationObserver` is a good way to destroy them before the application dies.

20.2.2 Multiple Documents

The `Application` class provides support (albeit rather limited) for multiple documents. This would allow you to create a word processor, for example, that could switch between one of several text files that are in memory.

Each document should be contained in its own instance of `Window` – the `containsDocument()` method is used to identify windows that contain a document. Any of these windows can be set to be the current document window using the application's `makeCurrentDocumentWindow()` method, which results in the window being passed the input focus and the `ApplicationObserver` being notified. Any part of the application can identify the current document window by calling the application's `currentDocumentWindow()` method. When a document window is closed, the application automatically passes focus to another document window (if one exists).

The `Window` classes provide methods that may be overridden to react to the current document being changed (`didBecomeCurrentDocument()` and `didResignCurrentDocument()`).

Note that this structure implies that there is a one-to-one mapping between documents and windows, which is not always the case.

20.3 `View` Classes

The `View` class is the IFC equivalent to the `Component` class – it is the superclass of every IFC component. Any view can contain other views as children – there is no distinction between components and containers as there is in the AWT. Every view is lightweight, which means that it is written in pure Java without an underlying native peer. Because everything must be drawn by the Java code, there is a potential for flickery displays. However, the `View` class provides a `setBuffered()` method that forces the view (and all of its children) to use double-buffering[2] when drawing themselves. This is all automatic – the drawing methods in the view will not be aware that they are drawing on an off-screen image.

The IFC views provide a great deal more flexibility than their equivalent AWT components. Most views can be completely customized without having to be subclassed.

As a simple example, let us have a closer look at the `Button` view.

20.3.1 The `Button` View

Listing 20.2 shows how to create an external window containing a simple button.

Listing 20.2 ·

```
import netscape.application.*;

public class IFCButtonApp extends Application
implements Target {
```

---

2   Double-buffering: all drawing operations are performed on an image in memory. This image can then be copied to the screen in a single operation, without any flickering. Note that this is slightly slower than drawing directly on the screen.

```
    // Initialize the application.
    public void init( ) {

        // Create a new button.
        Button b = new Button( 32, 8, 64, 28 );
        b.setTitle( "Close" );
        b.setCommand( "close" );
        b.setTarget( this );

        // Add the button to an external window.
        ExternalWindow window = new ExternalWindow( );
        window.sizeTo( 128, 72 );
        window.addSubview( b );
        window.show( );
    }

    // Perform a command, for the Target interface.
    public void performCommand( String command,
            Object data ) {

        // Stop the application in response to the close
        // command.
        if( command.equals( "close" ) )
            stopRunning( );
    }

    // Create and start the application.
    public static void main( String argv[] ) {
        IFCButtonApp app = new IFCButtonApp( );
        app.run( );
        System.exit( 0 );
    }
}
```

The setTitle() method sets the text that will be displayed on the button. The setTarget() method specified a target object that implements the Target interface. This object's performCommand() method will be called when the button is pressed with the command parameter set to the value specified with the setCommand() method.

The most significant difference from the AWT in Java 1.0 is that you no longer need to subclass a component in order to respond to events. This architecture also allows you to easily separate the interface controller code. The Delegation Event Model used in Java 1.1 is based on a combination of this approach and the Observer Model (as in the ApplicationObserver).

The example in Listing 20.2 is a simple one – the button view allows you to do much more. Table 20.1 shows most of the properties that are available. You should

Table 20.1

Property	Description
`title`	The text displayed on the button.
`altTitle`	The text displayed with the button is depressed.
`titleColor`	The colour of the text.
`disabledTitleColor`	The colour of the text when the button is disabled.
`font`	The font used to draw the text.
`image`	The image to display on the button.
`altImage`	The image to display on the button when it is depressed.
`imagePosition`	The position of the image on the button.
`bordered`	True if the button has a border.
`loweredBorder`	The border to use when the button is depressed.
`loweredColor`	The background colour when the button is depressed.
`raisedBorder`	The border to use when the button is not depressed.
`raisedColor`	The background colour when the button is not depressed.

note that the IFC does not conform to the JavaBeans naming convention (which did not exist when the IFC was created). The value of a property is read with a `propertyName()` method and set with a `setPropertyName()` method.

The `image` property allows you to specify an image that should appear on the button. The `Image` class is an abstract one – you need to use one of its descendants, such as `Bitmap` or `ImageSequence`. The latter class provides an animated image – yes, having animated images on a button is almost trivial!

You may also notice that you can set various borders for the button – having the border as a separate class makes it easier to modify the appearance of a view and easier to create new views with consistent borders.

20.3.2 Creating New Views

One of the major criticisms levelled at the AWT was its inflexibility in modifying and creating new components. In the previous chapter, we described, as an example, how it is impossible to modify the AWT `List` component to display images with the text. Let us consider how we would do this using the IFC. The IFC `ListView` displays a set of `ListItems`. Each `ListItem` has its own set of properties, which include `image` and `selectedImage`. We do not actually need to modify the `ListView` in order to display images with the text. This is fairly typical of the IFC components – they are flexible enough so that you rarely need to subclass them. However, to show how modifications of this nature can be done, let us create a list view that shows the selected item by using a bold font rather than a coloured background (Figure 20.2).

The code is shown in Listing 20.3. The `ListView` class is left unchanged, as we only need to subclass the `ListItem`. The `ListView` is created and 20 `BoldListItems`

Figure 20.2 Using bold to indicate list selection.

are added. The call to `sizeToMinSize()` ensures that the `ListView` is tall enough to display all of the items. The `ListView` itself does not have scrollbars, so a `ScrollGroup` is created to provide these.

In the `BoldListItem` constructor, we create a new bold font to use when the item is selected, based on the `ListItem`'s default font (obtained through the `font()` method). The `drawBackground()` method is overridden to do nothing, so that the item's background is not highlighted when it is selected. The `drawInRect()` method is the one that actually draws the item. This is overridden to call its inherited `drawInRect()` method if it is not selected. If it is selected, it changes the font before calling this method.

Listing 20.3

```
import netscape.application.*;

// The test application.
public class BoldListApp extends Application {

  // Initialize the application.
  public void init( ) {

    // Create a list containing 20 BoldListItems.
    ListView list = new ListView( 0, 0, 96, 0 );
    for( int i = 0; i < 20; i++ ) {
      BoldListItem item = new BoldListItem( );
      item.setTitle( "Item " + i );
      item.setImage( Bitmap.bitmapNamed("new.gif" ) );
      item.setSelectedImage(
        Bitmap.bitmapNamed("new.gif" ) );
      list.addItem( item );
    }
    list.sizeToMinSize( );

    // Put the list inside a scrollgroup to provide
    // a vertical scrollbar.
    ScrollGroup scroll = new ScrollGroup( 8, 8, 96,
      128 );
    scroll.setContentView( list );
```

```
    scroll.setVertScrollBarDisplay(
      ScrollGroup.AS_NEEDED_DISPLAY );

    // Add the scroll group to an external window.
    ExternalWindow window = new ExternalWindow( );
    window.sizeTo( 128, 180 );
    window.addSubview( scroll );
    window.show( );
  }

  // Create and start the application.
  public static void main( String argv[] ) {
    ImageListApp app = new ImageListApp( );
    app.run( );
    System.exit( 0 );
  }
}

// A list item that shows the selected item's text in
// bold, rather than with a coloured background.
class BoldListItem extends ListItem {

  // The font to use for the selected item.
  protected Font selectedFont;

  // During construction, create the font to use for
  // the selected item.
  public BoldListItem( ) {
    super( );
    selectedFont = Font.fontNamed( font( ).name( ),
      Font.BOLD, font( ).size( ) );
  }

  // Override the method that draws the background so
  // that it does nothing - we'll use a bold font
  // to indicate selection instead of colouring the
  // background.
  protected void drawBackground( Graphics g,
    Rect rect ) {
  }

  // Draw the list item.
  public void drawInRect( Graphics g, Rect rect ) {

    // If the item is selected, swap to the
    // bold font, and call the superclasses' method...
    if( isSelected( ) ) {
```

```
      Font normalFont = font( );
      setFont( selectedFont );
      super.drawInRect( g, rect );
      setFont( normalFont );

   // ...otherwise, draw the item as normal...
   } else {
      super.drawInRect( g, rect );
   }
 }
}
```

If you need to create an entirely new component, you will probably subclass the View class. Its drawView() method can be overridden to perform the drawing. The netscape.application.Graphics instance that is passed to the method adds a few useful features to its AWT counterpart. The pushState() and popState() methods allow you to save and restore the state of the graphics context which can be very useful if you want a method to leave the graphics context in the same state it found it. The setGraphicsDebugOptions() method provided by View can replace the Graphics object with an instance of its subclass DebugGraphics. This can cause each drawing operation to flash on and off, which can be invaluable when debugging drawing code.

Events are handled by overriding the various mouse and key methods provided by View. Note that unlike the original AWT in Java 1.0, unhandled events are not propagated up through the container hierarchy. This means that the event system has less overhead than the old AWT event system, although it is considerably less flexible than the newer Delegation Event Model.

The setBuffered() method in View provides buffered drawing without any further effort by the programmer. The View also provides support for drag-and-drop operations between views (although not between different applications). To help you create new views with a consistent look, the IFC also provides Border classes.

20.3.3 Choosers

Most GUI toolkits provide a set of common dialogs, and the IFC is no exception. Unfortunately, most of them are not terribly good. The FileChooser dialog is simply a wrapper for the AWT FileSelector, which means that the FileFilters still don't work, and its appearance is inconsistent with the IFC look and feel.

The standard mechanism for choosing colours is rather unintuitive. The application would have a dialog containing a ColorWell, which is a small rectangle filled with the current colour. To change this colour, the user clicks on the ColorWell, resulting in the appearance of the ColorChooser (see Figure 20.3). It provides a standard Red–Green–Blue slider mechanism for setting the colour. However, moving the sliders and closing the chooser does not update the

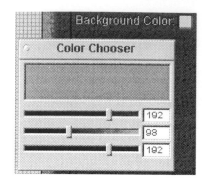

Figure 20.3 The IFC
ColorChooser.

ColorWell. To update the ColorWell, you have to move the sliders and then drag the coloured area in the ColorChooser back onto the ColorWell.

The FontChooser is pretty standard, although it does not show any example text in the font being chosen.

The Alert class provides an alert (or message) dialog that displays a simple message and icon, and allows the user to click on one of a number of buttons. This can be used to create an "Are you sure you want to quit?"-style dialog, for example.

20.4 Layout Managers

In the examples we have provided in this chapter, you will notice that we have set the size and position of the components explicitly in their constructors. This is the easiest way of constructing interfaces, but not the best. As with the AWT, the IFC provides layout managers to control the layout of interfaces. The GridLayout is equivalent to the AWT's class of the same name, and the IFC also provides the PackLayout, which is based on the TCL/TK[3] packer. This uses a PackConstraints instance (similar to the way in which a GridBagConstraints instance is used by the AWT's GridBagLayout). The PackLayout covers most of the functionality of the AWT's FlowLayout, BorderLayout and GridBagLayout, although it is rather less flexible than the latter. It is also rather easier to use than GridBagLayout.

The reason that the AWT introduced layout managers was that the dimensions of the components could change significantly between platforms, so that using absolute coordinates could result in misshapen components. In addition, layout managers allow an interface to respond to changes in the dimensions of its container (these issues are discussed further in Chapter 23). Do these reasons still hold true with the IFC?

IFC components are written in pure Java, and so have the same appearance whichever platform they are running under. This might imply that absolute coordinates are safe. In practice, there are small variations in the font size between platforms, and many of the IFC components display text. If a platform does not

3   A Unix-based scripting language and GUI toolkit.

support a particular font, it will have to substitute another one, which may have very different dimensions. These variations in font size mean that many IFC components require slightly different dimensions on different platforms.

The other argument for layout managers is that they allow an interface to respond to changes in the size of its container. The IFC makes provision for this without layout managers. The `View` class provides two methods: `setHorizResize-Instruction(int)` and `setVertResizeInstruction(int)`. These tell the view how to change its size or position when the size of its container changes. For example,

```
view.setHorizResizeInstruction(View.WIDTH_CAN_CHANGE)
```

will tell the view that as the size of its container changes, it can resize its width proportionately. The instruction

```
view.setVertResizeInstruction(View.
  TOP_MARGIN_CAN_CHANGE)
```

tells the view that it must maintain its height, but as its container resizes the view must maintain the distance between its bottom margin and the container, and move the top of the view to compensate. Although this approach feels a little unwieldy, in practice it works quite well, particularly when used with subpanels. Nevertheless, it can be difficult to understand how the interface responds to size changes by looking at the code.

In general, you can get away with using absolute coordinates with the IFC, which is one of the reasons for its popularity. Although this is not frowned on as much as with the AWT, we still feel that it is better practice to use layout managers: they can respond to changes in component size due to font variations; and using them to respond to changing container sizes results in clearer code than by using resize instructions. Using absolute coordinates also has implications for migrating to the JFC as we discuss later.

20.5 Windows

There are two types of window in the IFC – internal or external. External windows are the same as `Frames` in the AWT (or `Dialogs` if the window is set to be non-resizable). Internal windows appear as sub-windows inside an external one. The `ColorChooser` in Figure 20.3 is shown in an internal window. These windows do not attempt to mimic the look and feel of normal windows on the system, and cannot be minimized (or iconized).

Internal windows can be useful for implementing a Multiple Document Interface (MDI) style application. This is an application that allows several documents to be open at once, where each document is contained in an internal window.

They can also be useful for applets, so that they can use lots of windows that stay embedded in the Web page. The IFC Constructor tool is a good example of an applet (and an application) that uses internal windows.

20.6 Persistence

The IFC includes the precursor to Java's Object Serialization mechanism for making objects persistent. Because this is not integrated into the Java language, it is a little more unwieldy than Object Serialization. The `Archiver` and `Unarchiver` classes allow you to store and retrieve objects, which may be written in a binary or an ASCII form (the later is useful for debugging). Graphs of objects are correctly preserved, so that `Vectors` and `Hashtables` may be safely archived.

Any class that implements the `Codable` interface can be archived. This interface requires a class to provide a `ClassInfo` instance that describes the properties of the class. It must also define encode and decode methods to save and restore the class's properties.

20.7 IFC Constructor

Netscape also provide a tool called the IFC Constructor. This is an interface builder for the IFC that is deservedly popular. It is written using the IFC, and is a good example of what the toolkit can achieve.

The tool has three modes: build mode, wire mode and test mode. In build mode, you construct the interface by dragging components from a palette onto a view (see Figure 20.4). Each component can be moved and resized, and when it is selected its properties can be edited in a property sheet.

One of the components available is the `TargetProxy`. This component allows you to define a set of commands that can be executed. When the interface is used in an application, a class implementing the `Target` interface will replace the

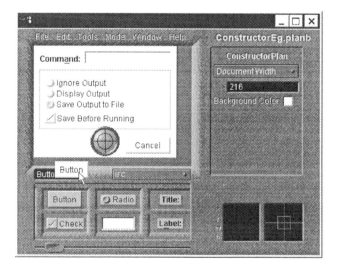

Figure 20.4 Building an interface using Constructor.

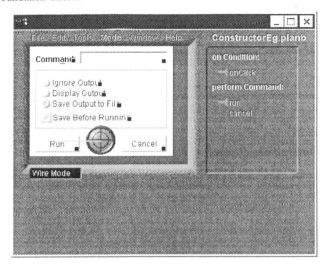

Figure 20.5 Wiring components in Constructor.

TargetProxy (the TargetProxy will not be visible when the interface is used in the application).

The value of this becomes apparent during the wiring mode. This allows you to connect an event generated by a component to a command provided by another component. For example, consider the interface in Figure 20.5. The TargetProxy has been defined with two commands: run and cancel. The "Run" button's onClick event is connected to the run command in the TargetProxy. When this interface is used in an application, the TargetProxy will be replaced with a class that can respond to the run and cancel commands.

Constructor does not create Java code for the interfaces. Instead, it creates a Plan object and archives this to a file. An application can unarchive the Plan and use its methods to turn the interface into a View (which may be created in a Window). This has a number of implications. Firstly, it is significantly slower than creating the interface in code – this makes it necessary to cache the interfaces rather than re-creating them each time that they are needed. Secondly, it makes it more difficult to get at the components in the interface – you have to go through methods in the Plan class. Finally, it is bad news if you are thinking of migrating the application to the JFC. The JFC does not support Plan files, and you will have no Java code to convert.

Users of the BeanBox will have noticed a striking similarity to Constructor – it seems likely that Constructor was the inspiration behind the BeanBox. Don't be put off by this – unlike the BeanBox, the constructor is a polished, robust application! It is possible to produce some good quality interfaces in a short time using Constructor. In fact, the Constructor is cited by many people as the main reason that they use the IFC.

We have already covered some problems related to Constructor's use of Plan files. There is another, quite important, limitation. Constructor positions and sizes components using absolute coordinates rather than using layout managers, which is generally bad practice, as we have already argued.

You need to ask the following questions before deciding to use the Constructor:

- Is the application is likely to be run on many different platforms?
- Does the interface need to respond flexibly to changes in the window size?
- Is the application likely to be upgraded to the JFC?

20.8 IFC and AWT

To a certain degree, the IFC and the AWT can be intermixed. This might be desirable if you have a particular AWT component that you need to use in an IFC application, or vice versa. The `AWTComponentView` is a wrapper class that allows you to embed AWT components in IFC interfaces. There is no equivalent that allows you to embed IFC components in AWT interfaces, but you can create new IFC external windows from within an AWT application. The IFC defines its own `Font`, `Window`, `Graphics`, `Menu` etc. classes. The `AWTCompatibility` class provides a set of static methods for converting between the IFC and the AWT versions.

The IFC also redefines several of the Java utility classes, such as the `Hashtable` and the `Vector`. These have been optimized for performance (see Chapter 15), mainly by removing the `synchronized` modifier. They also have a few useful methods added (for example, the `Vector` has a method `addElements(Vector)` that is useful for concatenating vectors). There is also a `Sort` class that works with vectors. These classes implement the `Codable` interface, allowing them to work with the IFC's persistence mechanism. Many of the IFC view classes use these classes, which generally means that you must use the IFC utility classes in your code.

The IFC's redefined classes use the same names as their AWT counterparts, which can cause clashes if you are writing an application that must use both. In these cases, you will be forced to use the full class names (e.g. `java.util.Vector`).

20.9 Migration to the Java Foundation Classes

The Java Foundation Classes (JFC) are based on the best parts of the IFC, and promise a "migration path" for IFC applications. This does not imply backward compatibility, or even semi-automated conversion to the JFC (as there was for converting Java 1.0 interfaces to 1.1). There are substantial differences between the two toolkits. However, the JFC provides most of the facilities found in the IFC, and that should make migration possible. How easy this is will depend on the complexity of the application.

Most of the components in the IFC have equivalents in the JFC. Note that the method names will be different, as the JFC uses JavaBeans-compatible names. Nevertheless, swapping IFC components for their JFC counterparts should not be too difficult.

If you are not using layout managers, you will have to convert your interface code to use JFC layouts. Although you can use absolute positioning with a null layout manager, this is really not on – a different look and feel could significantly change the dimensions of a component.

Applications that subclass IFC views to create new components are going to cause further difficulties. Although the JFC has equivalents to most IFC components, their internal structure will be quite different – the JFC components are based around a Model–View–Controller (MVC) architecture (see next chapter). In many cases, you will have to rewrite the new components more or less from scratch.

Finally, if you have been taking advantage of the IFC's extended utility classes (to sort a `Vector` for example), you may have to restructure this code. Although Java 1.2 provides most of these facilities, it is not directly compatible.

20.10 Summary

In this chapter, we have covered the most important features of the IFC. It is a replacement for the AWT that provides very real benefits – principally that of very flexible lightweight components. The API is fairly large and the online documentation is somewhat sketchy – this can make the initial learning curve a relatively steep one. Because of its size, there are one or two naming inconsistencies, although this charge could probably be levelled at most packages. You should also remember that the IFC has its own look and feel, which may be off-putting to some users.

The IFC has been superseded by the JFC. However, the IFC is in a complete and stable form today – past experience suggests that it will be some time before this can be said for the JFC. If you are writing an application that needs to be robust, using the IFC now and converting it the JFC at a later date may be the best approach. If you choose to do this, you should bear the following points in mind:

- There are significant differences between the IFC and the JFC – migrations to the JFC will not be a mindless process.
- Avoid using absolute coordinates to position components.
- Try to avoid creating subclasses of IFC components – if you do, be prepared to have to rewrite them for the JFC.
- Do not use the IFC Constructor, as you will be unable to use the Plan files it generates.
- Try to avoid using the extra features that the IFC utility classes provide (for example, the `Vector` sort routines), or at least check to see how they are implemented in Java 1.2.

20.11 Online References

Netscape's IFC and Constructor are available from:

```
http://developer.netscape.com/library/ifc/index.html
```

21 *Swinging with the Java Foundation Classes*

21.1 Introduction

The Java Foundation Classes (JFC) are an advanced framework of classes aimed at simplifying the development and deployment of commercial-quality applications. Parts of the JFC are already in Java 1.1 – they include the new Delegation Event Model and lightweight components. However, the core part of the JFC is Swing[1], the new GUI classes released as part of Java 1.2.

Developed by Sun and Netscape, Swing builds on the Internet Foundation Classes (IFC) to provide an unrivalled set of very flexible GUI components. It goes much further than the IFC, with a richer set of components, pluggable look and feel, and sophisticated component architecture. It also includes useful support services, such as the multi-level undo/redo framework. The new classes are 100% pure Java, and conform to the JavaBeans standard (see Chapter 4).

From the earliest stages, Swing was released to Java developers for feedback. Essentially, the aim was to give developers what they wanted. Indeed, the development team did respond to developer feedback, and Swing evolved significantly in that time.

In Chapter 19, we looked at the limitations of the Abstract Window Toolkit (AWT), and how these limitations led to the evolution of the Java UI classes through the IFC to the JFC and Swing.

In this chapter, we take at look at the important concepts behind Swing, and how they affect our application development. We start by looking at the underlying architecture of Swing (the Model–View–Controller (MVC) architecture), and how this is used to implement the pluggable look and feel. We then introduce the various GUI classes that make up Swing, before considering how easy it is to modify them, and to create new components from scratch. Finally, we look at some of the features that affect the development of applications with Swing: the new `Action` class, the `Undo` framework and Java Accessibility.

Please note that the examples in the text are compiled under the pre-release version (0.7) of Swing. In this release, Swing package names start with "`com.sun.java.swing`", whereas in Java 1.2 they will start with "`java.swing`". Please refer to our Web site for the most up-to-date versions of the example code.

---

1 Swing: apparently the choice of name was inspired by swing music playing during an early demo of the new components!

21.2 Model–View–Controller Architecture

Swing components use a modified version of the Model–View–Controller (MVC) architecture. The MVC architecture defines how the classes that make up a user interface should be structured, and was discussed in detail in Chapter 9. Its use is central in achieving the pluggable look and feel, although you do not need to understand it in order to use the new Swing components.

MVC separates a user interface (UI) into three classes (Figure 21.1). The model class encapsulates the data underlying the interface, and has no knowledge of how the data will be displayed, or how the UI will modify it. Not all components will have models –the `JScrollPane` is an example of one that does not.

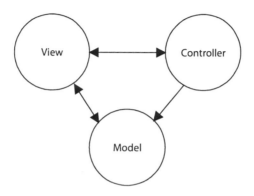

Figure 21.1 Model–View–Controller architecture.

The view class displays the data contained by a model. In the context of Swing, the separate view class allows us to change the look of a component without changing its underlying data model.

The controller class manages the interaction with the user. It modifies the data model in order to update its contents, and refers to the view in order provide feedback to the user. By changing the controller class, we can give a component a different feel, without disrupting its views or data model. For example, we could create an MS Windows-style menu controller that displays menus in response to a mouse click, or a Macintosh-style controller that displays menus only when the mouse button is held down.

The MVC is a very powerful architecture. However, in practice things are a little more complicated. In all but the simplest interfaces, there can be a great deal of interaction between the controller and the view classes. This means that views and controllers can become complicated, and closely bound to each other. The Swing team took the approach of combining the view and controller into a single class, referred to as the delegate class (Figure 21.2). As well as solving the problem, this also made changing the look and feel more convenient, as the new delegate encapsulates the look and feel in a single class.

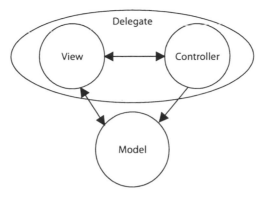

Figure 21.2 View and Controller are combined to form Delegate.

21.3 Pluggable Look and Feel

So how is the MVC and pluggable look and feel implemented in Swing? All Swing components are descendants of JComponent, which in turn is a descendant of Component. These classes are not models or delegates – they provide a sort of component context, in effect the glue between the model and the delegate.

Figure 21.3 shows the construction of a Swing component. The component is created by passing in a data model object to its constructor. Most components also provide constructors that accept data in a more convenient form – for example, a JList can be passed a Vector, the contents of which will be used to create a ListModel. Each model is described by an interface, and Swing also provides a default class that implements it.

The component then requests a delegate from the UIManager class, using its getUI(JComponent) method. The UIManager returns a delegate that is suitable for the current look and feel. Its setLookAndFeel() method can be used to change the current look and feel. For example, the following code snippet will change the look and feel to Motif:

```
try {
  UIManager.setLookAndFeel(
    "com.sun.java.swing.motif.MotifLookAndFeel" );
} catch( ClassNotFoundException e ) {
  e.printStackTrace( );
}
```

The various implementations of the LookAndFeel interface encapsulate the delegates that define a particular look and feel. Because the UI manager uses reflection[2] to find the look and feel class, the ClassNotFoundException must be handled. Note that the current look and feel is a bound property (see Chapter 5) of

---

2 Reflection: the ability to analyze classes at runtime (Chapter 5).

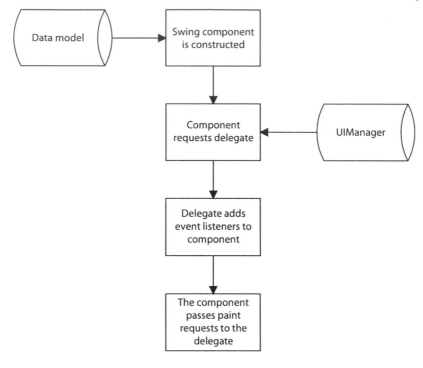

Figure 21.3 The construction of a Swing component.

the UIManager, which allows components to change their delegates automatically when the look and feel changes. Components are not forced to use the delegate provided by the UI manager, as JComponent provides a setUI() method that can be used directly.

When the delegate has been added to the component, it adds any listeners it may require to respond to events. This allows it to implement the Controller part of the MVC architecture. The delegate defines a paint() method, which is called by the component whenever the display needs updating. This provides the View part of the MVC. The data models support listeners that are notified when the model changes. The delegates add themselves as listeners so that they can update the view as necessary.

Swing currently comes with three look and feel styles. These are BasicLook-AndFeel which is for Windows 95 (Figure 21.4), MotifLookAndFeel for Unix (Figure 21.5) and JLFLookAndFeel (Java look and feel; Figure 21.6). The latter is not based on any operating system, and has been designed for people that want a uniform look across platforms. Unfortunately, there is some doubt over whether the Windows 95 look and feel can be legally used on other platforms, so this will only work under Windows 95 and Windows NT[3].

---

3   In the beta releases of Swing, you can trick a Unix Java VM into thinking it's on
    Windows by setting the "os.name" system property (-Dos.name="Windows NT"
    as a parameter to java)!

Figure 21.4 Basic (MS Windows) look and feel (from SwingSet demo).

Figure 21.5 Motif (Unix) look and feel (from SwingSet demo).

Figure 21.6 Java look and feel (from SwingSet demo).

21.4 Swing Components

Programmers need not be intimidated by the architecture of Swing components. Each component is a JavaBean, which means they plug into an interface as easily as an AWT component. However, understanding the underlying architecture is useful in understanding the design of the components, and later when we look at modifying them. We can now take a look at some of the GUI components included in Swing, starting with JComponent.

21.4.1 JComponent

All of the new Swing components are descendants of the JComponent class. If you look at the API documentation, you will notice that this is a large class with many methods. This is because much of the new functionality is common to all Swing components. For example, all components support tooltips (Figure 21.7). These are small messages that appear when the mouse is left hovering over a component, and act as a reminder of that component's purpose. They are particularly useful for reminding the user about graphical components that do not contain any text (toolbar buttons, for example). Adding tooltips is simply a matter of calling the setToolTipText() method with a string.

Figure 21.7 Tooltips.

JComponent is a subclass of Container rather than Component, which gives it the ability to add child components. This makes it easy to build up compound components using the existing Swing classes. JComponent's supports for keystroke handling is also useful in compound components. This is the ability to link keystrokes to actions in the component. The registerKeyboardAction() is used to link an instance of KeyStroke to an action in the component. This method accepts a condition as one of its parameters, which determines when the KeyStroke will be active. If the condition is WHEN_IN_FOCUSED_WINDOW, the KeyStroke will be active when the component is in a window that has the input focus. This would make it easy to link the Alt-C key to a "Cancel" button, for example. The condition WHEN_ANCESTOR_OF_FOCUSED_COMPONENT[4] makes the KeyStroke active if it contains the component with the input focus (at some level in the hierarchy). This would allow a component to define global KeyStrokes that are active when any of its subcomponents are active (for example, a tree component might trap the '+' key to expand all of its branches).

Any border may be set for a JComponent. These would normally be one of the standard borders provided by the BorderFactory class, but you can implement the Border interface to define completely new ones. JComponent gives you greater

---

4 We're all for meaningful identifier names, but this is getting silly!

control of the size of your components too, adding the getMaximumSize() methods to complement getPreferredSize() and getMinimumSize().

As with the IFC, most Swing components do not provide scrollbars. Instead, they automatically grow in size as needed, which lets them integrate with the JScrollPane class. The JScrollPane has a contentPane property, which can be set to any JComponent to provide it with scrollbars. In addition, JComponent can be configure to scroll automatically when the mouse is dragged outside the bounds of the visible area (see the setAutoscrolls() method).

JComponent supports graphics debugging through the DebugGraphics class, which is similar to the IFC's class of the same name. This slows down the drawing process, flashing each drawing operation on and off as an aid for debugging. Another powerful feature inherited from the IFC is automatic double-buffering, controlled through the setDoubleBuffered() method. When a component is double-buffered, it is drawn on an off-screen buffer, which is then copied to the screen. Although this is slightly slower than drawing directly on the screen, it prevents any flickering during the drawing operations. The double-buffering mechanism is intelligent, in that it ignores the setting if the component is contained within a component that is already using double-buffering.

JComponent also supports Java Accessibility – this is covered in a later section.

21.4.2 Buttons

Buttons in Swing are pretty much what you might expect. A button can contain text and an icon (and you can specify where the icon is positioned). You can also specify the icon to use when the button is disabled and when the mouse is over the button (the rollover icon).

The button classes JButton, JToggleButton, JCheckbox and JRadioButton all extend the AbstractButton class, which provides much of their functionality. Of course, they are all descendants of JComponent and inherit tooltips etc. They all use the ButtonModel interface (usually in the form of the DefaultButtonModel class) to store their state.

21.4.3 Menus and Toolbars

The JMenuBar class (Figure 21.8) provides Swing's menu system. JMenuBar is a component in its own right, and can be directly added to any container. In addition, the setJMenuBar() method in JFrame (the Swing equivalent to Frame) can be used to add it directly to a window.

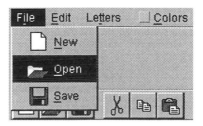

Figure 21.8 JMenu and JToolBar (from SwingSet demo).

Functionally, JMenuBar is similar to its AWT predecessor. A notable addition is that the JMenuItem class extends AbstractButton, which allows it to include icons with the text. If you intend to use icons on a menu, you will need to create a blank icon to add to the text-only items – otherwise the text will not line up. Usually you use menu icons to link the items with their toolbar shortcuts.

Macintosh users will notice that the new menus appear at the top of JFrames, rather than moving to the top of the desktop display. In this respect, Swing has less consistency with the Macintosh look and feel than the AWT. However, it is difficult to see how this could be avoided within the pluggable look and feel architecture.

Swing has good support for toolbars, although in the beta releases they were plagued with bugs. Any component can be added to an instance of JToolBar, but you would normally use JButtons containing only an icon. You can set the toolbar to use a vertical or horizontal orientation, but you need to access methods in the look and feel-specific UI class as follows:

```
BasicToolBarUI ui = (BasicToolBarUI)toolBar.getUI();
ui.setOrientation(BasicToolBarUI.VERTICAL);
```

Toolbars are normally added to one of the borders in a container using a BorderLayout. From here, they can be dragged outside the frame to appear in their own separate frame, or dragged to any of the other border positions.

In Section 21.9 we discuss how a single action can be added to a menu and toolbar in order to simplify application control.

21.4.4 Lists

The JList component does not provide as many features as the IFC's ListView class, but with a little more work the same effects can be achieved. For example, you cannot directly add icons to the elements in the list.

As with many of the Swing components, JList extends the encapsulation provided by the MVC architecture. The data model is provided by the ListModel interface, which allows programmers to define their own models containing exactly what they need (or use the DefaultListModel).

JList allows you to set a ListCellRenderer, which encapsulates the part of the View that draws each of the items in the list. It is not difficult to define ListCellRenderers that draw an icon with each item in a list – in fact, we look at this in Section 21.7.

You also have some control over the Controller part of JList. The type of selection that is allowed is encapsulated in an instance of ListSelectionModel. This gives you explicit control over selection, allowing you to prevent the user selecting more items than they can afford, for example.

Combo-boxes (edit boxes with drop-down lists) are also supported, in the form of the JComboBox class. Its data model extends ListModel, which means that you can define models that can be used by both classes. It also uses ListCellRenderers to draw its items. It is possible to set the style of combo-boxes to control how the user is able to edit the text directly.

21.4.5 Tables

The JTable class has seen the most changes during the development of Swing. It started evolving into a spreadsheet-like component before the development team decided it was getting too complex and needed cutting back. In its final form, it displays a tabulated set of data, with resizable column headings at the top (Figure 21.9).

Figure 21.9 JTable (from SwingSet demo).

The table data is encapsulated by an implementation of the TableModel interface, and a simple default is provided by the DefaultTableModel class (in the com.sun.java.swing.table package). This is essentially a 2D vector. See Section 21.4.8 for an example of a TableModel.

Each column has a class associated with it, representing the class of the data it is displaying. As with the JList component, JTable allows you to set a cell renderer (TableCellRender), this time for each column class. In addition, you may set a TableCellEditor that provides a component for editing any of the cells in the table. This is a very powerful feature, as it allows you to embed combo-boxes (for example) within the table.

21.4.6 Trees

The addition of tree components to Java user interfaces will be welcomed by many programmers used to MS Windows GUI development. The JTree component represents a hierarchical display of data, as in Figure 21.10.

The data model used by JTree (TreeModel) is reasonably complex, because it allows the tree structure to be determined dynamically. For example, if you had a tree representing a disk drive, you wouldn't want to build a tree for the whole drive. A

Figure 21.10 JTree (from SwingSet demo).

sensible approach would be to add nodes for the top-level directories, and fill in their children when they are opened.

You can create very simple (one-level) models by passing a Vector to the JTree constructor. Otherwise, the DefaultTreeModel provides a simple implementation of TreeModel for static data. It allows you to add nested instances of DefaultMutableTreeNode. All of the model classes are located in the com.sun.java.swing.tree package. The following code snippet constructs an instance of JTree from a model:

```
DefaultMutableTreeNode root =
  new DefaultMutableTreeNode( "Parent" );
root.add( new DefaultMutableTreeNode( "Child 1" ) );
root.add( new DefaultMutableTreeNode( "Child 2" ) );
DefaultTreeModel model = new DefaultTreeModel( root );
JTree tree = new JTree( model );
```

JTree also allows you to set selection models, cell renderers and cell editors.

21.4.7 Text Components

The IFC provided a TextView component that was capable of displaying styled text. Swing builds on this to give very sophisticated control of text. It is centred on the Document and StyledDocument interfaces, with their standard implementations PlainDocument and DefaultStyledDocument. These are found in com.sun.java.swing.text. Note that, in this case, document refers to the traditional concept of a text-based document, rather than being a generic term for application data.

The Document interface supports markup of styles and notification and tracking of changes, to allow for undo/redo functionality (see Section 21.10). Plain-Document is for very simple text, and does not implement the style and change functionality. DefaultStyledDocument does implement these features.

The simplest of the text components is JTextField. This is the equivalent of the AWT TextField component, designed to edit a single line of text. Like most of the text components, its constructor accepts a string and can create a default model automatically.

JTextArea is the Swing equivalent of the AWT's TextArea component. JTextPane extends this to support text styles. By using the DefaultStyle-Document class as its model, you are not far from having a fully functional word processor (see the StylePad Swing demo). By assigning attributes to sections of text, you can change its font, justification, colour and line spacing. JTextPane can save and load HTML and Rich Text Format (RTF) documents.

21.4.8 Database Connectivity

Sun are claiming that the Swing components are data-aware. This implies that the components provide support for displaying data held in remote databases. In fact, this is not quite true. Swing components have no direct provision for connecting to databases via JDBC or to `ResultSets` (see Chapter 7), but to do so is trivial. As most Swing components have data models, connecting them to a database is simply a matter of defining a model class that wraps around a JDBC query or `ResultSet`.

Listing 21.1 defines a simple data-aware implementation of `TableModel`. It subclasses `AbstractTableModel` so that we only have to define the relevant methods. Its constructor accepts a `ResultSet` as a parameter, as returned by a query executed by a `Statement`. All of the elements in the `ResultSet` are copied to a `Vector`. This is necessary, as the `ResultSet` cannot tell us how many rows it contains, and cannot provide random access to the rows. The `getRowCount()` and the `getValueAt()` methods refer to the `Vector` of results. The remaining `TableModel` methods simply wrap around calls to the `ResultSet`'s meta-data (which gives information about the number of fields and their names etc.).

Listing 21.1

```java
import java.io.*;
import java.sql.*;
import java.util.*;

import com.sun.java.swing.table.*;

// Map a ResultSet to a TableModel.
public class SQLTableModel extends AbstractTableModel
{

  // The ResultSet.
  protected ResultSet results;

  // A vector of vectors, containing each cell as a
  // String.
  protected Vector table;

  // Create a TableModel over a ResultSet.
  public SQLTableModel( ResultSet results )
  throws SQLException {

    // Copy the ResultSet values to a Vector.
    this.results = results;
    table = new Vector( );
    while( results.next( ) ) {
      Vector row = new Vector( );
      for( int i = 1; i <= getColumnCount( ); i++ ) {
        row.addElement( results.getString( i ) );
      }
      table.addElement( row );
    }
  }
}
```

```
  // Get the number of columns.
  public int getColumnCount( ) {
    try {
      return results.getMetaData( ).getColumnCount( );
    } catch( SQLException e ) {
      return 0;
    }
  }

  // Get the name of a column from the ResultSet meta
  // data.
  public String getColumnName( int col ) {
    try {
      return results.getMetaData( ).getColumnName( col
        + 1 );
    } catch( SQLException e ) {
      return "?";
    }
  }
  // Get the number of rows.
  public int getRowCount( ) {
    return table.size( );
  }

  // Get an element in the results.
  public Object getValueAt( int row, int col ) {
    return ((Vector)table.elementAt( row )).elementAt(
      col );
  }
}
```

The SQLTableModel does not allow editing. If you want to feed edits back into the database, you will have to do more work. This would involve maintaining a connection to the database and executing an SQL update command (through a Statement) in the model's setValueAt() method.

21.5 Windows

Swing provides two window classes, JFrame and JDialog, that correspond to the original Frame and Dialog classes in the AWT. Swing components can be added to a Frame or Dialog, but there must be a heavyweight component (e.g. Panel) higher in the container hierarchy. This is because Swing components are lightweight (i.e. do not have an underlying OS component) and need a heavyweight parent to draw on (sorry: although a Frame is heavyweight, it doesn't count as a component!).

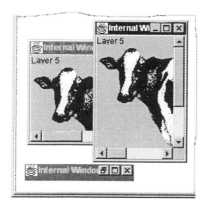

Figure 21.11 Internal windows (from SwingSet demo).

The Swing equivalents already have a heavyweight container, called a ContentPane, so you do not need to worry about this. All layout operations (such as setting the layout manager and adding components) must be performed on this object rather than the frame itself. The ContentPane is a property of the JFrame or JDialog. For example, in a JFrame constructor:

```
getContentPane( ).setLayout( new BorderLayout( ) );
getContentPane( ).add( new JButton( "OK" ) );
```

JFrame also differs from the AWT's Frame class in that Swing menus can be added to it directly. In addition, new instances have default WindowListeners added, so that the window will close automatically when the user clicks the close button. JFrame and JDialog are still based on the operating system's windows, and so will not be altered by the current look and feel (although the menu will be).

Swing provides internal windows in the form of the JInternalFrame class (see Figure 21.11). Unlike the IFC, it does not provide internal dialogs. However, Swing internal windows can be minimized, and they do match the current look and feel. Internal windows are useful for implementing Multiple Document Interface (MDI) style applications, where many documents can be open in an application at once.

Internal windows can be given a layer number. This affects how they occlude other internal windows – the highest number windows are always on top. This can be useful for creating palettes that always remain at the front.

21.6 Common Dialogs

Fortunately, Swing improves considerably on the "chooser" dialogs available in the IFC. The current implementation of the ColorChooser uses a Hue–Saturation–Brightness (HSB) colour space (Figure 21.12), and can be used to set a colour directly (in contrast to the rather obscure IFC colour chooser). The ColorChooser can be displayed as a modal dialog or embedded within a larger interface.

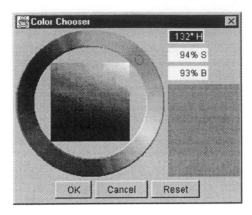

Figure 21.12 ColorChooser.

At the time of going to press, there is no news of a `FontChooser`, although it seems likely that it will be included in the final release of Swing. There is a `FileChooser`, however, which accepts file filters. These allow you to display only the relevant files in a directory (e.g. "`*.doc`"). Such a feature existed in the AWT's `FileDialog` but was never implemented – a pet hate for many programmers. `FileChooser` mimics the look and feel of native file dialogs closely (Figure 21.13). It cannot be embedded in a larger interface, but Swing does provide the `JDirectoryPane` for this purpose. This is the directory listing part of the `FileChooser`.

For general-purpose messages, the `JOptionPane` is a very useful class. It displays a message, together with an appropriate icon (such as a question mark for a confirmation dialog or an exclamation mark for a warning message) and a set of buttons. It can be used to get a simple text input as well. There are predefined constants for common icons and buttons, which make it easy to use. However, it also

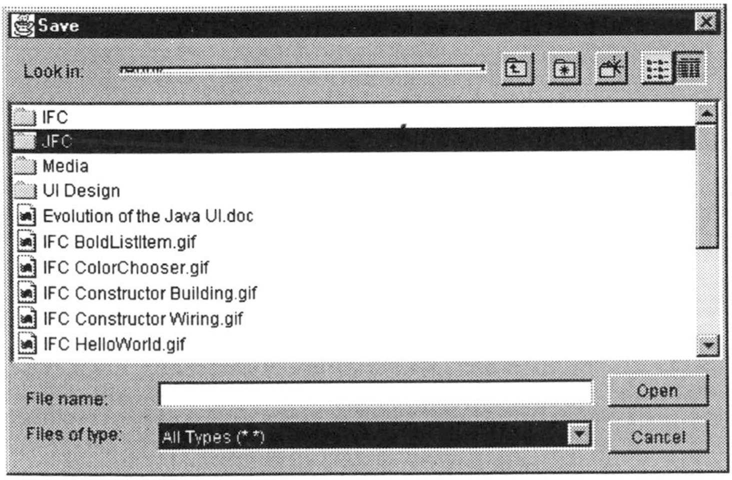

Figure 21.13 `FileChooser`.

allows you to specify any icon or button, making it very flexible too. Indeed, you can add any Swing component to the dialog to customize its behaviour.

21.7 Extending Swing Components

In the previous chapter we looked at how we could modify the IFC ListView component to display the items in a different way. This is something that cannot be done under the AWT. The JFC's equivalent of ListView is the JList class.

As mentioned previously, JList does not allow you to show images alongside the item's text. However, it does allow you to supply a ListCellRenderer that will be used to draw each item. Figure 21.14 is a screenshot of our implementation of a Swing list component that shows images with the items, and highlights its selected items using a bold font. The code for this is shown in Listing 21.2.

Listing 21.2

```
import java.awt.*;
import com.sun.java.swing.*;

// The test frame.
public class ImageListFrame extends JFrame {

  // Construct the frame.
  public ImageListFrame( ) {

    // Create a list containing 20 strings.
    Object data[] = {"Item 1", "Item 2", "Item 3",
        "Item 4", "Item 5", "Item 6",
        "Item 7", "Item 8", "Item 9",
        "Item 10", "Item 11", "Item 12",
        "Item 13", "Item 14", "Item 15",
        "Item 16", "Item 17", "Item 18",
        "Item 19", "Item 20"};
    JList list = new JList( data );

    // Tell the list to use a different renderer.
```

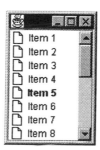

Figure 21.14 BoldImageList
uses a bold font to indicate selection.

```
      ImageIcon itemImage = new ImageIcon( "new.gif" );
      list.setCellRenderer(
          new ImageCellRenderer( itemImage ) );

      // Put the list inside a ScrollPane to provide
      // a scrollbar.
      JScrollPane scroll = new JScrollPane( list );
      scroll.setDoubleBuffered( true );
      getContentPane( ).add( "Center", scroll );
   }

   // Create and show the frame.
   public static void main( String argv[] ) {
      ImageListFrame frame = new ImageListFrame( );
      frame.pack( );
      frame.setVisible( true );
   }
}

// A ListItemRenderer that displays each item with an
// image, and highlights selection using a bold font.
class ImageCellRenderer extends JLabel
implements ListCellRenderer {

   // The font to use for unselected and selected
   // items.
   protected Font normalFont;
   protected Font selectedFont;

   // Construct the renderer, specifying the image to
   // use.
   public ImageCellRenderer( ImageIcon image ) {
      super( image, LEFT );
      normalFont = new Font( "Sans", Font.PLAIN, 12 );
      selectedFont = new Font( "Sans", Font.BOLD, 12 );
   }

   // Get a component that can draw a specified item.
   // We configure this object (a subclass of JLabel),
   // and return this.
   public Component getListCellRendererComponent(
      JList list, Object value, int index,
      boolean isSelected, boolean cellHasFocus) {

      // Set the text of the label.
      setText( value.toString( ) );
```

```
      // Choose the appropriate font.
      if( isSelected )
        setFont( selectedFont );
      else
        setFont( normalFont );

      return this;
   }
 }
```

The most important class is `ImageCellRenderer`, a subclass of JLabel. It implements `ListCellRenderer`, which requires that the `getListCellRendererComponent()` method returns a Component suitable for drawing an item. Our strategy is to always return *this*, the `ImageCellRenderer` itself, having initialized it correctly. In this way, we take advantage of the JLabel's ability to draw icons and text. In the constructor, we create fonts to use for selected and unselected items. Note that because we are subclassing JLabel, our renderer will be consistent with the current look and feel.

In the `getListCellRendererComponent()` method, we set the text of *this* (remember: it is a subclass of JLabel) and also its font, depending on whether or not the item is selected.

The `ImageListFrame` class simply creates a new JList with some sample data, sets its cell renderer to an instance of `ImageCellRenderer` and adds it to a double-buffered scroll pane to provide smooth scrolling.

Although this is marginally more involved than the IFC example, it is considerably more flexible. In particular, `ListCellRenderers` can be reused for other compatible components (such as JComboBox), and the separation of renderer and data values means that you can use the same renderer for a variety of underlying data types.

21.8 Creating New Swing Components

We have talked about how Swing provides a pluggable look and feel for components, and how Swing components can be customized relatively easily. But how can you define completely new components without violating the current look and feel? Clearly, extending the look and feel classes to provide new delegate types is not an option – the user might have any look and feel installed.

Visually, most new components can be divided into two kinds – compound components and those that paint themselves from scratch. Of course, a new component might use existing components and an area that draws itself from scratch – in this case, you are advised to break it down into two new components, one of which will be a compound one.

Compound components are not a problem – one of the container classes (JComponent or JPanel for example) can be subclassed. As each of the subcomponents is subject to the current look and feel, they will automatically help the component fit in.

If you are defining a component that paints itself from scratch, it is likely that it will have no parallel on the various look and feel platforms, and can look more or less the same for all of them. However, you can help it fit in by using the standard border types.

As well as providing component delegates, the look and feel classes also provide borders (implementing the `Border` interface). This helps you to delineate areas of the component in a visually compatible way. The `BorderFactory` class provides a number of static methods for accessing these borders (such as `createBevelBorder()`).

With the MVC architecture separating the interface into various classes, it can be confusing as to which ones should be subclassed. With compound components, it is simple: only the container class need be extended. There is no overall delegate, as the delegates are provided by the subcomponents.

If you are painting the component, you have a couple of choices. As mentioned earlier, `JComponent` is more-or-less glue between the component's model and its delegate. When you subclass it, you can choose to make it the view itself and do away with any "glue" by overriding its `paintComponent()` method. A better approach would be to create a new delegate class by extending `com.sun.java.swing.plaf.ComponentUI`. At least this will allow you to plug in new delegates of your own.

Most of the methods in `ComponentUI` are similar to those in `Component`, except that they have an extra parameter (the underlying component). For example:

```
public void paint(Graphics g, JComponent c)
```

In addition, there are three important UI-specific methods: `createUI()`, `installUI()` and `uninstallUI()`. The former is a static method that simply creates an instance of the UI class. It is provided so that the class can keep and reuse a single instance in a static variable. The install and uninstall method are called when the UI object is added to or removed from a component. It allows the UI to register any listeners that it requires on the component. It can also set the border of the component, rather than managing a border internally.

21.9 Actions

The `Action` interface extends `ActionListener`, and has an abstract implementation in the form of the `AbstractAction` class. It allows you to define classes for every action that your interface can perform. As well as defining the behaviour of the action (by implementing the `actionPerformed()` method inherited from `ActionListener`), you can also associate icons and text strings with the action. You would normally define `Actions` as inner classes within a component – this provides them with direct access to the class that they are acting on. An instance of `Action` can be added directly to a menu bar or toolbar, which will create a new item with the appropriate text and icon, and link it to the action. Actions can also be linked to keystrokes.

Using actions in this way leads to a number of advantages. Firstly, it breaks up the interface code nicely into manageable chunks. You no longer need long switch statements inside a single implementation of ActionListener. In addition, the Action interface allows you to enable or disable the action itself, which will be propagated to any components that register themselves as Property-ChangeListeners. Finally, the actions can be exported using Java Accessibility (see Section 21.11).

Consider the code in Listing 21.3. In the constructor, a Hashtable is created that maps action names to instances of the action. This is a convenient way of storing the actions, as we only want a single instance of each action. Next, a menu and a toolbar are created, and the actions are added to them.

Inside the ActionDemo class we define the actions. The ExitAction simply closes the frame. The DisableExit and EnableExit actions disable and enable the instance of ExitAction, respectively. Note how a single call to the action's setEnabled() method propagates to the menu and the toolbar.

Listing 21.3

```java
import java.util.*;
import java.awt.event.*;

import com.sun.java.swing.*;

// Demonstrate the use of the Action interface.
// Show a menu and toolbar linked to actions, where
// the ExitAction can be enabled and disabled.
public class ActionDemo extends JFrame {

    // Store a single instance of each action here.
    protected Hashtable actions;

    // Construct the frame.
    public ActionDemo( ) {

        // Create instances of all actions.
        actions = new Hashtable( );
        actions.put( "EnableAction", new EnableAction( ) );
        actions.put( "DisableAction", new DisableAction( ) );
        actions.put( "ExitAction", new ExitAction( ) );

        // Create the menubar.
        JMenuBar menuBar = new JMenuBar( );
        JMenu fileMenu = new JMenu( "File" );
        fileMenu.add( (Action)actions.get( "EnableAction"
            ) );
```

```java
    fileMenu.add( (Action)actions.get(
      "DisableAction" ) );
    fileMenu.add( (Action)actions.get(
      "ExitAction" ) );
    menuBar.add( fileMenu );

    // Create the toolbar.
    JToolBar toolBar = new JToolBar( );
    toolBar.add( (Action)actions.get(
      "EnableAction" ) );
    toolBar.add( (Action)actions.get(
      "DisableAction" ) );
    toolBar.add( (Action)actions.get(
      "ExitAction" ) );

    // Build the UI.
    setJMenuBar( menuBar );
    getContentPane( ).add( "North", toolBar );
    pack( );
  }

  // Enable the Exit action.
  protected class EnableAction extends AbstractAction {

    public EnableAction( ) {
      super( "Enable Exit Action",
        new ImageIcon( "check.gif" ) );
    }

    public void actionPerformed( ActionEvent e ) {
      ((Action)actions.get( "ExitAction"
        )).setEnabled( true );
    }
  }

  // Disable the Exit action.
  protected class DisableAction extends AbstractAction {

    public DisableAction( ) {
      super( "Disable Exit Action", new ImageIcon(
        "cross.gif" ) );
    }

    public void actionPerformed( ActionEvent e ) {
      ((Action)actions.get( "ExitAction"
        )).setEnabled( false );
    }
```

```
  }

  // Exit the application.
  protected class ExitAction extends AbstractAction {

    public ExitAction( ) {
      super( "Exit", new ImageIcon( "exclaim.gif" ) );
    }

    public void actionPerformed( ActionEvent e ) {
      System.exit( 0 );
    }
  }

  // Show the frame.
  public static void main( String argv[] ) {
    ActionDemo demo = new ActionDemo( );
    demo.setVisible( true );
  }
}
```

Unfortunately, there is no provision in the Action class for toggled actions (i.e. an Action that has a selected state). This would have been useful for keeping the state of menu items and toolbar buttons in sync – instead, you have to look after this yourself.

21.10 Undo Framework

One of the very useful features to be found in Swing is its Undo Framework (in the com.sun.swing.undo package). This supports a multi-level undo and redo facility that is surprisingly easy to use. The UndoManager class accepts instances of UndoableEdit through its addUndoableEdit() method. Each UndoableEdit encapsulates an edit that can be undone, and you must create new versions of these edits for your application. This is usually done by subclassing the AbstractUndoableEdit class and overriding its undo() and redo() methods.

Essentially, that's it! Having defined UndoableEdits for each of the editing operations that your application can perform, and having added them to an instance of UndoManager when they are performed, you can leave the rest to the UndoManager. Its undo() and redo() methods call the undo() and redo() methods of the UndoableEdit at the top of the undo and redo stack respectively.

Listing 21.4 shows a simple example. A list is shown, with buttons that add and remove items to and from it (they are linked to the AddAction and RemoveAction inner classes). Undo and Redo buttons are provided to undo these actions (linked to UndoAction and RedoAction). The AddItemEdit and

RemoveItemEdit classes encapsulate the editing operations. Their behaviour is very simple – they simply reverse the add or remove operation in their undo() methods, or reinvoke the operation in the redo() method.

In the frame's constructor, an UndoManager is created. The undo and redo actions call the UndoManager's undo() and redo() methods respectively. The buttons that add or remove items create a new instance of AddItemEdit or RemoveItemEdit and add it to the UndoManager.

Listing 21.4

```
import java.awt.*;
import java.awt.event.*;

import com.sun.java.swing.*;
import com.sun.java.swing.undo.*;

// Demonstrate the Undo Framework.
// Add or remove items to the list, then
// undo these operations.
public class UndoDemo extends JFrame {

  // The list and its model.
  protected JList list;
  protected DefaultListModel listModel;

  // The undo manager.
  protected UndoManager undoManager;

  // Create the frame.
  public UndoDemo( ) {

    // Use a flow layout, and create UndoManager.
    getContentPane( ).setLayout( new FlowLayout( ) );
    undoManager = new UndoManager( );

    // Create a list containing 2 strings.
    listModel = new DefaultListModel( );
    listModel.addElement( "Item 1" );
    listModel.addElement( "Item 2" );
    list = new JList( listModel );

    // Put the list inside a ScrollPane to provide
    // a scrollbar.
    JScrollPane scroll = new JScrollPane( list );
    scroll.setDoubleBuffered( true );
    getContentPane( ).add( "Center", scroll );
```

```java
    // Create Add, Delete, Undo and Redo buttons.
    JButton b = new JButton( "Add" );
    b.addActionListener( new AddAction( ) );
    getContentPane( ).add( b );
    b = new JButton( "Remove" );
    b.addActionListener( new RemoveAction( ) );
    getContentPane( ).add( b );
    b = new JButton( "Undo" );
    b.addActionListener( new UndoAction( ) );
    getContentPane( ).add( b );
    b = new JButton( "Redo" );
    b.addActionListener( new RedoAction( ) );
    getContentPane( ).add( b );

    pack( );
  }

  // Add an item to the list.
  class AddAction extends AbstractAction {
    public void actionPerformed( ActionEvent e ) {

      // Add an item to the list.
      String text = "New item";
      int index = listModel.getSize( );
      listModel.add( index, text );

      // Notify the undo manager.
      UndoableEdit edit = new AddItemEdit( text, index );
      undoManager.addEdit( edit );
    }
  }

  // Remove the selected item.
  class RemoveAction extends AbstractAction {
    public void actionPerformed( ActionEvent e ) {

      // Return if an item is not selected.
      int index = list.getSelectedIndex( );
      if( index < 0 )
        return;

      // Notify the undo manager.
      String text = (String)listModel.elementAt( index );
      UndoableEdit edit = new RemoveItemEdit(
        text, index );
      undoManager.addEdit( edit );
```

```
      // Delete an item from the list.
      listModel.removeElementAt( index );
    }
  }

  // Undo the last operation.
  class UndoAction extends AbstractAction {
    public void actionPerformed( ActionEvent e ) {
      if( undoManager.canUndo( ) )
      undoManager.undo( );
    }
  }

  // Redo the last operation.
  class RedoAction extends AbstractAction {
    public void actionPerformed( ActionEvent e ) {
      if( undoManager.canRedo( ) )
        undoManager.redo( );
    }
  }

  // An UndoableEdit that represents an add operation.
  class AddItemEdit extends AbstractUndoableEdit {

    // The item text and its index in the list.
    protected String text;
    protected int index;

    // Create the edit.
    public AddItemEdit( String text, int index ) {
      this.text = text;
      this.index = index;
    }

    // Undo the add operation.
    public void undo( ) {
      super.undo( );
      listModel.removeElementAt( index );
    }

    // Redo the add operation.
    public void redo( ) {
      super.redo( );
      listModel.add( index, text );
    }
  }
```

```
// An UndoableEdit that represents a remove
// operation.
class RemoveItemEdit extends AbstractUndoableEdit {

   // The item text and its index in the list.
   protected String text;
   protected int index;

   // Create the edit.
   public RemoveItemEdit( String text, int index ) {
      this.text = text;
      this.index = index;
   }

   // Undo the add operation.
   public void undo( ) {
      super.undo( );
      listModel.add( index, text );
   }

   // Redo the add operation.
   public void redo( ) {
      super.redo( );
      listModel.removeElementAt( index );
   }
}

// Show the demo.
public static void main( String argv[] ) {
   UndoDemo demo = new UndoDemo( );
   demo.setVisible( true );
}
}
```

Note that it is important that the overridden undo() and redo() methods in subclasses of AbstractUndoableEdit call the superclasses' methods. If you forget this, it can result in some obscure and seemingly unrelated behaviour in the UndoManager.

If you need to group several UndoableEdits together, the CompoundEdit class can be used. Sometimes, it will be useful to include UndoableEdits that do not modify any data. An example of this might be an edit that represents a shift of the input focus from one component to another. If you edit data in one component, then shift the input focus to another before invoking undo, it is desirable that the focus shifts back to the original component. You can do this by defining an UndoableEdit for the shift in input focus, whose isSignificant() method returns false. When the UndoManager's undo()

method is called, it will undo all insignificant `UndoableEdits` on the stack until it gets to a significant one.

21.11 Java Accessibility

Java Accessibility is a new framework from Sun that provides access to the inner workings of applications running on a Virtual Machine (VM). The primary application for this technology is to interface software that helps users with disabilities, although it will also be of interest to tool developers. It is quite separate from Swing, but all of the Swing components are compatible with this technology and it affects their design. It will be part of Java 1.2.

The sort of technologies that will take advantage of Java Accessibility include screen magnifiers, text readers (text to speech) and speech recognition for input and control. Many operating systems already support some of these technologies, and Sun are working on providing bridges that will let them be used with Java (MS Windows only at the moment).

Java Accessibility is divided into two main parts: the Accessibility API, and the Accessibility Utility classes. The API is contained in the `java.accessibility` package. Any compatible class implements the `Accessible` interface. Its only method, `getAccessibleContext()`, returns an instance of `AccessibleContext`. This interface provides access to the core accessibility features that every class should support, including its name, description, role, state, and its parents and children.

In addition, there are a number of other interfaces that the `Accessible-Context` object may implement as well. The `AccessibleAction` interface provides access to any actions that the class may provide (see Section 21.9). `AccessibleComponent` provides access to the graphical aspects of a component class. If a component provides the ability to select part of its contents, it should implement the `AccessibleSelection`. The `AccessibleText` interface provides access to any text that a component is displaying. Finally, `AccessibleValue` provides access to a varying numerical value. Because Sun want Java Accessibility to work with existing applications, they are working on providing Accessible translators for the AWT.

The Accessibility Utility classes expose the internal Java events so that tools can monitor the mouse moving, input focus changing etc. The API also exposes the `AccessibleContext` of components in a user interface. This would allow a speech control system to access actions within an application, for example. As well as being useful for the technologies outlined above, tool vendors will find these facilities useful for debugging applications.

Sun also include the pluggable look and feel under the Accessibility umbrella, as, potentially, look and feels could be developed that incorporated audio and tactile (e.g. braille) feedback.

21.12 Summary

The Java Foundation Classes aim to simplify the development and deployment of commercial quality applications. Swing is a major contribution towards this aim. Being 100% pure Java, the classes fit perfectly into the Java object model. In general, the design of the classes is excellent: they are easy to use, and yet still very flexible. This is probably due in part to the extensive feedback from the developer community.

Although it is not perfect, Swing is a great improvement on the IFC, and is in a different league from the original AWT. By using Swing with the Java Media frameworks (next chapter), developers will be able to create applications with interfaces as sophisticated (at least!) as those that are natively compiled.

21.13 Online References

Java 1.2 (including SwingSet demo) is available through Sun's JavaSoft Web pages:

```
http://java.sun.com/
```

Also, check out the Swing home pages:

```
http://java.sun.com/products/jfc/swingdoc-current/
   index.html
```

Accessibility pages:

```
http://www.sun.com/access/index.html
```

JavaSoft article on Swing, parts 1 and 2:

```
http://developer.javasoft.com/developer/
   onlineTraining/swing/
http://developer.javasoft.com/developer/
   onlineTraining/swing2/
```

22 *Graphical Java Media*

22.1 Introduction

The Swing user interface classes are not the only ones making an impact on the way we use graphics in Java. Java Media is a collection of class frameworks that enriches the way in which Java applications and applets can handle various types of media. In this chapter we look at the new facilities provided by Java 2D, Java 3D, and the Java Media Framework (JMF), although Java Media also includes telephony and speech APIs.

We start by considering Java 2D, which is part of the Java Foundation Classes (JFC) included in Java 1.2. It provides an enriched graphics context, capable of view transformations, bezier curves, etc.

Then we take a look at Java 3D, a 3D modelling API that makes it (relatively) easy to create advanced 3D worlds in Java. Finally, we explore the Java Media Framework, an API that supports playback of a variety of video and audio data formats.

Note that at the time this chapter was written, none of the APIs had seen final release –for this reason, there may be some small changes needed to the example code given here. Java 2D was tested with JDK 1.2 beta 2, Java 3D did not yet have an implementation, and the JMF was version 1.0 beta. For updated source code, please see our Web site.

22.2 Java 2D

The AWT's `Graphics` class represents a graphics context, and has a relatively poor set of graphics primitives. It was only designed to provide those features found on most platforms. For example, MS Windows programmers were able to able to set pen and fill styles, and set transformations to map from user-space to the display. In constrast, Java programmers were stuck with nothing more sophisticated than single-pixel lines and solid fills.

The Java 2D API set out to rectify this. Developed by Sun and Adobe, it is based around a new graphics context class, `Graphics2D`, which provides a number of sophisticated features. The API is not contained in a single package – some of its classes are in the original `java.awt` package, and the rest are in sub-packages:

- `java.awt` contains the new `Graphics2D` class; the `BasicStroke` class for creating pen styles; the `TexturePaint` and `GradientPaint` classes for creating fill styles; and updated `Color` and `Font` classes.

- `java.awt.color` provides classes for more sophisticated colour control.
- `java.awt.font` includes support for glyphs (rendered text strings); text with multiple fonts; and a greater range of font styles (such as superscript).
- `java.awt.geom` contains the classes concerned with geometric transformations.
- `java.awt.image` includes support for a range of image-processing tasks.

Note that with the beta-2 release of Java 1.2, Java 2D could not be used with the Swing components. This was because Swing components received a `SwingGraphics` object in their `paint()` methods which is a subclass of the original `Graphics` class.

22.2.1 Colour

A colour space describes a range of possible colours. The `Color` class uses a Red–Green–Blue (RGB) colour space as standard, whereby any colour can be described by its red, green and blue components. Although this is a convenient way of describing colour, there are other colour spaces designed to help you find colours with similar attributes, such as hue or saturation. A colour space such as Hue–Saturation–Brightness (HSB) might be more appropriate in this case. In addition, a number of devices use different colour spaces. Most colour printers, for example, use the Cyan–Magenta–Yellow–Black (CMYK) colour space.

All of the colour spaces mentioned above are device-dependent. Different devices have different colour capabilities, in particular the number of colours they can reproduce. The `java.awt.color` package provides a number of standard colour spaces and methods to convert colours between them. This is done through a colour profile that maps a colour space to or from the device-independent Commission Internationale de l'Eclairage X-Y-Z (CIEXYZ) colour space. If you want to convert colours between two device-dependent colour spaces, you must do so using the CIEXYZ colour space as an intermediate. The `java.awt.image.ColorConvertOp` class provides methods to convert the colours of whole images.

Java 2D also lets you define the *alpha* component of colours, which represents the transparency of the colour. If this sounds like a lot of hassle for just selecting colour, then don't worry. Although these features provide you with much more control over colours for different devices, you can still carry on using the `Color` class as before.

22.2.2 Pen and Fill Styles

The `Graphics2D` class provides properties that allow you to set the pen and fill styles to be used for subsequent drawing operations. The `setStroke()` method is used to set the pen style, and the `setPaint()` method is used to set the fill style.

The `Stroke` interface specifies the features provided by a pen, and the `BasicStroke` class is the only implementation that is provided. This class allows you to set the width of the pen, how the ends of wide lines are drawn, how wide lines are joined, and the dashed style of the line. Unfortunately, there is no provision for lines ending in arrowheads, although it would be possible to define a new class that implements the Stroke interface to provide this.

GradientPaint and TexturePaint are both implementations of the Paint class. The GradientPaint class allows you to specify a fill that graduates between two specified colours. The TexturePaint class uses an image as the fill. The image should be small, as it is copied by the TexturePaint instance. The setting of the Paint property in the Graphics2D class also affects the pen, as lines drawn with a wide pen style are filled using the current fill.

22.2.3 Transformations

The Graphics2D class allows you to set a transformation pipeline that is applied to all drawing operations in the graphics context, through the setTransform() method. This allows you to scale, translate and rotate anything that you can draw, including text, images and gradient fills.

A transformation is represented by the AffineTransformation class in the java.awt.geom package. An affine transformation is one that preserves the "straightness" and "parallelness" of lines. The class provides simple methods to scale, translate and rotate, as well as methods to set a transformation matrix. This range of methods makes it easy for someone without extensive graphics knowledge to use the class, without restricting those people who want more control, to define other transformations such as shears and flips. The concatenate() method makes it easy to concatenate transformations.

As well as being able to transform the whole graphics context, transforms can be applied to some drawing objects individually. For example, the BezierPath class can be transformed (this class represents a bezier curve).

22.2.4 Images

Java 2D provides the ability to apply filters to images, to transform them, and to adjust their colour look-up tables. These features are based around the new subclass of Image, called BufferedImage. This also provides methods to apply transformations, create sub-images and create a graphics context to draw directly onto the image.

22.2.5 Composition

The Graphics2D class includes a Composite property. A Composite object defines how new drawing operations are to be blended with the pixels already on the display. AlphaComposite is an implementation of the Composite interface, which blends colours based on their alpha (transparency) value. You can also increase the overall transparency of new drawing operations by changing the composite object's alpha value.

Images can maintain an alpha value for each pixel, which can lead to some very interesting effects!

22.2.6 Text

Java 2D completely updates font control, making a clear distinction between characters, glyphs and fonts. A character is a symbol that represents a letter or number in a writing system. When a character is displayed on the screen, it is represented by a shape. This shape is called a glyph. There is not always a one-to-one correspondence between characters and glyphs: the letter *á* might be represented by a glyph for the *a* and another for the acute accent. A font is simply a collection of glyphs.

Because the graphics system thinks of glyphs as being just like any other shape, they are affected by all of the properties of the graphics context. This means it is relatively easy to draw rotated text with a textured fill, for example.

The `java.awt.font` package includes a class called `GlyphSet`. This represents a set of glyphs that would usually represent a word or sentence, and is principally of use with the `TextLayout` class. This allows you define text using multiple fonts and justification styles, which can be drawn directly on the Java 2D graphics context. However, it goes further than this, allowing you to define selected areas of text, draw text cursors and perform character hit testing[1]. This makes it possible to create new text-editing components, or even to perform in-place editing within a canvas.

22.2.7 Anti-Aliasing and Quality

The `Graphics2D` object allows you to define "hints" that determine how the drawing operations are rendered. These hints currently cover anti-aliasing, and rendering quality. Anti-aliasing attempts to soften jagged edges by blending the colours of the surrounding pixels. This may be turned on or off (for faster performance), or left to the discretion of the underlying operating system.

Similarly, rendering may be performed with a bias for quality or speed, or left to the discretion of the operating system.

22.2.8 Example

Although the `Graphics` object in the AWT was very limited, it was also very easy to use. Java 2D is very flexible, and consequently a little more complicated. In practice, however, it is as complicated as you make it. Most of the features are relatively simple to use and it only gets complicated once you start delving deep into the system. The code in Listing 22.1 provides a simple example of many of the features discussed above. It displays an image surrounded by a border, with a title below. This image can be rotated and scaled using the appropriate buttons, or panned by dragging with the mouse. You can also set the quality through a checkbox –when selected, high-quality anti-aliased rendering is performed (see Figure 22.1).

The `Java2D` class extends `Frame` to provide the user interface. It is straightforward, simply mapping the buttons to methods in the `Canvas2D` class. In the `Canvas2D` constructor, the scaling, rotation and translation transforms are

---

1 Character hit testing: determining which character is below a point.

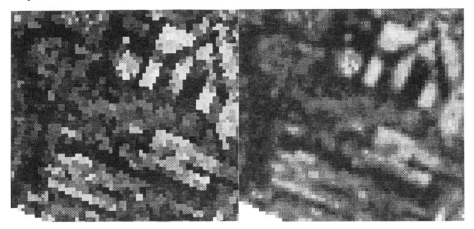

Figure 22.1 A transformed image, normal and high quality.

initialized, the image is loaded (ImageIcon is a convenient way of loading images), and a GeneralPath object is created that represents the border. A GeneralPath is similar to a polygon, except that it can include curves as well as lines.

Listing 22.1

```java
import java.awt.*;
import java.awt.event.*;
import java.awt.geom.*;

import java.awt.swing.*;

// A canvas that demonstrates some of the Java 2D
capabilities.
// A framed image is shown, which may be zoomed,
panned and rotated.
class Canvas2D extends Canvas
implements MouseListener, MouseMotionListener {

   // The indent between the image and its frame.
   protected static int indent = 8;

   // A geometric path that represents a frame around
the image.
   protected GeneralPath path;

   // The size of the canvas.
   protected Dimension size;

   // The image to be drawn.
```

```java
  protected ImageIcon image;

  // A scaling transformation.
  protected AffineTransform scale;

  // A rotation transformation.
  protected AffineTransform rotation;

  // A translation transformation.
  protected AffineTransform translation;

  // The point at which the mouse was pressed.
  protected Point mouseOrigin;

  // If true, use high-quality drawing.
  protected boolean quality;

  // Construct the canvas.
  public Canvas2D( ) {
    // Initialize the canvas.
    setBackground( Color.white );
    addMouseListener( this );
    addMouseMotionListener( this );
    size = new Dimension( 272, 256 );

    // Initialize the transformations.
    rotation = new AffineTransform( );
    translation = new AffineTransform( );
    scale = new AffineTransform( );

    // Load the image.
    image = new ImageIcon( "starry.gif" );

    // Create a geometric path to represent the image
    // frame.
    path = new GeneralPath(1);
    path.moveTo( 0, 0 );
    path.lineTo( image.getIconWidth( ) +
      2 * indent, 0 );
    path.lineTo( image.getIconWidth( ) + 2 * indent,
      image.getIconHeight( ) + 2 * indent );
    path.lineTo( 0, image.getIconHeight( ) +
      2 * indent );
    path.closePath();

    // Use speed over quality.
    quality = false;
```

```
  }

  // Paint the canvas.
  public void paint( Graphics g ) {

    // Cast the graphics object the the 2D version.
    Graphics2D g2 = (Graphics2D)g;

    // Concatenate the transformations.
    AffineTransform transform = new AffineTransform();
    transform.concatenate( translation );
    transform.concatenate( scale );
    transform.concatenate( rotation );

    // Create a stroke object to draw the frame with.
    Stroke stroke = new BasicStroke( indent / 2,
      BasicStroke.CAP_ROUND, BasicStroke.JOIN_BEVEL);

    // Create a paint object to give the graphics a
    // gradient fill.
    Paint paint = new GradientPaint( 0, 0, Color.red,
      image.getIconWidth( ), image.getIconHeight( ),
      Color.yellow, true );

    // Initialize the graphics object.
    g2.setTransform( transform );
    g2.setPaint( paint );
    g2.setStroke( stroke );
    // Set the quality of the drawing.
    if( quality ) {
      g2.setRenderingHints( Graphics2D.ANTIALIASING,
        Graphics2D.ANTIALIAS_ON );
      g2.setRenderingHints( Graphics2D.RENDERING,
        Graphics2D.RENDER_QUALITY );
    } else {
      g2.setRenderingHints( Graphics2D.ANTIALIASING,
        Graphics2D.ANTIALIAS_OFF );
      g2.setRenderingHints( Graphics2D.RENDERING,
        Graphics2D.RENDER_SPEED );
    }

    // Draw the frame, image and text.
    g2.draw( path );
    g2.drawImage( image.getImage( ), indent, indent,
      null );
```

```
    g2.drawString( "Java 2D!", (float)(indent +
      image.getIconWidth( ) / 2), (float)(indent * 4 +
      image.getIconHeight( )) );
  }

  // Return the preferred size of the canvas. This is
  // required to prevent the layout manager giving the
  // canvas a size of (1,1).
  public Dimension getPreferredSize( ) {
    return size;
  }

  // Zoom in by adjusting the scaling transformation.
  public void zoomIn( ) {
    scale.scale( 2.0, 2.0 );
    repaint( );
  }

  // Zoom out by adjusting the scaling transformation.
  public void zoomOut( ) {
    scale.scale( 0.5, 0.5 );
    repaint( );
  }

  // Rotate clockwise by adjusting the rotation
  // transformation.
  // Note that angles are in radians.
  public void rotateClockwise( ) {
    rotation.rotate( -Math.PI / 16,
      size.width / 2.0, size.height / 2.0 );
    repaint( );
  }

  // Rotate anticlockwise by adjusting the rotation
  // transformation.
  // Note that angles are in radians.
  public void rotateAnticlockwise( ) {
    rotation.rotate( Math.PI / 16,
      size.width / 2.0, size.height / 2.0 );
    repaint( );
  }

  // Set the quality of the drawing (true=high
  // quality).
  public void setQuality( boolean b ) {
    quality = b;
    repaint( );
```

```
    }

    // When the mouse is pressed, note its coordinates.
    public void mousePressed( MouseEvent e ) {
      mouseOrigin = new Point( e.getX( ), e.getY( ) );
    }

    // Pan the display, responding to the mouse being
    // dragged.
    public void mouseDragged( MouseEvent e ) {
      // Determine how far the mouse has been dragged.
      int dx = e.getX( ) - mouseOrigin.x;
      int dy = e.getY( ) - mouseOrigin.y;

      // Adjust the translation transformation.
      translation.translate( dx, dy );
      repaint( );

      // Note where the mouse is now.
      mouseOrigin = new Point( e.getX( ), e.getY( ) );
    }

    // The following methods are not used, but are
    // required by the
    // MouseListener and MouseMotionListener interfaces.
    public void mouseEntered( MouseEvent e ) { }
    public void mouseExited( MouseEvent e ) { }
    public void mouseReleased( MouseEvent e ) { }
    public void mouseClicked( MouseEvent e ) { }
    public void mouseMoved( MouseEvent e ) { }
  }

// A frame to contain the Java 2D demo canvas. It
// links buttons to the zoom and rotate methods in the
// canvas.
public class Java2D extends Frame
implements ActionListener, ItemListener {

  // The 2D demo canvas.
  protected Canvas2D canvas;

  // Construct a new Frame.
  public Java2D( ) {

    // Initialize the frame.
    setLayout( new FlowLayout( ) );
    setBackground( Color.lightGray );
```

```java
    // Add the canvas.
    canvas = new Canvas2D( );
    add( canvas );

    // Add the zoom buttons.
    Button b = new Button( " + " );
    b.setActionCommand( "zoomIn" );
    b.addActionListener( this );
    add( b );

    b = new Button( " - " );
    b.setActionCommand( "zoomOut" );
    b.addActionListener( this );
    add( b );

    // Add the rotation buttons.
    b = new Button( " Rotate + " );
    b.setActionCommand( "rotate-" );
    b.addActionListener( this );
    add( b );

    b = new Button( " Rotate - " );
    b.setActionCommand( "rotate+" );
    b.addActionListener( this );
    add( b );

    // Add the quality checkbox.
    Checkbox check = new Checkbox( "Quality" );
    check.addItemListener( this );
    add( check );

    pack( );
  }

  // When a button is pressed, call the appropriate
  // method in the
  // 2D canvas.
  public void actionPerformed( ActionEvent e ) {
    if( e.getActionCommand( ).equals( "zoomIn" ) )
      canvas.zoomIn( );
    else if( e.getActionCommand( ).equals( "zoomOut" ) )
      canvas.zoomOut( );
    else if( e.getActionCommand( ).equals( "rotate+" ) )
      canvas.rotateClockwise( );
    else if( e.getActionCommand( ).equals( "rotate-" ) )
      canvas.rotateAnticlockwise( );
  }
```

```
  // When the checkbox is changed, update the 2D
  // canvas.
  public void itemStateChanged( ItemEvent e ) {
    // Assumption that there is only one checkbox.
    canvas.setQuality( e.getStateChange( ) ==
ItemEvent.SELECTED );
  }
  // Create and show the 2D demo.
  public static void main( String argv[] ) {

    Java2D frame = new Java2D( );
    frame.setVisible( true );

  }
}
```

All of the interesting stuff happens in the paint() method. First, the Graphics parameter is cast to a Graphics2D instance. Next, we concatenate the scaling, rotation and translation transforms to get a single transformation to use. The three transformations are kept separate, as transformation concatenation is non-commutative.

We then create a thick Stroke object and a gradient Paint object to use in drawing the border. The graphics context is then initialized with these objects, and the quality of the rendering is set. All that remains is to draw the border, the image and the text. In the few lines of this paint() method, we have defined a scaling, rotating and translating image display, drawing a geometrical shape and text using a gradient fill.

22.3 Java 3D

Java 3D is a high-performance 3D graphics API, produced through a collaboration between Sun, Silicon Graphics International, Intel and Apple. It provides a platform-independent, object-oriented API with a rich set of 3D features. It is aimed at a wide range of applications, from 3D animated logos in Web pages to 3D games and CAD packages. It is very flexible, including support for Head Mounted Displays (HMDs) and sound.

The API is implemented on top of the operating system's low-level 3D facilities, such as Direct3D or OpenGL. This means that it is not limited to the "lowest common denominator", and yet will be able to take advantage of any hardware 3D acceleration available. As the underlying hardware increases in speed and sophistication, Java 3D is designed to scale up to meet this increase in hardware performance.

Java 3D does not attempt to replace the Virtual Reality Markup Language (VRML), the 3D system used on the Web. However, Sun expects many browsers to implement VRML support in Java 3D.

Java 3D is a Java extension, rather than being a core part of Java. A Java Extension (new with Java 1.2) contains a library of Java classes (which may include native code) that may be automatically downloaded and installed when an application tries to use it.

There is a certain amount of overlap between the Java 2D and Java 3D geometry classes – for example, the class `java.awt.geom.Point2D.Float` is the same as `java.vecmath.Point2f`. This is probably due to them being developed in parallel, and it would be nice if they could be integrated at some point in the future.

22.3.1 Immediate or Retained Mode

The API may render scenes using three different modes. At the lowest level is the immediate mode API. In immediate mode, the programmer maintains a world model and draws to the screen using points, lines and polygons. This mode is only likely to be used if the application has been converted from one that already maintains a world model, or if there are particular performance reasons (in terms of maintaining the world model) for doing so.

At a much higher level are retained mode and compiled retained mode. With these rendering modes, the API maintains the world model itself (referred to as a scene graph). Nodes in the scene graph define the appearance and position of objects, how they may change and how they behave. Some parts of the scene will never change, which allows Java 3D to optimize the graph by compiling some of its branches. In most situations, using the retained modes will give better performance than immediate mode (and with considerably less work).

22.3.2 World Model

Figure 22.2 shows the structure of the world model for a simple scene containing a rotating cube. This example and the associated code is taken from the JavaSoft White Paper on Java 3D.

The world is represented by a scene graph – a directed acyclic graph containing nodes that define the contents of the world. At the top level is an instance of the `VirtualUniverse` class. This defines a named universe. Most applications would only define one of these, although it is possible to create more.

Below this is a locale object, which provides an origin within the universe. There are two `BranchGroupNodes` beneath this. These act as the root of a sub-graph or branch in the scene, and are the only objects allowed to connect to a locale. One branch defines the view platform. The other defines the cube object in terms of its behaviour, transformations and shape. This code is shown in Listing 22.2.

Listing 22.2

```
// A "Hello World" for 3D.
// From the Java 3D White Paper.
public class HelloUniverse extends Frame {
```

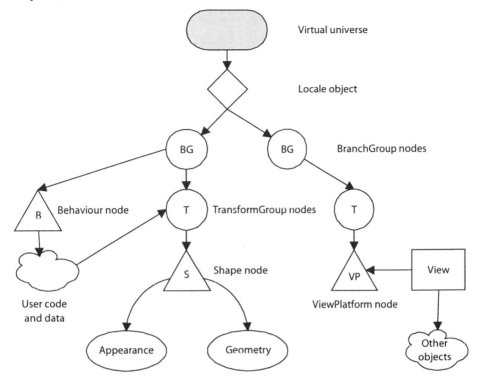

Figure 22.2 Java 3D scene graph.

```
// Create the Scene Graph containing a spinning
// cube.
// c is the canvas that will display the 3D view.
public void createSceneGraph(Canvas3D c) {

    // Establish the virtual universe, with a single
    // hi-res Locale
    VirtualUniverse universe = new VirtualUniverse("My
        Universe");
    Locale locale = new Locale(universe);

    // Create a View and attach the Canvas3D to the
    // view.
    View view = new View();
    view.addCanvas3D(c);

    // Create two branch group nodes: one for the view
    // platform and one for the object
    BranchGroup vpRoot = new BranchGroup();
    BranchGroup objRoot = new BranchGroup();
```

```
// Create a ViewPlatform object, and its
// associated TransformGroup object, and attach it
// to the root of the subgraph. Attach the view to
// the view platform.
Transform t = new Transform();
t.setTranslation(new Vec3f(0.0f, 0.0f, -3.0f));
ViewPlatform vp = new ViewPlatform();
TransformGroup trans = new TransformGroup(t);
trans.addChild(vp);
vpRoot.addChild(trans);
view.attachViewPlatform(vp);

// Create the transform group node and initialize
// to the identity.
// Enable the TRANSFORM_WRITE capability so that
// our behavior code can modify it at runtime. Add
// it to the root of the subgraph.
Matrix4d mat = new Matrix4d();
mat.setIdentity();
Transform t1 = new Transform();
t1.setTransform(mat);
TransformGroup objtrans = new TransformGroup(t1);
objtrans.setCapability(TransformGroup.
  ALLOW_TRANSFORM_WRITE);
objRoot.addChild(objtrans);

// Create some simple geometry (without an
// appearance node).
// Create a new shape leaf node using the
// specified geometry and add it into the scene
// graph.
QuadArray g = new ColorCube();
Appearance a = new Appearance();
Shape s = new Shape(g,a);
objtrans.addChild(s);

// Create a new Behavior object that will perform
// the desired operation on the specified
// transform object and add it into the scene
// graph.
MyBehavior rotator = new MyBehavior(objtrans);
BoundingSphere bounds =
  new BoundingSphere(new Vec3d(0.0,0.0,0.0),
    100.0);
rotator.setSchedulingRegion(bounds);
objtrans.addChild(rotator);
```

```
        // Attach the subgraphs to the universe, via the
        // Locale. The scene graph is now live!
        locale.addGraph(objRoot);
        locale.addGraph(vpRoot);
    }
}
```

22.3.3 View Platform

Traditionally, 3D APIs provide a "camera" that may be positioned in the scene to represent the display. Java 3D goes further than this, cleanly separating the virtual and physical world. A view platform may be positioned in the scene, but this does not generate the display directly. The renderer decides what view to render based on the position of the view platform and the user's position and orientation within the physical environment.

This is a very powerful abstraction which allows a Java 3D application to work unchanged with a monitor display, with 3D goggles, or even with a head-mounted display (HMD) that tracks the position of the head. For the application programmer, the idea of a view platform is no more complicated that than of a camera.

22.3.4 Geometry and Appearance

The geometry of an object is defined, as you might expect, in terms of lines, vertices and polygons. Note the clear separation between the geometry and appearance of an object – this allows the same geometry to be reused between different objects. Listing 22.3 shows the code for the spinning cube example.

Listing 22.3

```
// User-extended class to create a cube out of Quads
public class ColorCube extends QuadArray {

    // The vertices.
    private static final float[] verts = {
        // front face
        1.0f, -1.0f,  1.0f, 1.0f,  1.0f,  1.0f,
       -1.0f,  1.0f,  1.0f,-1.0f, -1.0f,  1.0f,
        // back face
       -1.0f, -1.0f, -1.0f,-1.0f,  1.0f, -1.0f,
        1.0f,  1.0f, -1.0f, 1.0f, -1.0f, -1.0f,
        // right face
        1.0f, -1.0f, -1.0f, 1.0f,  1.0f, -1.0f,
        1.0f,  1.0f,  1.0f, 1.0f, -1.0f,  1.0f,
        // left face
       -1.0f, -1.0f,  1.0f,-1.0f,  1.0f,  1.0f,
       -1.0f,  1.0f, -1.0f,-1.0f, -1.0f, -1.0f,
```

```
    // top face
    1.0f,   1.0f,   1.0f, 1.0f,   1.0f,  -1.0f,
   -1.0f,   1.0f,  -1.0f,-1.0f,   1.0f,   1.0f,
    // bottom face
   -1.0f,  -1.0f,   1.0f,-1.0f,  -1.0f,  -1.0f,
    1.0f,  -1.0f,  -1.0f, 1.0f,  -1.0f,   1.0f };

  // The colours.
  private static final float[] colors = {
    // front face (red)
    1.0f, 0.0f, 0.0f, 1.0f, 0.0f, 0.0f,
    1.0f, 0.0f, 0.0f, 1.0f, 0.0f, 0.0f,
    // back face (green)
    0.0f, 1.0f, 0.0f, 0.0f, 1.0f, 0.0f,
    0.0f, 1.0f, 0.0f, 0.0f, 1.0f, 0.0f,
    // right face (blue)
    0.0f, 0.0f, 1.0f, 0.0f, 0.0f, 1.0f,
    0.0f, 0.0f, 1.0f, 0.0f, 0.0f, 1.0f,
    // left face (yellow)
    1.0f, 1.0f, 0.0f, 1.0f, 1.0f, 0.0f,
    1.0f, 1.0f, 0.0f, 1.0f, 1.0f, 0.0f,
    // top face (magenta)
    1.0f, 0.0f, 1.0f, 1.0f, 0.0f, 1.0f,
    1.0f, 0.0f, 1.0f, 1.0f, 0.0f, 1.0f,
    // bottom face (cyan)
    0.0f, 1.0f, 1.0f, 0.0f, 1.0f, 1.0f,
    0.0f, 1.0f, 1.0f, 0.0f, 1.0f, 1.0f };

  ColorCube() {
    super(24, QuadSet.COORDINATES | QuadSet.COLOR_3F);
    setCoordinates(0, verts);
    setColors(0, colors);
  }
}
```

Java 3D also allows you to define the appearance of an object in terms of its texture and its colour.

22.3.5 Behaviour

If you refer back to Figure 22.2, you will notice that part of the definition of the object is a behaviour node. Behaviours define how objects react to changes in inputs or over time. In the example, the behaviour modifies the transformation node in order to rotate the cube over time. A behaviour could be linked to the ViewPlatform that monitors a joystick, allowing us to move the ViewPlatform through the virtual universe. This would have to modify the transformation node above the ViewPlatform.

Clearly, in a large universe there might be a large number of objects and behaviours. Java 3D attempts to minimize the overhead this might impose by restricting rendering and behaviour execution to a view cone from the ViewPlatform. Anything outside this cone is not visible and so need not be considered. In addition, each behaviour defines a wakeup condition that determines when the behaviour code should be executed.

The Behavior object is initialized in the initialize() method (Listing 22.4). This is where it specifies the initial wakeup condition. When the behaviour is within the view cone and the wakeup condition is realized, the stimulus() method is executed.

Listing 22.4

```
// User-extended Behavior to rotate the cube.
class public class MyBehavior extends Behavior {

   TransformGroup objectTransform;
   Matrix4d rotMat = new Matrix4d();
   Matrix4d objectMat = new Matrix4d();
   WakeupOnElapsedFrames w = new
WakeupOnElapsedFrames(1);

   // Override initialize method to setup wakeup
   // criteria
   public void initialize() {
     // Establish initial wakeup criteria
     wakeupOn(w);
   }

   // Override Behavior's stimulus method to handle the
   // event
   public void stimulus(WakeupCondition arg) {

     // Rotate by another PI/120.0 radians
     objectMat.mul(objectMat, rotMat);
     objectTransform.setTransform(new
       Transform(objectMat));

     // Set wakeup criteria for next time
     wakeupOn(w);
   }
   // Constructor for rotation behavior.
   // tg is the transform group node to be modified.
   public MyBehavior(TransformGroup tg) {
```

```
    objectTransform = tg;
  objectMat.setIdentity();

    // Create a rotation matrix of PI/120.0 radians
    // about Y
    rotMat.rotY(Math.PI/120.0);
  }
}
```

22.3.6 Light and Sound

As well as containing graphical objects and viewing platforms, a 3D scene may contain other types of object too. Lighting is an important part of many 3D scenes, and Java 3D provides a selection of lights.

The forthcoming Java Sound API will be responsible for generating high-quality sound in Java applications. However, Java 3D includes specific provision for sound within the 3D environment. Sound sources can be positioned within a scene just like any other object, and the system can handle advanced sound features, such as Doppler shifts from fast-moving sources. By integrating sound into the 3D scene, it should be relatively easy to create convincing immersive virtual reality.

22.4 The Java Media Framework

The Java Media Framework API (JMF) provides Java applications (and applets) with the ability to play most popular media files. This currently includes video (MPEG-2, QuickTime, AVI) and sound (WAV, AU, MIDI). Keeping to the Java ideals, it aims to do so in a platform-independent manner, although the API itself is implemented in native code and can take advantage of any hardware acceleration the platform provides. Again, it is not a core part of Java, but is provided as a Java Extension.

The JMF can operate on local files or across a network using protocols such as HTTP or Real-Time Transport Protocol (RTP is a protocol under development for broadcast data). It is extensible, so that new media types can be integrated through the provision of new media players and controllers.

22.4.1 Data Sources

The location of the medium to play and the protocol required to access it are encapsulated within a `DataSource`. A JMF player identifies its data source through either a Universal Resource Locator (URL) or a `MediaLocator` object. A `MediaLocator` is similar to a URL, except it is not restricted only to the protocols recognized by the system.

JMF distinguishes between two types of data source. Pull data sources represent media that are transferred under the control of the client application. The protocols for this include HTTP and FILE. Push data sources represent media under the control of a server, such as broadcast media and Video-On-Demand (VOD).

Clearly, the type of data source affects how much control the client application can exert over the media player. For example, an MPEG file might allow random access into the video, something that would not be possible for broadcast media.

22.4.2 Players

A Java media Player reads data from a `DataSource` and renders it at a precise time. Each player has a `TimeBase` variable that defines the flow of time for that player, and also a media time that represents the current position in the media stream. For players to be synchronized, they must use the same `TimeBase`.

A Player's user interface may be divided into two parts: the visual component that plays the media and the control panel that provides components for controlling the player. Applications are free to define their own control panel to use with a Player.

A media player can be in one of six states:

1. Unrealized state: the player has been created, but does not yet know anything about its media.
2. Realizing: in response to the `realize()` method, the player determines its resource requirements and acquires any non-exclusive resources. This may include downloading data over the Net.
3. Realized: a realized player knows how to render its data and so can provide its visual components and control panels. In this state, the player still does not own any exclusive resources that could stop another player starting.
4. Prefetching: in response to the `prefetch()` method, the player does everything it needs to do in order to prepare itself to play. This includes preloading the media data, and acquiring exclusive use resources.
5. Prefetched: the player is ready to play!
6. Started: the player has started, although it may be waiting for a particular time to begin presenting its data.

By providing these separate states in the player, the JMF allows an application to control explicitly how exclusive and non-exclusive resources are allocated, preventing deadlock between players. You should note that not all `Player` methods can be called in all states. For example, it would not be appropriate to call the `getControlPanelComponent()` method until the player was in the realized state and was aware of its media type.

22.4.3 Events

The JMF uses the standard Delegation Event Model as used by JavaBeans. Most of the events are generated by the `Controller` class (`Player` is a subclass of `Controller`), and are subclasses of `ControllerEvent`. These events may notify the application that some attribute of the player has changed, that the state of the player has changed, or that the player has closed or stopped due to an error.

Monitoring the state of the player is the only way to determine when an asynchronous method call has finished.

To listen for `ControllerEvents`, a class must implement the `ControllerListener` interface. In addition to controller events, a `GainControl` object can post events in response to the gain (volume) setting changing.

22.4.4 Example

Figure 22.3 shows a screenshot of an example application, from the code in Listing 22.5. Given a URL locating a media file, the application will play it – the figure shows a movie (.MOV) file playing.

When the frame is constructed, the player is created and the `Media` class is added as a `ControllerListener`. The player's `realize()` method is then called. This causes it to analyze the media type and download it if it is not local. It then dispatches a `RealizeCompleteEvent`, which is directed to our `realizeComplete()` method. Here, we ask the player for a visual component and for a control panel, both of which are added to the frame. The player's `prefetch()` method can now be called to prepare it for playing. When prefetching is complete and the `PrefetchCompleteEvent` has been sent, the application calls the player's `start()` method.

Listing 22.5

```
import java.awt.*;
import java.io.*;
import java.net.*;

import javax.media.*;

// Demonstrate the Java Media Framework (JMF).
```

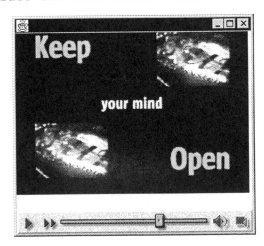

Figure 22.3 Java media demo.

```java
// Play a media file specified from the command line.
public class Media extends Frame
implements ControllerListener {

  // Create the demo.
  public Media( String urlName )
  throws MalformedURLException, NoPlayerException,
    IOException {

    // Create a URL for the media file.
    URL url = new URL( urlName );
    if( url == null ) {
      System.err.println( "Can't create URL for " +
        urlName );
      return;
    }

    // Create a player for this media file
    Player player = Manager.createPlayer( url );
    if( player == null ) {
      System.err.println( "Can't create player for " +
        url );
      return;
    }

    // Add this as a listener and start to realize the
    // player.
    player.addControllerListener( this );
    player.realize( );
  }

  // Dispatch a Controller event to appropriate
  // methods.
  public synchronized void controllerUpdate(
ControllerEvent e ) {
    // RealizeCompleteEvent occurs after a realize()
    // call.
    if( e instanceof RealizeCompleteEvent )
      realizeComplete( e );
    else if( e instanceof PrefetchCompleteEvent )
      prefetchComplete( e );
    else if( e instanceof EndOfMediaEvent )
      endOfMedia( e );
    else if( e instanceof ControllerErrorEvent )
      controllerError( e );
  }
```

```
// When the player has been realized, add its visual
// and control components to the panel, and ask it
// to prefetch.
protected void realizeComplete( ControllerEvent e ) {

// Get the visual component, if any, and add it to
// the frame.
Component visualComp = null;
if (( visualComp = ((Player)e.getSource
    ()).getVisualComponent()) != null) {
  add("Center", visualComp);
}

// Get the control component, if any, and add it to
// the frame.
Component controlComp = null;
if ((controlComp = ((Player)e.getSource
    ()).getControlPanelComponent()) != null) {
  add("South", controlComp);
}

  invalidate( );
  pack( );

// Ask the player to prefetch data and prepare to
// start.
((Player)e.getSource( )).prefetch();
}

// When the player has prefetched its data, play it.
protected void prefetchComplete( ControllerEvent e ) {
((Player)e.getSource( )).start();
}

// When we have come to the end of the media,
// play it again from the beginning.
protected void endOfMedia( ControllerEvent e ) {
((Player)e.getSource( )).setMediaTime(new Time(0));
((Player)e.getSource( )).prefetch();
}

// Display a controller error.
protected void controllerError( ControllerEvent e ) {
  System.err.println("Received controller error: "
    + e );
}
```

```
    // Run the demo.
    public static void main( String argv[] ) {

      if( argv.length != 1 ) {
        System.err.println( "Usage: URL" );
        System.exit( -1 );
      }
      String urlName = argv[0];

      try {
        Media media = new Media( urlName );
        media.setVisible( true );
      } catch( Exception e ) {
        e.printStackTrace( );
      }
    }
  }
```

22.5 Summary

The Media frameworks provide a valuable addition to Java's graphical capabilities. Once again, the development teams have come up with systems that are easy to use, and yet offer a great deal of flexibility.

Java 2D's more flexible graphics context will be appreciated by most Java developers –in particular its ability to draw thick lines! However, it also opens the door to much more sophisticated Java applications, such as desktop publishers, image editors and drawing tools.

Java 3D's appeal is a little more limited. However, with the backing of all of the major players in 3D graphics, it has advanced the state of the art. For this reason, it seems likely to take over from the less sophisticated libraries such as OpenGL to become the standard for 3D development, which is good news for Java in general.

The Java Media Framework makes it very easy to integrate various media types into Java code. It will probably make the most impact in Web pages, although it does have great potential for remote conferencing style applications (see Chapter 1).

22.6 Online References

Java 1.2 (including Java 2D) is available through Sun's JavaSoft Web pages:

```
http://java.sun.com/
```

Also, check out the Java 2D home pages:

```
http://java.sun.com/products/java-media/2D/index.html
```

The Java 3D home pages (including Java 3D White Paper):

```
http://java.sun.com/products/java-media/3D/
```

The Java Media Framework pages:

```
http://java.sun.com/products/java-media/jmf/index.html
```

JavaSoft technical article on Java 2D:

```
http://developer.javasoft.com/developer/
    technicalArticles/monicap/2DGraphics/Intro/
    simple2D.html
```

JavaSoft technical article on colour:

```
http://developer.javasoft.com/developer/
    technicalArticles/monicap/2DGraphics/Color/color.html
```

23   *User Interface Design Issues in Java*

23.1 Introduction

There are many books describing how to create graphical user interfaces (GUIs) in Java. Unfortunately, the vast majority of these describe how the classes and packages *can* be used, with no discussion of how they *should* be used. Although we enthused over various advanced UI features of the Java Foundation Classes (JFC) in the previous chapter, it is still possible to create a very poor interface with the JFC and a very good one with the humble AWT.

User interface design is a very important issue – it affects the users' perception of quality, ease of learning, performance, error rates and overall satisfaction with the system. A good UI can be a matter of life and death in some safety-critical systems (such as in the Three Mile Island nuclear disaster).

Developing user interfaces is a sufficiently important topic to warrant several books. This chapter does not attempt to replace these books; rather we provide a discussion of the most important concepts for Java developers, and provide some practical guidelines for designing UIs using Java classes.

We focus on aspects of UI design that have particular importance for Java, either because of the unique qualities of the language (such as its portability), or because Java makes specific provision for overcoming a problem (e.g. internationalization).

23.2 Users and Tasks

Focusing on the person that will be using the application and the tasks that they are trying to achieve is essential when designing a good user interface. Many programmers make the mistake of focusing their efforts on the features of the application itself.

A sensible first step in creating a user interface is to try to determine what is wanted from it. The requirements in terms of software engineering are fairly easy to define. To start with, a well-engineered application must provide the correct level of functionality. Inadequate functionality will frustrate the user (particularly experienced users) and may lead to the application being discarded. Conversely, an application with excessive functionality can bewilder the user, making learning and use of the application more difficult (to say nothing of the extra implementation and maintenance difficulties). It is difficult to choose the most appropriate level of functionality, and it is particularly tempting to add excessive functionality when competing with similar applications.

An application must also achieve an appropriate level of reliability. Even if the application's interface makes interaction easy, if it is unreliable or provides incorrect results the user's trust in the system will be damaged. A user's trust is fragile, and once lost it is not easily regained.

A good application will use appropriate standards and maintain consistency. Slight differences between applications (or parts of the same application) will increase the learning time and may lead to annoying or dangerous errors. Substantial differences may require complete retraining. We consider user interface consistency in more detail later. An application should try to conform to standards for storage formats as well as standards for the UI, as this affects the usability of the application as part of a larger system. For example, Java's object serialization is certainly the easiest way to make objects persistent, but may not be the best way if the data may be used in other systems. For example, text would be more useful saved as ASCII rather than as serialized `String` instances.

The requirements in terms of the quality of user interaction are rather less obvious. The key to designing a good user interface lies in a good understanding of the people that will be using the system. The cultural background, the physical abilities, the motivation and the experience of the users will all affect their interaction with an application. A design that is good for one group of people may be quite unsuitable for another. Before we take a closer look at some of these influences, we need some criteria that will help us target and evaluate our design efforts.

23.2.1 Human Factors

Schneiderman identifies five measurable human factors that are central to evaluating a user interface:

1. *Time to learn*: how long does it take a typical user to learn how to use the application to perform a set of tasks?
2. *Speed of performance*: how long does it take an experienced user to perform a benchmark set of tasks?
3. *Rate of errors by users*: how many (and what kind) of errors are made when carrying out the set of tasks?
4. *Retention over time*: how well do users maintain their knowledge after a period of time? This is related to the time to learn and to the frequency of use.
5. *Subjective satisfaction*: how much did the users enjoy using the system?

How we design for these factors depends on the type of person that will be using the application. Ideally, we could create an interface that would succeed in all of these categories, but they can often conflict. For example, we could introduce complex shortcuts to increase speed of performance at the expense of a longer learning time. By considering the needs of the eventual users, we can assign priorities to these factors when designing.

23.2.2 User Knowledge

A part of understanding the users of an application is to appreciate the knowledge that users have. The Syntactic–Semantic Object–Action (SSOA) model of user behaviour can be useful for this. Syntactic knowledge concerns device-dependent details of how to interact with the computer. This might include knowledge that the arrow keys move the cursor through text, or that the disk icon is used to save the current document. Learning, use and retention of syntactic knowledge may be difficult, because it is often arbitrary and system-dependent. It must be acquired by rote learning and retained by repetition. By maintaining consistency within an application and the other applications on the system, and by reducing the amount a user must remember (menus can help here), novice users will find the syntactic knowledge needed to use an application easier to acquire and retain.

Semantic knowledge is concerned with the concepts behind the application, and may be divided into computer concepts and task concepts. It is stored in long-term memory, and may be learned by showing examples of use, offering a general theory or model, or by relating concepts to previous knowledge by analogy.

Computer concepts include a hierarchical set of objects and actions. For example, the concept of data storage may be refined into concepts of files and directories, and the action of creating a new file can be decomposed into creating a new document in memory and then saving it. Users must acquire semantic knowledge about computer concepts, but they are relatively stable in memory and transfer across different computer systems.

Task concepts are used to decompose large and complex problems into smaller ones, until each sub-problem is manageable (again using objects and actions). Each of these types of knowledge must be integrated in order to use an application. Schneiderman gives the example of writing a letter on a word processor, for which the user must have the high-level concept of writing (task action) a letter (task object), recognize that the letter must be stored as a file (computer object), and know the details of the save command (computer action and syntactic knowledge).

23.2.3 User Context

Looking at the context in which the system is used can help us to assign priorities to the human factors. Operators working on safety-critical systems (such as ambulance control systems) require rapid, error-free performance. Lengthy training periods are acceptable to achieve this, and retention is through frequent use. Users are normally well motivated, so subjective satisfaction is not paramount.

Industrial and commercial applications (such as a system that supports telephone-based ordering) are primarily concerned with cost. Training is expensive and should be minimized, but performance is important. Again, subjective satisfaction is less important, and retention is through frequent use.

With office and home users, subjective satisfaction is important, which is usually achieved though ease of learning and low error rates. If users cannot succeed quickly, they may abandon the application. Use of the application may be intermittent, so aids for retention, such as online help, are useful.

23.2.4 Cultural Background

The cultural background of users can affect their interaction with an application. For example, a dialog layout that shows information logically from left to right would appear illogical to oriental users, who scan displays differently. "1/10/1997" would be interpreted as 1 October 1997 in Britain but as 10 January 1997 in the USA. The former example is difficult to overcome, but Java 1.1 directly supports localized date and currency conversion (as well as localized text). We look at this in Section 23.8. A failure to internationalize an application can increase the time to learn as well as leading to a higher error rate.

23.2.5 Physical Abilities

Users of an application may have disabilities of varying severity. The designer can help those with poor sight (such as the elderly) by allowing the use of larger fonts. Users with poor motor control can find it difficult to control a mouse, and are helped by providing keyboard alternatives. The JFC introduces Java Accessibility. This is a mechanism for bypassing an application's GUI to provide access to its data and actions. This would allow a text-to-speech converter to read the contents of a text field, or a speech recognition system to save the current file. We discussed accessibility in greater depth in the previous chapter. In the worst cases, applications are unusable by people with disabilities.

23.2.6 User Profiles

We have discussed how users' experience, knowledge, abilities, and place of work can affect their interaction with an application. A useful method of bringing all of this together, in order to assign priorities to the human factors mentioned above, is to create a user profile. Table 23.1 provides an example of user profiles for an address book application.

Establishing the type of user for an application is often difficult. Doing so for an applet may well be impossible – it could literally be accessed by anyone with a networked computer. Even when we can isolate the users, there may be several communities of them, each with different requirements. How can we deal with this? Some applications provide separate interfaces for the different types of user. The popular compression application WinZip provides a wizard[1] interface for novices and a classic interface for more experienced users.

Many applications provide dialogs that display only the basic information, with an "Advanced" button that reveals the more complicated options. Also, providing the ability to configure the application is valuable for experienced users. This might allow them to turn off confirmation dialogs for example, in order to speed up the interaction. The sections that follow aim to help you create interfaces that meet the needs of as wide a selection of people as is possible. Nevertheless, you will still need

---

1 Wizard: a style of dialogue that takes the user step-by-step through the actions needed to achieve a task.

Table 23.1 User profiles for an address book application

Type of user		User interface requirements
Home	Novice	No syntactic and little semantic knowledge. Restrict the number of actions possible, and allow the user to carry out a few simple tasks to build confidence. The user does not have access to knowledgeable colleagues, so informative feedback and helpful error messages are essential.
	Intermittent	Because use is intermittent, the user has difficulty in retaining the syntactic knowledge. Providing a simple and consistent structure to the interaction helps overcome this. The provision of an Undo facility helps the user explore partially forgotten commands without danger. The user does not have access to knowledgeable colleagues, so online access to help is also valuable as a reminder.
Office	Intermittent	Has similar requirements to the intermittent home user, except that the user may have access to knowledgeable colleagues, which makes online help less important. The office user may require consistency and interaction with other office applications.
	Frequent	The frequent office user is familiar with the syntax and semantics, and wants to get the job done quickly. This may be helped by rapid response times, brief, less distracting feedback and shortcuts. The user may require consistency and interaction with other office applications.

to make compromises, and understanding the users' needs is essential to making the right decisions.

23.2.7 Tasks

A common mistake for application designers is to base the structure of the interface on the structure of the code. However, design or implementation convenience should never dictate the structure of the interface.

Interfaces that are structured around the task that the user is trying to perform are easier to learn and provide faster performance. UI designers should consider the tasks that the user is trying to achieve. High-level tasks can be decomposed recursively into atomic actions that can be executed with a single command. Decomposing tasks to the correct level is difficult – if the atomic actions are too small, a high-level task may require a large number of actions. On the other hand, if the atomic actions are too large the application must provide a large number of them to provide the necessary functionality.

A good designer will consider the frequency of the tasks and design the interface so that frequently performed tasks are simple and fast, even at the expense of lengthening the more infrequent tasks.

As a simple example of designing around tasks, consider a class timetabling application. The user needs to enter the details of a module, in terms of its name, its teachers and its class size. The application can then create a timetable. We could design the code for this so that it provided one class for a module, and a separate class

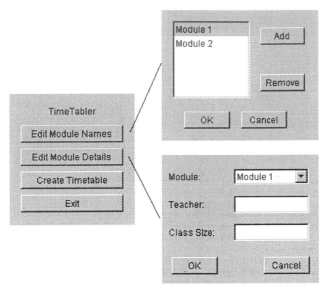

Figure 23.1 A code-based interface design.

for the module requirements. We might then use this structure as the basis for the interface design in Figure 23.1.

The problem with this design is that it forces the user to enter the module names separately from the module details. If we decompose the task, we can see that this does not fit in with the way that most users will work, and so is less intuitive and slower.

- Enter modules
  - Add each module
    - Specify name
    - Specify teacher
    - Specify class size
- Create timetable

A better design (one that fits in with this task decomposition) is shown in Figure 23.2.

23.3 General Guidelines for Good Design

Schneiderman proposes eight "golden rules of dialogue[2] design":

---

2 In this case, he means the more general form of dialogue, in terms of communicating with the computer, rather than the restrictive idea of a dialog box (the Java class `Dialog`) getting input from the user.

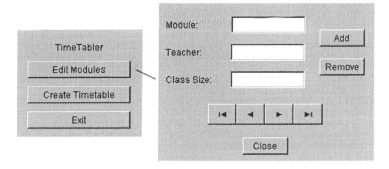

Figure 23.2 A task-based interface design.

1. Strive for consistency.
2. Enable frequent users to use shortcuts.
3. Offer informative feedback.
4. Design dialogs to yield closure.
5. Offer simple error handling.
6. Permit easy reversal of actions.
7. Support internal locus of control.
8. Reduce short-term memory load.

We consider these in more detail below.

23.3.1 Strive for Consistency

Consistency is probably the most important aspect of a user interface. A good interface will be consistent throughout, from the layout of dialogs, the layout of menus, the terminology used, and the way tasks are performed. By maintaining consistency, the interface becomes easier to learn, retention is better, and the users will make fewer errors.

Schneiderman said of consistency, "This principle is the most frequently violated one, and yet the easiest one to repair and avoid (violating)". We look at this further in Section 23.4.

23.3.2 Shortcuts

Experienced users want to perform their tasks as quickly as possible, without being hampered by parts of the interface that make it easier to learn. For this reason, a good interface will provide shortcuts to allow these users to quickly access the required commands.

Java supports shortcuts to menu items that can be accessed from any component in the Frame that accepts the input focus. These are particularly useful as they allow fast typists to access the commands without having to leave the keyboard. Toolbars also provide shortcuts to menu items for the most commonly used commands.

Swing provides direct support for toolbars, but if you must use the AWT you will have to write your own or use a commercial library.

MS Windows applications usually provide Alt-key shortcuts to sections of a dialog (for example, Alt-O for the OK button). The AWT did not support this, but Swing does through the KeyStroke class.

23.3.4 Informative Feedback

For every command that a user performs, there should be some form of feedback. This may mean updating the display, or even just showing a message in a status bar. This helps give the users a feeling of control over the computer, and provides them with the information necessary to assess the effects of their actions. It is quite easy to create a status bar component – essentially it is one or more TextFields contained within a Panel.

23.3.5 Design Dialogs to Yield Closure

If, during the course of completing a task, a user has to open a multitude of windows and swap between them, and can finish the task with many of them left open, it can become very confusing. The user has not been given a clear path through the interface. When we design dialogs to yield closure, there is a clear beginning and end to the dialog.

The key tool in achieving this is the modal window, provided in Java by the Dialog class. A modal window is one that blocks all input to other windows until it is closed. Consider a simple text editor, with modal dialogs for opening and saving a file, for printing, and changing options. Even at this level of simplicity, if the dialogs were made modeless (so that you could open a file without closing the FileSelector, for example), it could become very confusing when many of the dialogs were open at once.

23.3.5 Offer Simple Error Handling

A good user interface will try to prevent errors as much as possible. If errors are made, the system should provide intelligible error messages and simple mechanisms for handling the error. Erroneous commands should leave the state of the application unchanged, or the application should give instructions for restoring the state. We look at this further in Section 23.7.

23.3.6 Permit Easy Reversal of Actions

Some form of Undo mechanism is a very valuable addition to a user interface. Because users know that errors can be undone, it encourages them to explore unfamiliar actions, or to attempt an action that they cannot completely remember. Swing includes an excellent Undo mechanism – in many cases it is relatively easy to add multi-level undo/redo to your application. We discussed this in the previous chapter.

23.3.7 Support Internal Locus of Control

In general, users are happier with an application when they feel in control: the locus of control must be with the user (internal to the user rather than the application). A good interface will be designed to support this, rather than leaving the users feeling that they are merely responding to the computer.

23.3.8 Reduce Short-Term Memory Load

Research has shown that we can retain about seven chunks of information in short-term memory at once (depending on how familiar we are with the type of information). You can make life easier for the users by keeping the displays simple, minimizing the amount of information a user has to remember between dialogs, and by providing online access to information.

23.4 Consistency

Consistency should run throughout most aspects of an application. Why is this important? By sticking to a small and predictable terminology, new users have less to take in, and it becomes easier to learn how to use the new application. For all users, there is much less scope for confusion, and this syntactic information is easier to retain.

23.4.1 Consistency in All Areas

Terminology

The terminology used should be the same – if your menu item is "Add Image", the title of the resulting dialog box should be "Choose Image to Add" rather than "Choose Picture to Insert". The menu item "Delete Table" matches with "Delete Image", but not with "Remove Image". You should also carefully choose the complements of words. For example, "Add" complements "Remove", and "Insert" complements "Delete".

The style of messages should be kept consistent. Consider the following confirmation messages from a file manager program, each accompanied by a "Yes" and "No" button:

● Confirmation: do you want to copy this file?
● Confirmation: do you want to move this file?
● Confirmation: do you want to delete this file?
● Confirmation: do you want to abort formatting your hard disk?

The first three messages consistently abort the operation with the "No" button, whereas the final message is negated and aborts the operation with the "Yes" button. This inconsistency is dangerous, because an experienced user might scan through the message quickly and choose the wrong button.

A loose interpretation of terminology might include images and shortcut keys too – images on buttons and toolbars and shortcuts to menu items must also be used consistently.

Layout

Keeping to a consistent layout in your interface is also important. As well as giving the application a more polished look, it helps users locate items in the display. As a simple example, consider the "OK" and "Cancel" buttons in a dialog. If they always appear at the bottom of the dialog, with the "OK" button at the left, then the user can find them immediately, without really having to look at the dialog. This can speed up performance when dismissing confirmation dialogs, as an experienced user will expect them. The grouping of components within a dialog should also be logical and consistent.

The layout of menus is also important. If the layout is consistent with other applications, new computer-literate users will find it much easier to locate items.

Tasks

The way in tasks are performed should be kept consistent. For example, consider an address book program that can contain entries for people and companies. To print a person's details, the user must first select the person, and then the "Print" item in the menu. To print a company's details, the user must double-click on the company's entry and select the print button from the dialog that appears. In this case, two similar tasks have been implemented differently. The user must remember two separate methods of achieving a similar task, and remember which method is required for each type of entry.

23.4.2 Internal vs. External Consistency

There are two classes of consistency: internal and external. Internal consistency means that your application is consistent within its own internal code. This is relatively easy to achieve, because the application is under your control. External consistency means that the application is consistent with code external to it, as found in the operating system, and with other applications that are being used. Clearly, this is a more difficult prospect, as the other applications are not under your control.

For example, an externally consistent interface will use a menu layout that is standard for its operating system (for example, an MS Windows application will normally contain "File", "Edit", "View", "Window" and "Help" top-level menus). In fact, it should be externally consistent in all of the areas discussed above. External consistency is significant, because users that are experienced with a particular platform will find it much easier to learn how to use your application, and will retain that knowledge longer.

But wait a minute! Java applications are platform-independent, which can make maintaining external consistency problematic. A consistent look and feel is provided by the graphical toolkit, but that does not cover layout and terminology, never mind images and tasks.

One solution to the problem is to ignore it, which is certainly what most Java applications do. It is possible to come up with interfaces that make a reasonable compromise between various platforms' standards.

Another solution is to create different versions of your application for each platform, although this is rather defeating the point of multi-platform development. A better approach is to tailor your applications dynamically to suit the host platform. Having defined a `StdDialog` class that contains "OK" and "Cancel" buttons, together with a Panel, you can read the "`os.name`" system property to determine which operating system is being used and tailor the layout accordingly. Subclasses of `StdDialog` can add their own contents to the Panel that it contains, while still taking advantage of platform-specific layout.

If you want to go further than this, and adapt the layout of menus, use different icons etc., it is best to store this information in one or more configuration files. A configuration file might look something like Listing 23.1. You should define a default configuration file, and then define files for each platform that differs from this. The `Properties` class is a useful way of reading configuration files, particularly as it stores the data in a text file. You can determine which operating system is being used by checking the "`os.name`" system property, and use this to locate the correct configuration file. For example:

```
String osName = System.getProperty( "os.name" );
String configName = osName + ".config";
```

This is a similar approach to handling language internationalization (Section 23.8.1) using the `PropertyResourceBundle`. In fact, the `Property-ResourceBundle` can be used for adapting to different platforms, but it is probably better practice to keep language and platform configurations separate.

Listing 23.1

```
#
# Configuration file for MyApp.
# Base configuration for MS Windows.
#

mainMenuBar=fileMenu editMenu viewMenu helpMenu

fileMenu=newItem openItem saveItem closeItem -
exitItem

editMenu=cutItem copyItem pasteItem

viewMenu=toolBarItem statusBarItem

helpMenu=aboutItem

mainToolBar=newItem saveItem - cutItem copyItem
pasteItem
```

```
newItem.icon=new_win.gif
newItem.shortcut=n

openItem.icon=open_win.gif
openItem.shortcut=o
```

23.4.3 Breaking Consistency

Rules are made to be broken, and there are times when it is appropriate to be incon-sistent. Inconsistency can be used to draw attention to a dangerous operation (for example, colouring a "do you want to format your hard disk" message in red). Sometimes, you want to make life awkward for your users – there are a number of shareware programs that bring up "Please register" panels with the "OK" and "Cancel" buttons in a random order. This prevents the user from dismissing the panel automatically.

Sometimes, you may find a better way of performing a task that makes your interface externally inconsistent. In this case, you must carefully weigh up the advan-tages your new interface gives against the extra difficulty associated with learning how to use it and retaining that knowledge.

23.5 Menus

Menus provide an excellent way of accessing the commands of an application. Novices can search the menus for the items they want without having to learn any new syntax. More experienced users that are unfamiliar with a particular application can browse the menus to discover the functionality that the application provides. Menus that provide shortcuts allow experienced users to work faster.

When designing a menu, we must consider how the items are to be organized, how they are to be phrased, and how we provide shortcuts. At the same time, we must bear in mind our commitment to external consistency. This actually helps us in many cases, as we can model our terminology and layout on existing applications. For example, most applications with have a menu based on the one shown in Figure 23.3.

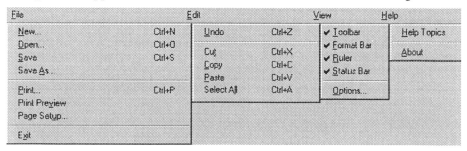

Figure 23.3 Typical MS Windows menu layout.

This section talks about the issues in relation to menu bars, but most of the principles apply to selections provided by a set of radio buttons or items in a `Choice`, etc.

23.5.1 Organization

Items on a menu should be arranged logically and grouped functionally or by tasks. The grouping can be achieved by separating items onto their own menus (or cascading submenus), or within a menu by using separators. For example, the "File" menu usually contains all of the items concerned with storing the current document. Separators are used to group the items that access a document on disk and those to do with printing the document.

The groupings that are used are important – a good choice results in a menu structure that allows items to be located very quickly. A poor structure can leave the user more-or-less searching through every item. Organizing a menu can be difficult and requires careful thought. For example, the MS Word item to insert a table appears under the "Table" menu, but it could just as well appear under the "Insert" menu.

Java supports cascading menus, but they should be used sparingly. Research shows that users find it much easier to find items in large shallow menus than they do in smaller, deeper menus. The items in the menu should be phrased concisely using familiar terminology. The items must be distinct and not overlapping, so that the user does not have to choose between two vaguely worded items. For example, if I wanted to insert a picture (stored as a file) into a document, would I choose "Add Picture" or "Insert File"?

Making the most significant word in the menu item appear at the left will help users scan through a menu quickly. The ordering of the items within a menu is also important in helping users find a desired item – they should be consistently ordered, usually by function, or chronologically.

Finally, if there is a shortcut to the menu item, this should be included in the item as an aid for reminding the user of the faster syntax. Swing also allows menu items to contain icons, which are a useful way of reminding the user of items available through the toolbar.

23.5.2 Shortcuts

Shortcuts to menu items are essential for experienced users to achieve faster performance. They allow fast typists to select menu items without having to leave the keyboard. Java supports key combinations as shortcuts to menu items, although a component in the `Frame` containing the menu bar must have the input focus for the shortcut to work. You should try to choose keys that are easy to remember – sticking to establish conventions will help this. For example, the save item is usually linked to Ctrl-S.

Most applications also have a toolbar, providing direct access to the most frequently used menu items. The standard icons should be used whenever possible, but you should not change the generally accepted meaning behind them (for example, don't use the undo icon to represent the screen redraw item). If you have to create a new icon, use a consistent style and try to avoid localized concepts that would not be understood by other cultures.

Tooltips (see Figure 23.4) are very useful for reminding users of the meaning behind the icons when they are not familiar, and are supported by all of the Swing components.

Figure 23.4 Tooltips.

23.5.3 Popup Menus

Many modern applications use popup (or context-sensitive) menus. These menus usually contain items relevant to the component (or selected data in the component) that currently has the input focus. For example, an object-based drawing program might allow the user to right-click on an object to select it and display a popup menu containing "cut" and "copy" items.

It is important that the popup menu items are duplicated in the main menu, as the main menu is used to browse through the functionality in an application. The popup menu items must be relevant to the current component (or selected objects), and the type of items that appear for a component (or object) must be consistent with others of a similar nature, to avoid confusing the user.

Java directly supports popup menus with the `PopupMenu` class. The `MouseEvent` class provides the `isPopupTrigger()` method – you should use this to ensures that the popup menu is invoked in a manner consistent with the operating system. For example:

```
public void mousePressed( MouseEvent e ) {
   if( e.isPopupTrigger( ) ) {
      // Show popup menu...
```

23.6 Dialogs

Dialog boxes are generally used to present information, or to get information from a user. A dialog should have a meaningful title, so that the user can be reminded of the task in hand, and a neat layout. Ideally, the layout will be familiar to the users, perhaps based on a paper layout that was used previously. The input components should be in a logical sequence, and grouped logically also.

An example of poor layout of a simple dialog is shown in Figure 23.5 and a good layout is shown in Figure 23.6. In the first layout, there is no logical grouping (the address fields are mixed with the name fields), and no logical ordering (the postcode field is always last but one in an address).

If some of the inputs to the dialog may be left undefined, this should be clearly marked. All components should be clearly labelled, and values such as dates and currency should be displayed in a localized form. Java 1.1 allows the user to use the Tab key to traverse through the components in a dialog. A common mistake with

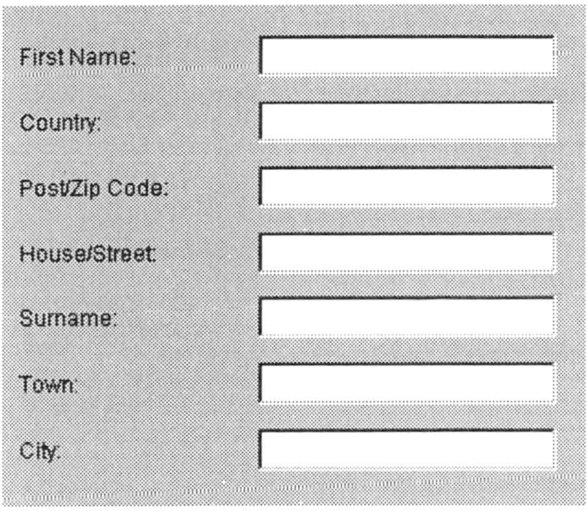

Figure 23.5 Illogical layout for a dialog.

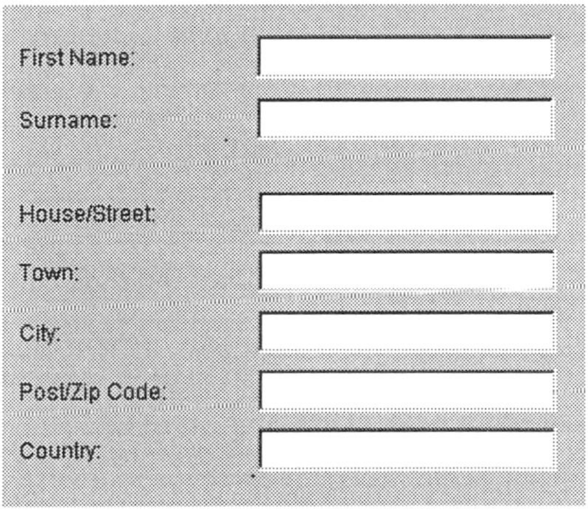

Figure 23.6 Logical layout for a dialog.

programmers is not to consider the traversal order of components within a dialog. It is quite annoying when each press of the Tab key jumps to a completely different part of the dialog, rather than traversing the components in a logical order. The Tab order in Java is defined by the order in which you add components to a panel (although you can insert a component at a particular position in the panel).

Often some components in a dialog are disabled, because they are incompatible with a selection made elsewhere. For example, in a printing dialog, the page number field might be disabled if the user has chosen to print the whole document. It can be frustrating for users to see an option that they want to change, only to find that it is disabled and they don't know why. It must always be clear why something is disabled – logical grouping of components can help this.

Dialogs should try not to require the user to remember information from elsewhere in the application – if possible, the information should be available in the same dialog. Although selection components, such as Choices and ComboBoxes, are easier for novices and prevent erroneous inputs, they slow down experienced typists – you need to decide which of these considerations has priority.

You should try to avoid the user having to enter data more than once – apart from being inefficient, it provides another opportunity for errors to creep in. If fields must appear in more than one dialog, copy the first entry across.

Be careful not to cram too much information into one dialog, as it can get messy and confusing. Tabbed panels are a good way of breaking up complex dialogs, but don't overdo it, as too many tabs can leave you with the same problem. Swing provides a tabbed panel in the form of `JTabbedPane`.

23.7 Error Handling

Errors are inevitable in any application, and how the application handles errors is an important part of the user interface. Errors occur due to a lack of knowledge, poor understanding or simply through a slip-up. The user may well be feeling confused, out of his or her depth, or angry, and the response from the computer should try to relieve these anxieties rather than exacerbate them.

23.7.1 Prevention

As with illness, prevention is better than cure. Good interfaces prevent (as much as possible) the user from making errors in the first place. A very simple example is a text field used to input someone's age. A robust interface would check the contents of the field before attempting to convert its value into a number, just in case the user had entered letters or punctuation. A better interface would disable the letter and punctuation keys for that field. In Java, this is relatively simple: Listing 23.2 shows a `KeyListener` implementation that can be added to a `TextField` (using its `addKeyListener()` method) for number-only fields. It also disables the "–" key to prevent negative ages being given. Listener objects are called before the component itself responds to the event. The `consume()` method in `Event` allows the `AgeKeyListener` class to prevent the `TextField` responding to invalid key presses. Note that when you use this sort of technique, it should always be clear to the user why the keypresses are not getting through – in this case it is clear that an age field should only contain numerals.

There are many ways in which you can help the user input correct values. If there are a limited number of values for a field, then use a `Choice` (or ComboBox in Swing). Buttons and menu items can be disabled when an action is not appropriate (e.g. saving should be disabled when there is no document open). Slider bars can be used to select a number in a fixed range, and a calendar could be used to pick dates in the year.

Listing 23.2

```java
import java.awt.*;
import java.awt.event.*;

// A KeyListener suitable for age fields: it only
// allows numbers to get through.
class AgeKeyListener extends KeyAdapter {

  // When a key is typed in a component.
  public void keyTyped( KeyEvent e ) {

    // If the key pressed was not a digit, consume it
    // to prevent the field using it.
    // Character.isDigit( ) provides an
    // internationalized test for digit characters.
    if( ! Character.isDigit( e.getKeyChar() ) ) {
      e.consume();
    }
  }
}

// A Frame to test the AgeKeyListener.
public class ErrorPrevention extends Frame {

  // Construct the new frame.
  public ErrorPrevention( ) {

    // Set a 2 column layout, and background.
    setLayout(new GridLayout(1,2));
    setBackground(Color.lightGray);

    // Add a label.
    add(new Label("Telephone:"));

    // Add a field with an AgeKeyListener.
    TextField field = new TextField();
    field.addKeyListener(new AgeKeyListener());
    add(field);

    pack( );
  }

  // Create and show the frame.
  // Use Ctrl-C to kill this application.
  public static void main(String argv[]) {
    ErrorPrevention frame = new ErrorPrevention( );
```

```
        frame.setVisible( true );
    }
}
```

23.7.2 Error Messages

Even if you try to prevent errors through your user interface, it is likely that there will be occasions when errors occur and the user must be informed. It is important to consider carefully the style and content of your error messages, so that they help the user understand what went wrong (and hopefully how to overcome the problem). In general, the user interfaces of applications have improved enormously over the last few years, but many still have poor error messages. Good error messages should be specific, positive in tone and constructive.

The user needs to understand what has gone wrong, in order to correct the error and to avoid it in the future. The more specific the error message is, the easier this becomes. Consider the following error messages, increasing in specificity, from a compiler:

- Syntax error
- Syntax error in `Test.java`
- Syntax error in `Test.java`, line 34
- Syntax error in `Test.java`, line 34: method `getElement()` not found in class `Vector`

The first message gives you no help whatsoever in finding the error, whereas the final message lets you pinpoint the error exactly.

In order to calm the user's frayed nerves, error messages should be positive in tone. A message that condemns the user is likely to increase that user's anxiety, making it more difficult to correct the error and increasing the chance of introducing more errors later on. Wherever possible, the message should give constructive guidance on how to resolve the problem. Consider the condemning and unhelpful message "That doesn't make sense: don't try to print before you've defined a customer". This can be rewritten positively and helpfully as "Please define at least one customer before trying to print: this can be done from the 'Edit' menu".

Although it is good to include constructive help in an error message, this must be balanced against the need for concision. Verbose error messages are distracting for experienced users, and too much information can confuse novice users too. Probably the best approach is to keep the error message clear but concise, and include a "Help" button in the message dialog that links to more detailed information about the error.

Error messages should not contain complex error codes, as this can help reinforce novice users' feelings of confusion and distrust. It is better to use mixed case characters, as this can seem less intimidating that upper-case text.

There are a few programs whose interface gives the feel of interacting with another human being. For example, it might use an error message like "Sorry, I'm confused: please tell me about a customer before you ask me to print". The idea is that novice computer users will feel more at home interacting with a "sentient" computer. However, UI experts generally accept that this is not a good idea. Computers are not sentient, and leading users to think as if they are will lead to unrealistic expectations. Users should think of computers as a tool and learn how to control them, accepting responsibility for their behaviour.

23.8 Internationalization

The world market for programs is now more accessible than ever before – applets may be browsed from any country in the world. Internet distribution allows this sort of global access to applications too. It has become important for applications to be aware of the locale in which they are operating, displaying messages in an appropriate language and formatting dates and currencies correctly.

Java 1.1 added a number of features in support of internationalization. Once you have used these features a few times, it really doesn't take much extra effort to create internationally aware applications. Internationalization is based around the `Locale` object. It isn't useful in itself, but it is used by all of the locale-dependent methods in other classes. You would normally create a locale object using its static method `getDefault()` to get the locale based on the OS settings. Locale defines a set of constants for the most commonly used locales, but you can also specify an ISO country and language code to construct a specific locale.

23.8.1 Changing Languages

Changing the language of the text used in a UI is relatively easy, using the `PropertyResourceBundle` class. Listing 23.3 shows an example of how it can be used. In the `testMessage()` method, a new instance of `PropertyResourceBundle` is created that contains the localized text. Whenever we need a text string, the bundle's `getString()` method is used with a key value.

The name passed to the `PropertyResourceBundle` constructor is used to locate one or more resource files. The first file that is loaded provides the default mappings between key values and localized text strings (in this case, it will be called "`Internationalization.properties`", located somewhere in the `CLASSPATH`). The `PropertyResourceBundle` will also look for a properties file whose name ends in the specified locale's ISO language code – in this example we provided a resource file for French called "`Internationalization_fr.properties`". This property file inherits all of the values from the default file, so it need not redefine every value (for example the "`title`" value is not defined). Property files can be created for even more specific locales by appending a country code –"`Internationalization_de_CH.properties`" would be for the German-speaking Swiss locale.

Listing 23.3

Internationalization.java:

```
import java.util.*;
import java.text.*;

// A class to demonstrate internationalization of text
// and time.
public class Internationalization extends Object {

  // A method that displays an internationalized
  // message indicating the current time.
  public static void testMessage( Locale locale ) {

    // Create a Date/Time formatter for the given
    // locale.
    DateFormat formatter =
      DateFormat.getDateTimeInstance(
      DateFormat.LONG, DateFormat.LONG, locale );

    // Create a resource bundle for the given locale.
    ResourceBundle resources =
      ResourceBundle.getBundle(
      ".Internationalization", locale );

    // Get and format the current time.
    Date date = Calendar.getInstance( ).getTime( );
    String timeString = formatter.format( date );

    // Display the internationalized message.
    System.out.println( "" );
    System.out.println( resources.getString( "title" ) +
      locale.getDisplayCountry( ) );
    System.out.println( resources.getString
      ( "time_is" ) + timeString );
  }

  // Display information about the current locale, and
  // print an internationalized message for two
  // locales.
  public static void main( String argv[] ) {

    // Display information on the current locale.
    Locale defaultLocale = Locale.getDefault( );
    System.out.println( "The default locale is:" );
```

```
        System.out.println(
          defaultLocale.getDisplayCountry( ) );
        System.out.println(
          defaultLocale.getDisplayLanguage( ) );
        System.out.println(
          defaultLocale.getDisplayVariant( ) );

        // Display the test message for the UK...
        testMessage( Locale.UK );

        // Display the test message for France...
        testMessage( Locale.FRANCE );
    }
}
```

Internationalization.properties
```
#
# Base Properties File for International English.
#

title=Internationalization:
time_is=The current time is
```

Internationalization_fr.properties
```
#
# Properties File for French.
#

time_is=Il est
```

Sample output:
```
The default locale is:
United Kingdom
English
Internationalization: United Kingdom
The current time is 17 January, 1998 15:24:14 GMT

Internationalization: France
Il est 17 janvier 1998 16:24:14 GMT+01:00
```

23.8.2 Dates and Time

The Calendar class stores a GMT time for a particular date. This can be converted into a format suitable for any locale using one of the static methods in the java.text.DateFormat class. For example, DateFormat. getDateInstance().format(myCalendar.getTime()) might return

"10-Jan-98" for a British locale, or "10.1.98" for Germany (following the German convention). The `getTimeInstance()` and `getDateTimeInstance()` methods work in the same way for times of the day and date and time, respectively. `DateFormat` also provides methods for parsing strings to create new `Calendar` instances.

23.8.3 Currency and Numbers

Clearly, currency symbols differ between countries, but the way in which numbers are formatted differs also. For example, the number 1234.56 would be formatted as "1,234.56" in the UK, but as "1.234,56" in Denmark. The `java.text.NumberFormat` class provides a set of static methods for formatting numbers. The example above would be coded as `NumberFormat.getInstance().format(1234.56)`. Currency is formatted in a similar way using the `getCurrencyInstance()` method, and again there are methods for parsing strings to create numbers.

Unfortunately, there are no components in the Swing that allow internationally safe editing of dates and currency: either you have to create one yourself, or use a text field and parse the string it returns.

23.9 Response Time

The more experienced users become, the higher their expectations and the more impatient they become (generally!). The time that your interface takes to respond can seriously affect their subjective satisfaction. In addition, an unresponsive interface can result in annoying errors – we have seen a number of people clicking on buttons, waiting for a few seconds with no response, then clicking madly on the button, which results in about 10 new windows opening! Excessive delays will also make it less likely that users will experiment with features in your application.

You should always provide some response within about two seconds. Ideally, this response will be the results of the user's action, but if this is not possible, you should (as a bare minimum) change to a "busy" mouse cursor (use the `setCursor()` method in `Component`). Many programs these days show a progress bar during slow operations, so that at least the user has something to look at and can gauge how long there is to wait. You should also try to include a button somewhere that cancels the operation – there is nothing more frustrating than accidentally starting something and then having to wait for ages while it finishes!

The ideal way to handle slow operations is to display the results as they become available (although this is not appropriate for all operations). A familiar example is a Web browser loading a page – as the page is loaded, you can see the page build up on the screen. This allows you to start reading things before the loading operation has finished (and possibly cancel it when you have the required information). Java's multi-threading capabilities would help in creating an interface like this.

23.10 Screen Design and Colour

Most displays these days support colour – its use can help make a display more inter-esting, and it can be used to convey information. However, you can have too much of a good thing: poor use of colour can result in unreadable displays, and can imply relationships between things that do not exist.

The most important thing to remember is to use colour conservatively. Too many colours can make the display look messy and difficult to read. In any case, you should design your display so that it is usable in monochrome, as there are a significant number of people that are colour-blind. Some colours go badly together, and you should try to avoid these combinations (for example red text on a blue background).

Colour can be used to make displays easier to read, by picking out titles and labels for example. This is particularly useful when there is a lot of information in the display. It is important to use these colours consistently between different displays – otherwise it can end up disorientating the user rather than helping.

You can indicate relationships between items in a display by the use of colour coding. For example, the names of Welsh rugby players could be in red, and New Zealand players in black - their national teams wear these colours. You shouldn't have to look for these relationships – if they are irrelevant to the task in hand then they are probably a distraction. You should also be wary of implying relationships between items that do not exist. For example, if you had a list of rugby players and used a random colour for each one, it might lead the user to assume that players with the same colour came from the same team.

Colour can also be used to draw the users' attention to items of interest in the display –for example overdrawn customers or changing values can be highlighted. When choosing colours, you should be aware of people's common associations with them – red is normally associated with stopping or danger, and green with going or safety.

23.11 Help!

Online help is an important part of a modern application – it teaches beginners how to use the system and reminds occasional users of the system syntax. The most useful form of help is context-sensitive help. This means that when you invoke help, the page it displays depends on the context in which it was invoked. For example, if you click on the help button in a dialog box, the help system displays help on that dialog (rather than requiring you to look through the contents for it).

23.11.1 Help Under Java

One of the simplest (but still useful) forms of help is the tooltip: if the mouse hesitates over a component, it can display a short message explaining its purpose. This is supported directly by the `JComponent` class in the Swing, through the `setTooltip()` method.

There is no standard help browser in Java yet, although the JavaHelp API is in the early stages of development. It will be based around an HTML browser, with a searchable index, history list and a full-text searching facility. Until this becomes part of the JDK, you could use one of the commercially available Java help systems, or write a simple one of your own. The IFC contains its own HTML text component, and the HotJava HTML component can be used under the AWT or Swing. These could form the basis of a viewer for applications' help text. Applets can use the Web browser (in which they are displayed) to create new windows containing help as HTML text (through the `AppletContext` instance).

23.11.2 Writing Help Files

As when designing a user interface, a good understanding of the users is essential in creating good online help. The terminology used should be familiar to the user. If the information is too simple, experienced users are unlikely to find it helpful. If more complex information is included, then novice users are likely to be intimidated and confused. HTML allows us to present a relatively simple overview of a topic with links to explanations of unfamiliar terminology and concepts for novices, and to more in-depth information for power users. Pictures of dialogs and explanatory diagrams are often useful, particularly when describing the function of parts of the interface.

For the help pages concerned with introducing the user to the system (as opposed to help linked to a particular dialog or error), you should organize the text around the tasks that the user is trying to perform. This helps present a coherent picture of how the user can achieve a task. Adding examples to the text will help reinforce the more abstract discussions, and is particularly useful for novices.

23.12 Configuration

Many applications allow users to configure aspects of the user interface. This is particularly popular with experienced users, as it allows them to adapt the application to suit the way in which they already work. Allowing users to change the menu shortcuts can be useful to help maintain external consistency with other applications. Many text editors, for example, offer keyboard mappings for other editors such as BRIEF, so that experienced users do not have to relearn another convention. Toolbars usually offer the most commonly used actions as buttons, but these actions are bound to vary between users. The ability to customize the toolbars can be useful.

It is not just experienced users that can benefit from this sort of configuration. Users of slow machines may welcome the ability to turn off fancy interface features (such as animated icons) in favour of better performance. Users with poor eyesight would welcome the ability to choose larger fonts for the display, and most of us like control over the colours used by an application.

Of course, there is a downside to such flexible configuration – different installations may become inconsistent with each other. A novice user might become completely disoriented trying to use an expert user's customized version of an application. This sort of problem can be minimized by storing separate configuration files for each user. The system property "user.home" specifies the user's home directory. On Windows this is always "C:\", but you can wrap the application in a batch file that sets this property (using the -D command-line option for java) to the value in the USERPROFILE environment variable.

The easiest way to implement configuration files is with the Properties class. This allows you to associate string values with keys, and to save to and restore from a text file.

23.13 Platform Independence

Although Java is a platform-independent language, it is still possible to create platform-dependent interfaces. The biggest problem is people using absolute positioning of components, rather than using Java's layout managers. Many people will be doing this without realizing it, as most of the Java GUI builders default to absolute positioning (some don't support anything else).

It is easier to create interfaces using absolute positioning, but they are inflexible. If the application runs on a system with larger fonts, text components may not be large enough to display the text (even different installations of the same OS can use different system fonts). This problem can be even worse with the different types of look and feel, as components can have significantly different shapes and sizes on different platforms. In addition, an interface constructed using absolute positioning will not be able to respond to changes in the window's size, which is important, particularly for systems with large screens.

You should try to avoid depending on UI features that may not be supported on all systems, such as colour and sound. They may still be included, but make sure that the interface remains usable without them.

23.14 Summary

We have discussed a variety of issues in this chapter, including, among other things: the need for consistency; logical task/user-oriented design; and error prevention. None of this is written in stone, but it will help you make careful, informed decisions when designing your interface. The most important point to remember is to try to understand your users and their tasks, and adjust your designs accordingly. Prototyping can be a useful way of iteratively evaluating and updating your designs.

Take a look at the applications that you use yourself. Which ones do you find easy to use, and which ones are hard? More importantly, why? Try to reassess them from a different perspective, such as a novice user. By becoming more aware of the issues that affect the usability of an interface, you will become a better designer.

23.15 Further Reading

Schniederman B. (1992) *Designing the User Interface: Strategies for Effective Human-Computer Interaction*, 2nd edn. Addison-Wesley, Reading.
Newman W. and Lamming M. (1995) *Interactive System Design*. Addison-Wesley, Reading.
Kletz T. (1995) *Computer Control and Human Error*. Institution of Chemical Engineers, London.

23.16 Online References

JavaHelp home page:

```
http://java.sun.com/products/javahelp/index.html
```

Index